The State as Defendant

Recent Titles in
Contributions in Political Science
Series Editor: Bernard K. Johnpoll

The State as Defendant
GOVERNMENTAL ACCOUNTABILITY AND THE REDRESS OF INDIVIDUAL GRIEVANCES

Leon Hurwitz

Contributions in Political Science, Number 51

Greenwood Press
WESTPORT, CONNECTICUT

Library of Congress Cataloging in Publication Data

Hurwitz, Leon.
    The state as defendant.

    (Contributions in political science; no. 51
ISSN 0147–1066)
    Bibliography: p.
    Includes index.
    1. Government liability. 2. Administrative
remedies. 3. Administrative responsibility.
4. Civil rights. I. Title. II. Series.
K967.H87   342'.088   80–657
ISBN 0–313–21257–0 (lib. bdg.)

Library of Congress Catalog Card Number: 80–657
ISBN: 0–313–21257–0
ISSN: 0147–1066

First published in 1981

Greenwood Press
A division of Congressional Information Service, Inc.
88 Post Road West, Westport, Connecticut 06881

Printed in the United States of America

10 9 8 7 6 5 4 3 2 1

To the memory of my father,
Saul Hurwitz

CONTENTS

FOREWORD

> We hold these truths to be self-evident, that all men are created equal: that they are endowed by their Creator with certain unalienable rights; that among these are life, liberty, and the pursuit of happiness. That to secure these rights, governments are instituted among men, deriving their just powers from the consent of the governed. . . .
>
> *Declaration of Independence*

America is a country proud of its history of providing for and protecting the rights and the freedoms of its people. It is a system forged by our forefathers to ensure the innate rights of every American. These men knew only too well what it was like to live under a system that lent a deaf ear to their cries for justice and the right to choose their own form of government. The result of this burning desire for freedom and justice led the colonies into a violent revolution.

The Revolution of 1776 was only the first step in a continuing battle to safeguard the just rights of all Americans. Throughout the last two hundred years, those who felt their rights had been violated have turned to our system of courts for justice. During these last two centuries, our judicial system has been successful in maintaining a standard of justice that has become a model for the rest of the world. Even though our country has achieved this high standard, the continued preservation of a fair system of justice is a very delicate, arduous, and vigilant task. In order to preserve and improve our superior tradition, we must constantly strive to update our methods of justice through the diligent study and review of our own system as well as other systems, past and present.

Leon Hurwitz has provided us with a fine study of the judicial relationship between the individual and the state. Through his writings on the various methods of judicial redress, he has illustrated the tremendous obligation of the state to protect the human rights of each of its members. Furthermore, he states that this problem of safeguarding the rights of the individual citizen, with a just form of redress, is compounded by a world that is becoming every day more complex and impersonal. Mr. Hurwitz has successfully presented us with a very thorough study of one of the paramount issues that face every government in our modern world.

As our forefathers found, the preservation of justice is a formidable task. But with the aid of contributions such as this volume, we may learn and benefit from our past experiences and improve and perpetuate our future freedom.

Frank D. Celebrezze
Chief Justice
Ohio Supreme Court

PREFACE

This book examines the different processes and methods at the disposal of a private citizen in various selected countries to complain against his or her government and have a reasonable expectation that the complaint will be heard and acted upon without prejudice. Such complaints concern either an alleged violation of a central personal liberty by the state or the insensitivity of the faceless bureaucratic structures. It is also a cross-national comparative analysis of an individual's ability to have his or her basic human rights protected against governmental or bureaucratic interference. The main theme and unifying element of this study is the question of how one can bring some measure of justice and sensitivity to bear on the relationships between an ever-growing, impersonal administrative technology in the nuclear world—the modern postindustrial state—and the individuals who comprise this state.

This book supports the belief that a system of redress against the state is needed. The need for such a system can be seen on two levels, both equally important. The first level—the macrolevel—is the public policy argument concerning political goals, and it is approached from the perspective of the political system. The second level—the microlevel—is the philosophical argument approached from the perspective of the individual.

Approached from the perspective of a democratic political system, it is simply "good" politics to provide avenues of redress against the state. An individual who believes his rights have been violated or has a complaint against the impersonal bureaucratic apparatus—an apparatus that permeates daily life in a postindustrial society—is all too frequently ignored or shunted aside. The American expression "you can't fight city hall" is an attitude of resignation in the face of official (and officious) attitudes of nonresponse. The individual thus feels increasingly alienated from a nonresponsive political system that refuses to grant avenues of redress. Alienation in a democratic society can have drastic, and often fatal, consequences for the system if it is widespread. The demands directed at the system's decision-making units become more numerous and vocal, and they may far outstrip the capacity of the decision-making unit to handle the increased input. An alienated society does not view its political system, and certainly not its political personnel, as legitimate or as right and proper. Such a society is often characterized by instability and violence.

By providing a system of redress against itself, the state may be able to strengthen the level of support and feelings of legitimacy among the population. The state might then be able to maintain its stability in the face of constant pressures and continue its basic societal patterns by adapting to the changing environment. The fact that the British political system, as an analytical concept, can be traced at least as far back as 1066, if not earlier, is in some measure due to its record of providing some institutionalized avenues of redress for its population.

But this public policy argument should not be overstated because its applicability *is* limited. The above remarks are valid only in a fully functioning and authentic democratic political system in which the democratic processes are not mere facades for underlying nondemocratic governing patterns. A system of redress against the state is necessary in a society where the population at large has the free and unhindered power to overthrow the decision makers. In such democratic systems—and these systems constitute a minority of all political entities in the world—it is the people who govern through the electoral process. The state's decision makers, if only to maintain themselves in office as presidents or prime ministers, must ultimately pay heed to those who have the ability to substitute one set of decision makers for another. In systems where the population does not yet possess such abilities—in authoritarian political systems such as the Soviet Union, Iran, Chile, or South Africa—the decision makers need only satisfy or pay heed to that very small segment of the population that does have the ability to overthrow and replace the ruling elite.[1]

These small groups who have the ability to overthrow the ruling elite are invariably the army, secret police, bureaucracy, and, in certain societies, large landholders and the church establishment. The population at-large in these societies—the blacks in South Africa, for example—lies outside the political system. Of course, periodical and well-orchestrated demonstrations of support exist in many of these societies ("elections" in the Soviet Union are excellent illustrations of orchestrated but meaningless demonstrations of mass support), but avenues of redress against the state need not be provided for most of the population. To be sure, the army, secret police, bureaucracy, landholders, and the religious establishment have such avenues available to them, but these groups represent only a very small percentage of the population. But if an authentic and effective democratic political system wants to maintain high levels of legitimacy and system support to reduce alienation, it is good politics for the maintenance of systematic stability to institutionalize a system of redress against itself.

The second argument in favor of a system of redress against the state is on the philosophical level, and it is approached from the perspective of the individual. This argument is briefer than the political one, and it is not circumscribed by the type of political system that may exist. This argument is (should be) valid in totalitarian systems as well as democratic societies, for it concerns the individual and *not* the configuration of his or her political system. This position can be stated quite simply: each person has dignity and worth and is to be valued for his or her intrinsic existence as an individual. People ought—a moral "ought"—to be respected because each person possesses inviolable human rights.[2]

The Western idea of human rights tends to reflect its political (liberalism) and socioeconomic (capitalism) outlook.[3] Although it is sometimes clothed in a somewhat collectivist appearance, the individual is still the focus of Western images of, and approaches to, human rights. This basic dignity and worth of the *individual* is deeply rooted in the Western Judeo-Christian philosophic tradition and cultural heritage. This second argument in favor of a system of redress against the state simply posits the absolute necessity and right of the individual to complain against insensitive or callous treatment by the bureaucracy on grounds that each individual has basic human rights regardless of the form of government that may exist.

This study is thus concerned with some political attempts to make available such avenues of redress. It is *not* concerned with what others may term more direct and immediate action to secure redress against the state for alleged wrongs, that is, anomalous behavior such as violence and revolution. I do not want to de-emphasize the sometimes excellent efficacy that violence has had in securing redress for past grievances against an oppressive and nonresponsive state. The problem, however, is that one's point of view is invariably influenced by whether the people engaged in violence against the state are categorized as "freedom fighters" or as "terrorists." *Freedom fighters* are honorable people who, after exhausting all peaceful methods to secure redress, employ limited acts of controlled violence against an oppressive state to secure a just end. *Terrorists*, on the other hand, are irrational gangsters who afflict unlimited and indiscriminate violence upon innocent people.

History provides too many examples of this duality in perceptions to separate the different types, even from one single national point of view. An illustration of this problem is found in a recent book by Michael Walzer (*Just and Unjust Wars*).[4] Walzer attempted to apply (his) moral principles to particular cases of war and terrorism to sort out the *just* ("honorable freedom fighters in a great moral crusade") from the *unjust* ("gangster terrorists engaging in deviant psychopathic behavior"). Unfortunately, not everyone will agree with Walzer's categorization. It is sufficient here to conclude that violence is indeed an often-employed avenue of redress, and it has had a long, and sometimes honorable, history in the relationship between an individual or groups of individuals and the state. But this study is concerned with the peaceful, accepted, and institutionalized processes that contribute to the stability of the system, increase the level of system support and legitimacy, and protect individual human rights.

Underlying this entire process of protecting the individual from society's excesses, of redressing valid grievances against the state, of providing incentives for polite and humane treatment from the bureaucracy, is the clash between two opposing conceptions of the standing of the individual vis-à-vis the sovereign national state. One conception is the classical tradition of *sovereign immunity*, which holds that the king and/or the king's agents can do no wrong. This view derives from the politico-philosophic concept of *rex gratia dei* ("king by the grace of God"), and it elevates the state to a position of primacy over the individual. *Rex gratia dei* is no longer a viable precept in the majority of countries, but sovereign immunity has far outlived it. To be sure, even the contemporary content of sovereign immunity is quite different from that existing during the feudal age, although it is still a viable concept and enforced doctrine even in some of our modern postindustrial democracies.

A second and more "modern" view of the relationship between the individual and the state says that the king and/or the king's agents *can* do wrong, that they can err, and that they are to be held responsible for their actions. If one describes sovereign immunity as deriving from and resting upon the notion of *rex gratia dei*, this alternative conception rests upon the general notion of *rex gratia populi* ("king by the grace of the people"). The entire concept of sovereign immunity and the question of the standing of the individual vis-à-vis the state are complex issues; they are explored in greater detail in chapter 1.

The following chapters examine, in a historical and descriptive context, some of these avenues of redress and some of the political attempts to recognize the fact that the king and/or his agents can do wrong. Although dealing with essentially legal questions—the capacity and limitation of law in affecting the behavior of individuals and organizations, the role of law in the settlement of disputes and conflict management and resolution, the operation of informal systems for settling legally relevant disputes, how legal systems are modified in response to economic and social changes—this book is not written in a legal framework. I am a political scientist, and the following remarks are thus written in a social and political public policy framework.

The specific functional areas of redress that are discussed include a country's regular court system, specialized administrative tribunals such as the French *Conseil d'État* ("Council of State"), the office of ombudsman or "citizen's protector," parliamentary oversight processes, public intergovernmental institutions such as the European Commission on Human Rights, and private nongovernmental avenues such as Amnesty International.

Not all of these processes are available to everyone, since several are specific to individual countries, and some have much more efficacy than others in conflict management and the resolution of disputes. Each procedure is intimately linked to the political culture and values of the society in which it operates, and each reflects the society's past record in providing avenues of redress against the state. But common to all is the crucial recognition that the state is (or should be) liable for its actions; that the individual can demand sensitive treatment; and, finally, that the state, in its technocratic and bureaucratic costume of the twentieth century, is dealing with individuals and that these individuals should not be wronged by the king.

NOTES

1. Arthur S. Goldberg presented a mathematical probability analysis of the likelihood that any one regime will be displaced by another. Goldberg conceived stability as "... a function of the extent to which decisions are made on the basis of power weighted preference orderings ... [and] to what extent ... the regime makes decisions which do not offend those who have the ability to displace it." His theory is presented as descriptions of the preference orderings of the components of the system (army, church, warlord, party) that could displace the regime, as well as estimates of the probability of success for each component that opts to move against the regime. See Arthur S. Goldberg, "A Theoretical Approach to Political Stability" (Paper presented at the Sixty-fourth Annual Meeting of the American Political Science Association, Washington, D.C., September 2-7, 1968).

2. One of the most eloquent statements of such individual dignity was put forth by John Locke almost three hundred years ago, and his remarks are especially relevant in the twentieth century: "[F]or man, being all the workmanship of one omnipotent, and infinitely wise master; all servants of one sovereign master, sent into the world by his order, and about his business; they are his property, whose workmanship they are, made to last during his, and not another's pleasure . . . there cannot be supposed any such subordination among us, that may authorize us to destroy one another, as the inferior ranks of creatures are for ours." John Locke, *Two Treatises of Government*, ed. Peter Laslett (New York: The New American Library, 1963), p. 311.

3. For a discussion of Western images of human rights, see Leon Hurwitz and Alan Rosenbaum, "European Images of Human Rights: The Impact of Third World Views on European Conceptions" (Paper presented at the Seventy-fourth Annual Meeting of the American Political Science Association, New York, August 31-September 3, 1978).

4. Michael Walzer, *Just and Unjust Wars: A Moral Argument with Historical Illustrations* (New York: Basic Books, 1978).

ACKNOWLEDGMENTS

Several people gave me aid and comfort while I was writing this book, and I would like to acknowledge their gracious assistance. For most efficient secretarial services, my thanks go to Leslie Bowman, Katy Hanrahan, Raynette Boggins, Karen Holder, and to the Word Processing Center at Cleveland State University, so ably administrated by Charles Urbancic.

Carol Patrick of The Cleveland State University Libraries helped with specific research problems as did Maud Buquicchio of the Office of the Secretary to the European Commission of Human Rights in Strasbourg. For permission to use previously copywritten material, I would like to thank Amnesty International-USA and the *Cleveland State Law Review*.

The entire editorial and production staff at Greenwood Press have been most helpful, especially James T. Sabin, Margaret Brezicki, and Mildred Vasan. I would also like to thank Bernard K. Johnpoll, editor for Greenwood's Series Contributions in Political Science.

My thanks go to my colleagues in the Department of Political Science at Cleveland State University, and especially to Ev Cataldo, for providing an atmosphere conducive to research which hastened the completion of this study. I also want to thank several administrative levels at Cleveland State University, especially Jack Soules, dean of the College of Arts and Sciences, and John Flower, provost, for facilitating a leave from teaching duties during the fall of 1979 and thus enabling me to finish this book.

Finally, as always, the support and encouragement of my wife, Fran, and my children, Elise and Jonathan, were appreciated.

The State as Defendant

INTRODUCTORY ESSAY:
A Historical Overview of Governmental Accountability

1

The ability of a private citizen to complain against his or her government, and have a reasonable expectation that the complaint will be heard and acted upon in an impartial manner, is a relatively new development in the Western historical and political fabric. This ability to complain (other than by violence) about alleged violations of a central personal liberty, for maladministration by the state's agents, or for insensitivity by the bureaucratic structures, is a process that has not yet arrived in the majority of cultures and political systems, including both modern postindustrial states such as the Soviet Union and traditional developing societies in Africa and Asia. It is also a development that is not yet fully understood and implemented in many of what are here termed the *modern democratic regimes* that at least pay outward homage to the rights of individuals and to the primacy of the individual over the state.

The concept of an individual's right to complain and place the state in the role of defendant has changed greatly in the past one hundred years. The traditional view was that the state was protective but passive—protective in that it would punish individuals who attempted to violate another individual's position, but passive in that, essentially, the state did not provide any real encouragement or tools to the individual to extend his position. This protective nature of the state was, of course, not always evident—the lack of governmental protection of blacks in the United States from white exploitation and oppression is but one example—but, traditionally and generally, one of the prime functions of any organized state was to protect individuals from each other within the confines of that society and to protect the entire society from external threats. This function of maintaining "law and order" is not difficult to accept, because part of the modern definition of the *state* is that entity or organization that has a "monopoly of force" within a certain geographical area and that (usually) has the legitimate authority to exercise that monopoly to protect one individual from another.

The usual view that the state is protective but passive has changed in two crucial aspects. The protective but passive function has been altered, at least in some of the democratic systems, into a more positive and assertive role. Now the state is seen to have the obligation not only to protect people from each other (the traditional passive role), but also to provide individuals with the means with which they can attain and enjoy certain rights and benefits (for example, affirmative action programs and equal opportunity legislation). David H. Bayley presented an excellent discussion of this important change, and the following example is from *Public Liberties in the New States*.[1] Bayley recognized a major difference between the statement "A man has the right to freedom of speech" and "A man has a right to education." For the first statement, all the state has to do is to protect the individual from other individuals' attempts to limit that speech; for the second statement, however, the state also has to provide the right (establish and fund an educational system). Bayley employs a good descriptive analogy: "The collectivity [the state] is no longer simply the bank guard which sees to it that the individual may cash his check; it is now the bank itself which must provide the wherewithal demanded."[2]

The second change away from the traditional view of the state as protective but passive—a more important change, and its nature is the focus of this book—has been the gradual implementation of procedures to protect the individual from the state itself (the state has always maintained procedures to protect *it* from the people). It is a much more difficult and complex question to provide not redress for one individual against another with the state as referee but, rather, redress for one individual against the state. The protection of rights *may* be an easy matter when only private citizens are involved but not when such rights have to be enforced against the state itself. This "monopoly of force" is now expected to turn upon itself and control the monopoly, for law and order no longer exists solely to enforce the king's law on his subjects but also to enforce that same law on the king and his agents. Unfortunately, complaints against the state have not been as successful as complaints directed at individuals by the state because the former are often simply denied permission to complain.

The unadorned and unamended doctrine of "parliamentary supremacy" in the United Kingdom, for example, was a pristine illustration of this situation in previous times. British society, through its democratically elected representatives sitting in Parliament, devised an admirable body of law to protect the individual from other individuals and to protect society at-large from the actions of antisocial or antigovernmental groups. But the tenets of parliamentary supremacy deny the third and possibly the most important relationship—the individual versus the state. The state, seen as Parliament in its collective wisdom, was not liable for review. The substance of a parliamentary decision simply could not be questioned by any formal, organized review process, and it was not relevant whether the decision in question was wise or silly, just or unjust.

This view of British parliamentary supremacy is exaggerated in relation to the latter half of the twentieth century because it ignores some limitations on the doctrine. These limitations are both long-standing internalized constraints on parliamentary behavior as well as some recent external constraints. Although external controls over the scope and content of parliament's decisions may not have existed in the past, the British Parliament for the most part did not engage in arbitrary, capricious, or authoritarian behavior. Traditional British culture to which the member of Parliament (MP) wholly adhered, provided sufficient internalized constraints on what Parliament could or could not do. The tenets of democracy and the dignity of the individual were deeply etched into this culture, and the lack of an external control did not by itself mean that the British state oppressed its citizens.

Some external controls to this doctrine of parliamentary supremacy have occurred recently, both for the United Kingdom and other members of the Council of Europe. The European Convention on Human Rights, discussed in chapter 6, has effectively placed certain areas beyond the reach of Parliament—Parliament *cannot* legislate violations of the convention. But the existence of an external control—the United States Constitution as interpreted by the Supreme Court, for example—does not by itself automatically lead to authentic avenues of redress against the state for maladministration and/or insensitivity. Even with the Constitution and Supreme Court, the American version of "sovereign immunity," at least until the post-World War II period, effectively diluted an individual's ability to complain against the U.S. government.

The comments above—that an institutionalized avenue of redress against the state is a relatively new process in Western culture—apply more to the implementation of and not to the philosophical foundations of the view that the state is liable for its actions. Such a philosophical view has had a long and honorable history in Western thought, but, essentially, it has been only in the post-World War II period that such tenets have been transformed in the population's perception and expectations: the state is no longer just the bank guard but has become the bank itself with a fistful of money to distribute to its customers. In addition, the state's monopoly of force has been turned inward upon itself in cases where the population does not receive as much money as it wants—the guard now directs his firearm at the teller to help the customer get the money. This introductory essay traces the historical development of this right to complain against one's government—placing that state in the unaccustomed and unwelcomed role of defendant—and it also provides a foundation for subsequent chapters.

The usual point of departure in most discussions of the relationships between the individual and the state or the state's administrative bureaucracy has been the classical pre-Christian Greek city-state system. In fact, most Western political scientists begin with the Greek *polis* in any discussion of politics or political science when approached from a philosophical or historical framework. For example, Sir Ernest Barker, a highly respected and eminent scholarly authority on political thought, once wrote that "political thought begins with the Greeks," and Andrew Hacker, another scholar, remarked that "Plato was the first writer to address himself to political philosophy."[3]

As much as Barker and Hacker are to be respected, they are probably mistaken with their praise of Greeks. The pre-Christian Greeks were not the first to wonder about, and then attempt to provide answers to, questions such as "How should a person behave in society?" "How are society's resources to be distributed?" "What particular rules or standards of behavior should be enforced?" "Who enforces these standards or rules?" "What are the penalties for violating these norms?" "What entity is to be supreme—the society as a collectivity or the individual?" It was probably the first cave person in prehistoric times, thousands of years before the Greeks, who first thought about "political" relationships when he or she wondered about the cave society's structures, elites, and decision-making processes. The cave society most certainly was a "political" system: it generated leaders and established lines of authority and organizational structures, and decisions were made that affected and bound the entire population.[4]

Of course, some element of conjecture arises in this argument, because cave people did not leave sytematic written material or treatises as Plato and Aristotle did, and it is always possibile that the cave people only thought about which animal was going to provide (or have) the next meal. But we do have written records from cultures that predate the Greeks: the ancient Egyptians, Old Testament Biblical literature, and the classical Chinese and Hindu civilizations all have left documentary evidence. These peoples and societies were active participants in a highly developed political process, complete with administrative bureaucracies to carry out the will of the decision maker(s). Thus this introductory essay does not begin with the Greeks (the Greeks, in fact, are not mentioned further) but, rather, with the ancient Chinese and Hindu civilizations. The philosophical conception of the standing of the individual vis-à-vis the state and the actual bureaucratic behavior in these ancient cultures reflected the specific variables of their own time and space. However, these cultures also contained several characteristics common to our modern Western democracies, at least until the latter half of the twentieth century.

The usual state of affairs regarding the relationship of the individual vis-à-vis his government and the right of this individual to complain about the actions of the administrative bureaucracy is well evidenced in Confucian China over twenty-five hundred years ago. For almost all of its history, including that of the current system, China has been guided by the Confucian concept that an individual's right always is secondary to an individual's duty. The Chinese individual was not expected to have an independent existence outside the state, nor was he encouraged to complain about state behavior. The individual had the duty to be loyal, obedient, and subservient to the state.[5] The need and reverence for "harmonious relations" among the various groups in society effectively reduced an individual's standing and placed the Chinese state—and the state's agents—in a position of primacy over the individual. Repression as a tool of control was sanctioned, for it was a most effective way of dealing with opposition, and the law served the function of preserving the social order rather than protecting the individual.

The philosophy of the group called the "Legalists" raised this doctrine of the primacy of the state to a very high level in ancient China during the fourth and third centuries B.C.[6] As Herrlee Creel wrote, the Legalist conception of the law was that it was seen simply as an instrument of control by the bureaucracy, and its objective was not to protect the individual. The Legalist conception of the law was akin to the Marxian view of bourgeois law: it was simply a tool of the ruling class(es) to maintain themselves in power and to oppress other classes in society. The Legalist regimes in ancient China really should not be termed *totalitarian*, for, compared to the modern varieties of the species, they lacked the all encompassing ability to penetrate every aspect of society; terror as a method of control was not as institutionalized, and mass thought control was not practiced. The term *authoritarian* is a much better descriptive category for those Legalist regimes. As a statement of the lack of a system of redress against the state, however, ancient China presents an excellent example, and it would not have been until recently that some of the processes in classical China would have appeared alien to some modern democratic regimes.

The ancient Hindu civilization in what is now India presents the same motif as does classical China with the Hindu conception of the caste system.[7] The concept of caste encompassed *all* aspects of behavior, and the doctrine did not encourage or allow individual complaints to be lodged against the state. Basic to the Hindu belief system of caste is the tenet of rebirth and the reincarnation of the soul. For those individuals who lead a "good" life—a life that conforms to the traditionally expected behavior patterns of a particular level or caste—subsequent rebirth will be at a higher level. Conversely, those who do not lead the "good" life will be reincarnated into a lower level. The ultimate goal is not to be reborn at all; that is, the soul finally will be freed from its earth-bound material existence and it will join the unconscious cosmic universe.

Thus under the Hindu caste system, the "law" did not emphasize individual rights or protect the individual from the state. Rather, the law defined the minute and stringent duties and obligations each individual had at various stages on the long and tortuous path toward the cosmic universe. The individual was stoically to accept his position and hardships and to endure these hardships without complaint. To be overly ambitious—to actively strive to better one's position—or to complain against governmental action would be resistance and nonacceptance of one's current life, and this would surely be a blot on the next reincarnation. But as D. Mackenzie Brown wrote, no real injustice to the individual is possible, given the logic of reincarnation.[8] Brown explained that the circumstances and situation of one's present life are only the ethical consequences of the individual's past life, and, to be reborn at a higher level (or, ideally, not to be reborn at all), the individual is expected to embrace and tolerate whatever may be inflicted upon him, whether the mistreatment is from other individuals (individuals who will be reincarnated at a lower level) or from the state. One cannot complain about perceived injustices because they do not exist: mistreatment is only the ethical consequences of one's past life, and life must be endured to be eligible for a higher rebirth.

But the ancient Eastern societies and the philosophies of classical Chinese and Hindu cultures are not the only such views that limit the accountability of the state in its dealings with the population. In an immense temporal and spatial leap from China and India, one can see that the practices of the Soviet Union also present an excellent illustration, albeit in modern terminology, of a system in which effective grievance procedures are absent. It is sufficient to read Alexandr Solzhenitsyn's *The Gulag Archipelago* (any of the three volumes will do) for the distinct impression that, at least during Stalin's regime, complaints against governmental or bureaucratic behavior caused drastic, and mostly fatal, consequences for the individual daring or misguided enough to complain.

More leeway concerning complaints in the Soviet Union may be evident in the 1970s, but only when the complaints are positive or what is here termed *constructive*. That is, complaints about the inefficiency of state organs are received and acted upon by the Soviet apparatus, and the pages of *Pravda* frequently report some shortcomings or serious faults of various officials. These rebukes are given because it serves the party's purpose: such public reprimands and exhortations are to increase production and to reinforce the political socialization process. But if an individual's complaint concerns rights that can be satisfied only at the expense of the state and/or party, the Soviet citizen has little effective protection. To complain against official policies and one's treatment by the bureaucracy most assuredly provokes the wrath of the state. The individual in the Soviet Union is reduced to the strange position of being grateful for what the state does not do *to* one's person rather than attempting to get the state to do something *for* the individual.

Valery Chalidze[9] presented an excellent description of the standing of the Soviet citizen vis-à-vis the state and the doctrine of state supremacy in the Soviet Union. Chalidze wrote that Soviet law has become an instrument to maintain the primacy and supremacy of the state over the rights of the individuals, and he cited a paragraph from the Soviet criminal code: "Although coming under the indicia of an act specified in criminal law, an act is not criminal if it was committed in a state of extreme necessity; that is, to eliminate a danger threatening the interests of the Soviet State. . . ."[10] Soviet law thus allows the concept of "extreme necessity" in protecting the interests of the state without any measure of accountability. Chalidze noted that this concept is very convenient for those officials who, under the guise of protecting the interests of the state, have violated the rights of the individual.

The entire concept of an impartial grievance procedure against bureaucratic mistreatment is totally absent in the Soviet Union, and the Soviet citizen does not have access to an effective avenue of redress. The Soviet state simply does not allow itself to be placed in the position of defendant and it does not recognize its liability. The concept of sovereign immunity—deriving from the czars and *rex gratia dei* but now with an independent existence—is well entrenched in the Soviet Union, and its application far surpasses the use of sovereign immunity in the Western democracies. The current Soviet treatment of dissident intellectuals and prospective Jewish emigres are examples of the inability of Soviet citizens to be protected from administrative mistreatment when their actions run counter to national interests. The simple and legitimate request for an exit visa opens the individual to a series of administrative sanctions: loss of job, demands for financial reimbursement for the "cost" of one's education, and psychological harassments. Complaining about these privations and harassments only leads to greater mistreatment by the bureaucracy. Finally, to retaliate against those individuals who do not have enough sense to stop pursuing their rights, the Soviet state has increasingly turned to prosecutions on trumped-up criminal charges and, in some instances, by simply declaring the complaining individual to be a psychotic and locking him away in an insane asylum.[11]

The above comments on China, India, and the Soviet Union are but three examples that demonstrate the *usual* state of affairs regarding the lack of standing of the individual vis-à-vis the governmental apparatus and the primacy of the state over the individual. Although not very supportive of the individual, this doctrine is engrained in the sociopolitical fabric of most societies. The list of cultures similar to the above three, with only slight variations, is almost endless: Germany under the Nazis, Franco's Spain, Salazar's Portugal, South Africa, the military juntas of South and Central America, the less developed countries of Africa and Asia. The historical and contemporary norm is to deny the liability of the state and not to permit effective avenues of redress.

This book, when it discusses the processes in the Western democracies, is in a real sense discussing the exceptions to the historical norm, the outliers, the abnormal and atypical cases. But the West's abnormality is only of recent vintage, because for most of their history, even the Western democracies refused to permit the state to be placed in the uncomfortable position of defendant. Much of the European experience (and by extension, the American experience) leading to the contemporary avenues of redress was basically a process of overcoming the doctrines of *rex gratia dei* and sovereign immunity. Although not rooted in a Confucian philosophy or in a Hindu caste system or even in a Stalinist terror regime, the West's record in the past is very spotty in providing effective redress. The rest of this chapter traces the development of these redress processes in relation to *rex gratia dei* and sovereign immunity in some Western democracies.

The concept of *rex gratia dei* and the related doctrine of sovereign immunity, although having their roots in prehistory, perhaps reached their purest expression and application during the feudal age in Western Europe. The entire feudal system, resting upon a code of personal rights and obligations among the different levels of society, was a pyramidical structure with the serfs on the bottom and the king at the apex. The serfs owed allegiance to the lord of the manor, and in return for the lord's protection, the serfs tilled the land for, and delivered most of the crops to, the manor lord. The collection of local knights would fight for the lord in exchange for upkeep, and the services of these knights could be used to fulfill the lord's obligations to the regional duke. The regional duke, in turn, owed allegiance to the king and had to provide the king with the necessary economic and military support. The king, although at the apex of this temporal feudal pyramid, was not entirely free of personal obligations: the feudal king, being king by the grace of God—*rex gratia dei*—was obligated to abide by God's law, just as the dukes abided by the king's law and the serfs abided by the manor lord's law.

The above is a very simplified description of the feudal organization, but it is sufficient for this discussion. The pyramidical structure of feudalism was of pristine inambiguity, because all segments and classes in society "knew their place," and the lines defining superiors and inferiors were not blurred. The doctrine of *rex gratia dei*, or king by the grace of God, was a necessary component in this structure. The divine right of kings theory says, in effect, that the king receives his power to rule from God and not from the people. With this view, little if any popular input goes into the decision-making process, and the king is subject to no power on earth, but he is subject to God's law. One could not complain against the king's actions, for this in essence would be a revolt against God. Thus "sovereign immunity": the king can do no (temporal) wrong and cannot be held accountable or tried in any temporal tribunal.

But the king's behavior had some limits, because the baggage of *rex gratia dei* included the obligation to obey God's law. During the Middle Ages and throughout the feudal system, it was the pope who (sometimes) attempted to exert a tempering influence upon the king's actions. Europe was Catholic, and although the kings received their authority from God, the pope, as interpreter of God's law and will on earth, was often successful in maintaining some semblance of ethical behavior on the part of the sovereigns. Of course, much of the popes' intercessions were based more on *realpolitik* and the political interests of the papacy than on any pious devotion to morality; nevertheless, the feudal kings were seen to be obligated to God through the pope. It was the pope who crowned the kings and emperors, and thus the pope formally legitimized *rex gratia dei*.[12] The Protestant Reformation freed many sovereigns from the pope's titular control, and in several countries, *rex gratia dei* did not then have whatever tempting or civilizing input the pope may have been able to employ. The Protestant version of *rex gratia dei* allowed the kings to interpret God's law themselves, and in these societies, the quasi-control of the pope was removed.

Rex gratia dei gave moral and religious justification to sovereign immunity, although each has an independent existence. The pyramidical feudal organization, similar in structure at each level, did not allow one's inferiors to complain about the actions of those in a position of dominance. The situation at the national level—the king and his court—was a mirror image of the serfs in the fields. The feudal ideology created and legitimized a complex network of courts but imposed severe restrictions on its use. The local manor lord established a "court" to adjudicate disputes and enforce whatever legal codes applied to his serfs, but the lord, obviously, could not be tried in his own court. That is, the manor lord was immune from suits or complaints from those below him, for example, the serfs. The local manor lord had sovereign immunity—he was the judge and he could not be held liable for his actions or be a defendant in his own court. The lord was, of course, liable for judicial proceedings in his superiors' courts—the duke's and the king's court—but he maintained sovereign immunity vis-à-vis those "below" him.

Sovereign immunity continued and flourished up the pyramid until the king was reached: since everyone in society was below the king, the king's court could bring action against anyone, and thus everyone was liable and a possible defendant; since no temporal being was superior to the king, the king could not be a defendant in any temporal court. The king, according to the feudal ideology, might have been subject to God's law, but this gave little solace to those individuals who felt wronged by the king. Since this ideology held that the king could do no wrong, it was a very small and easy step to say that the king could not authorize others to do wrong. The king's agents were acting for the king in an official capacity, and the king's personal immunity extended to his agents. Sovereign immunity thus evolved from the king's own person to his household to his agents and then to the modern bureaucratic apparatus (even if there were no longer a king). The bureaucracies of the Western democracies are only the logical outgrowth of the king's household, and even today, many civil servants are "servants of the crown."

This concept of sovereign immunity is complex and can affect the individual in two ways. First, the state can simply *refuse* to permit the existence of any avenue of redress, claiming that the king can do no wrong and thus cannot authorize his agents to do wrong. As shown above, this refusal in the past was based upon *rex gratia dei* and, after *rex gratia dei* was discredited, upon the unadorned doctrine of sovereign immunity and the inherent power and supremacy of the state when in conflict with an individual. In this situation, the individual had no standing to bring a complaint against the bureaucracy. The second application of sovereign immunity came much later, and it is still in effect in several countries: the state may permit avenues of redress to operate, but such processes cannot be used until and unless the state grants to the individual prior permission or the right of access to these procedures.

This later version of sovereign immunity slightly alters the classical conception but does not change it in any fundamental manner. By requiring the state's prior permission before redress can be sought simply means that the king and/or his agents (the bureaucracy) determine whether the state should be held accountable for its actions and placed in the position of defendant. The necessity of "prior permission" severely limits the individual's right to redress, and there is little practical difference between this version of sovereign immunity and the one that claims the king can do no wrong: it is easy to conclude that the state will not grant permission to pursue avenues of redress if any indication exists that the individual's claim might have some validity. Any system of redress that requires the future "defendant's" approval *before* redress can actually be sought, however impartial the subsequent procedure may be, still places the state in a position of dominance over the individual, and the individual, at least on one level of analysis, is no different from the feudal serf who pleads hat-in-hand with his manor lord.

The individual, to be able to seek redress against the state, thus had to overcome three successive obstacles: (1) *rex gratia dei*, (2) the traditional version of sovereign immunity, and (3) prior approval, the most recent version of sovereign immunity. The following remarks trace the transformation of the standing of the individual vis-à-vis the state by a discussion of the dismantling of *rex gratia dei*; the arrival of the notion that the king can do wrong, but only if he admits it and allows the individual to complain; and the contemporary doctrine and practice in several Western democracies that freely place the state in the role of defendant and make it accountable for its actions.

The doctrine of sovereign immunity, deriving from *rex gratia dei* but not dependent upon it, was one of the political foundations of the European feudal system, and it remained unaltered for centuries. It was not until the seventeenth century that cracks began to appear, for during the 1600s, at least in England and by extension in the other Anglo-Saxon cultures, two violent assaults on *rex gratia dei* occurred, bringing about the beginning of the slow erosion of sovereign immunity. These assaults were primarily philosophical arguments, although actual behavior in the 1600s was an additional attack. The two English philosophical assaults came from Thomas Hobbes (1588–1679) and John Locke (1632–1704). The writings of Hobbes and Locke, along with the actual events in England during the seventeenth century—especially the execution of Charles I in 1649 and the Glorious Revolution of 1688–1689—demolished the concept of *rex gratia dei* in England and, with hindsight, was the beginning of the slow dismantling of sovereign immunity. Hobbes argued against *rex gratia dei* but did not reduce the significance of sovereign immunity; Locke delivered the final blow against *rex gratia dei*, and he began the assault on sovereign immunity, a process that was not completed until the twentieth century.

Hobbes and Locke lived and wrote during a turbulent period of English social and political history. Elizabeth I (the second of Henry VIII's three children) died in 1603 without any direct heirs, and the crown passed to a cousin, James of Scotland. James I (1603–1625) was a firm believer in the divine right of kings theory and acted upon the belief that he was indeed king by the grace of God. He ruled for several years with the embryonic Parliament dissolved, and he also alienated both Catholics and the various Protestant sects with his policies. James I was intolerant in matters of religion, and various sects were severely discriminated against. (In fact, one such sect, the Puritans, left England and landed at Plymouth in 1620.)

James I was followed by Charles I (1625–1649), and Charles I had the same notions about the divine right of kings as did his predecessor. Charles I was continually at odds with Parliament (*rex gratia dei* does not admit input from the people into the decision-making process), but Parliament retaliated in 1628. One of the most famous and enduring components of the English constitutional system and behavior patterns was voted by Parliament in 1628, and this document was specifically directed at Charles I. Called the "petition of right," it stated, in part, that all taxes not debated, voted on, and approved by Parliament were illegal, null, and void. Accepted by Charles I, the petition of right gave effective control of the purse and all public revenue bills to Parliament. But Parliament was soon dissolved by Charles I, and the king continued to disregard Parliament until 1642 when war credits and funding—a military appropriation bill—were needed for a military campaign in Scotland. Called into session after a long absence, Parliament reacted against Charles I by not only refusing to vote the money but also by passing a resolution forbidding the king to dissolve Parliament again without the consent of Parliament. The lines were drawn, the proposed military campaign in Scotland became irrelevant, and a civil war ensued between the forces loyal to the king and the parliamentary forces.

The civil war was bitterly although intermittently fought from 1642 to 1649, and this period witnessed the effective erosion of legitimate state authority. The parliamentary side was victorious, and Charles I was publicly beheaded in 1649. This beheading was a massive and bloody blow struck against *rex gratia dei*, but it did not entirely remove the concept from England. However, Charles I's execution was a major watershed in the transformation from *rex gratia dei* to *rex gratia populi* ("king by the grace of the people"). The following decade, 1649–1659, was also a turbulent period. Oliver Cromwell, head of the victorious Parliamentary Army, ruled as "protector of the Commonwealth" and abolished both the House of Lords and the position of monarch. Cromwell died in 1659, and his son Richard attempted to follow his father as protector but was unable to maintain himself in office. The position of protector disappeared, the Commonwealth system disintegrated, and Parliament returned to traditional authority after the charismatic interlude.

In 1659 Parliament *invited* (another blow at *rex gratia dei*) Charles II to rule as king, and the House of Lords was organized anew. Charles II ruled from 1660 to 1685, and he was aware that it was Parliament, and not God, that invited him to rule. But in 1685 James II followed his father, and it appears that James II either was unaware of the past eighty years or simply chose to disregard the changes. James II was an avowed Roman Catholic in what was by then a predominantly Protestant England, and he perceived nothing wrong with the divine right of kings. Fearful of an extension of royal power at the expense of the prerogatives it had gained and fearful of a reemergence of Catholicism, the Protestant Parliament demanded that James II abdicate, and Parliament then invited William and Mary of Orange to accept the titles of king and queen and to rule jointly.

This invitation issued to William and Mary (William III and Mary II) in late 1688-early 1689 is known as the Glorious Revolution. This event may not have appeared very glorious to James II and his supporters, but it was a bloodless, nonviolent palace coup d'état. James II probably realized that he might have suffered the same fate as Charles I had he resisted the abdication order, so he left for France. The Glorious Revolution of 1688–89 finally put an end to the divine right of kings theory in England and the rest of the Anglo-Saxon cultures. No monarch since James II has dared resurrect the view that he or she was chosen by and therefore was responsible only to God and not the people. England was thus in the forefront of demolishing *rex gratia dei*. France had to endure exactly one hundred more years of *rex gratia dei* until the guillotine struck another massive blow in 1789; Russia endured until 1917, but Czar Nicholas too, went to his death proclaiming God's authority.

The philosophical assaults by Hobbes and Locke are as important as the physical assaults on *rex gratia dei*. Hobbes's *Leviathan* was published in 1651, two years after Charles I was beheaded and during the second year of Cromwell's protectorate, although the book was written before 1651, most likely during the civil war of 1642–1649. Hobbes studied at Oxford and "graduated" in 1609 at age twenty-one. He came from a well-to-do family; he traveled widely, especially in France, and had a comfortable existence in the aristocratic circles of England and France. He was a Royalist and spent several years in self-imposed exile in France over fears to his safety from the parliamentary forces. But he returned to England in 1651 because his views on religion—he was an outspoken atheist—ran into severe opposition from the French church. He "recanted" his past associations with and allegiance to the Royalists and accommodated himself to Cromwell's protectorate as well as to the subsequent restoration of the Stuarts with Charles II in 1660.

It is important that Hobbes argued against the divine right of kings doctrine but *not* against sovereign immunity. In fact, Hobbes's defense of sovereign immunity far surpassed any defense offered for it during the feudal age. However, his attack on *rex gratia dei* was the first coherent attack on the primacy of the king and set the stage for subsequent writers (especially Locke) to begin the assault against sovereign immunity itself. Hobbes's assault on *rex gratia dei*—and his defense of sovereign immunity—derived from his concept of the contract theory of government.

The *Leviathan* presents Hobbes's philosophical description of his version of the origins of government and organized civil society, based upon the contract theory. Of course, competing theories on the origin of the state deny the social contract view that the people, willingly and rationally and voluntarily, come together and establish a state. Fascist doctrine, especially the Nazi variety, held that the state's origins evolved from the irrational, mystical spirit of the people, and Marxist theory held that the state was created (and would eventually disappear) through the operation of mechanistic and deterministic economic laws. Both were also violent attacks on *rex gratia dei* but *not* on sovereign immunity. The discussion here, however, is limited to the contract theory.

Hobbes's basic assumption was that man is nasty and life in the "state of nature" is a perpetual condition of interpersonal violence. The term *state of nature*, favored by many political philosophers, refers to that period, eons ago, when things such as governments, states, kings, and organizations did not exist—the only things that existed in the state of nature were people and the natural environment. For Hobbes, life in that state of nature was a struggle for survival, with continual fear and danger of death; the life of man was "solitary, poor, nasty, brutish, and short." The way out of this morass was seen to be man's fear of the violent death awaiting him, and this fear separated man from animal in the state of nature. Man began to see the need for some sort of organization (government) with enough power and authority to protect each person from harm. This, for Hobbes, was the origin and reason of governments and political institutions: government was established to manage conflict, and only the existence of this government prevented a return to the anarchial state of nature. Thus it is the people who create a government to protect themselves from violence.

The mechanism of this establishment is Hobbes's version of the social contract and the contractual foundation of government. The people, acting together, cede all power to an individual, and this individual, who does not sign the contract but is its creation, is then expected to protect the people. The people become subjects and create the sovereign, and then the sovereign exercises legitimate power over the subjects. Government is thus created by a voluntary agreement among the people, and the sovereign is also created. In a direct and immediate sense, this view denies *rex gratia dei* and, in its place, says *rex gratia populi*—king by the grace of the people. The sovereign and the people are now more or less on an equal footing rather than having the sovereign claim an exalted heritage. The very essence of the contract theory, whatever its particular content, refutes *rex gratia dei*, and the king no longer has an obligation only to God but also to the people who created him. Hobbes's writings were an influential attack on *rex gratia dei*, and the doctrine was never quite the same, at least for the Anglo-Saxon cultural societies, after the publication of *Leviathan* and, of course, after the events in England from 1642 to 1688.

But for every single stone that Hobbes demolished in the edifice termed *rex gratia dei*, he unfortunately erected two stones in the sovereign immunity edifice. For Hobbes, the sovereign had no obligations whatsoever (except, of course, to prevent the reemergence of anarchy); he had rights. The people now have the obligations—follow the directives of the sovereign. The sovereign cannot act illegally, for he alone is the source of all laws, and it is he who determines what is legal. Thus the people-turned-subjects cannot complain that the sovereign has acted illegally or outside the bounds of the contract. The only "law" that existed for Hobbes was man-made positive law, and he denied the existence of ethical principles. Hobbes's sovereign could not act unjustly or authorize unjust acts—no higher ethical standards existed; the sovereign could not act illegally or authorize illegal behavior—the sovereign was the sole source of the law, and the law was therefore whatever he said it was. Hobbes thus raised sovereign immunity to a new level, although it was now divorced from *rex gratia dei*. The people, after the voluntary and rational cession of all rights to the sovereign, had no standing to complain against the acts of the sovereign or his agents. It is not relevant whether the sovereign power was one person acting as king—as Hobbes preferred—or a representative parliament—which Hobbes grudgingly admitted—since it was the nature of the sovereign that carried immunity and not its specific form. The doctrine of "parliamentary supremacy" in present-day Great Britain has a direct and immediate link to Hobbes's views.

Whatever stones Hobbes might have left standing with *rex gratia dei* were demolished by John Locke and the events of 1688–1689, and, fortunately, Locke began to chip away at the mortar holding sovereign immunity intact. Locke also ascribed to the contract theory of government, although his version was distinct from Hobbes's. Locke was a contemporary of Hobbes and thus wrote during the same turbulent period of English political upheaval. Except for a four-year period, 1679–1683, Locke spent from 1675 to 1689 in political exile, first in France and then in the Netherlands. Locke returned to England soon after James II abdicated and served in a variety of government posts from 1689 until his death in 1704. Locke's major work is *Two Treatises of Government*, published in 1690 but written before the Glorious Revolution.

For Locke, governments were established to achieve two goals: to make the content of natural law clear to every member of society and to ensure that violations of the law do not remain unpunished. Locke, like Hobbes, was a firm believer in the contractual foundation of government: the people, willingly and voluntarily, come together and agree to establish a civil society with a sovereign and a government. But Locke's contract is the opposite of Hobbes's. Whereas Hobbes's contract was signed only by the people, and these people gave up all of their rights to the sovereign (they in a sense said "rule us and we will submit without complaint"), Locke's contract was a trust arrangement, and the sovereign existed only to carry out the will of the people. The sovereign had to perform what the people decided, and if he refused to abide by the population's mandate, the people could remove him from office. The change from James II to William III in 1688–1689 can be interpreted simply as a situation where the people removed the sovereign because the terms of the contract were not followed. This trust arrangement is organized similar to any modern fiduciary trust agreement with a trustor, a trustee, and a beneficiary.

According to Locke, the *trustor* is the people, the *trustee* is the government and the sovereign, and the *beneficiary* is also the people. The sovereign as trustee is created by the people-trustor through the contract, and the sovereign must sign the agreement containing all the clauses and stipulations. Moreover, the people and not the sovereign determine what the people's best interests are. The people as trustor create the contract, decide upon its terms and content, decide how the resources are to be used, and then they hire the sovereign-trustee to do the everyday and mundane work of administering the agreement. The sovereign must abide by the terms of the contract and pursue the best interest of the people as defined by the people or be fired (voted out of office, exiled, beheaded).

The bitter conflict between former President Nixon and the press, Congress, the special prosecutors, and the Supreme Court can be approached through the contract and the nature of the sovereign's power. Nixon was arguing the Hobbesian position: the president as sovereign had the sole right to determine what the best interests of the people and society were and the surrender of subpoenaed tapes was not in the "best interests" of society. The special prosecutor argued the Lockean approach: the president is only a hired hand (the trustee), and it is for the people and the people's representatives to determine their own best interests. The Lockean conception that the sovereign is a hired hand who has no claims to the nation's resources and no special insights to the people's best interests and who can be fired at will was given practical application during those weeks in July and August 1974.

Locke's view of the contract as a trust arrangement was the final blow, in England, against *rex gratia dei*. His *Treatises* were also the beginning of the slow erosion of sovereign immunity. Since Locke was a firm believer in natural law and ethical principles (life, liberty, and property), his sovereign was not the sole source of law as was Hobbes's. Locke's sovereign was bound by natural law, and thus the sovereign's power had definite limits. With Locke, the sovereign could do wrong and could authorize his agents to do wrong: either an act that was prohibited by the contract or an act that was prohibited by natural law.

Although it is an exaggeration to argue that Locke actually stripped away sovereign immunity, he did argue that the king could do wrong, a concept Hobbes did not accept, and this set the stage for a slow process that culminated in a formal avenue to force the king to make amends for such wrongs. Thus, in England, from a combination of the events of 1642 to 1688 and the writing of Hobbes and Locke, the concept of *rex gratia dei* was put to rest, and it was recognized that the king could err. What remained was to transform this crucial recognition of the state's ability to do an individual wrong to a functioning system of redress. This transformation did not occur until the twentieth century.

The legal status of an individual in the United Kingdom who wanted to pursue a complaint against the state was practically nonexistent until the mid-twentieth century.[13] Individuals with complaints against the state (that is, the king) would meekly and humbly present their claims to the sovereign, and if the king so ruled, the matter would then be referred to a court. This process of requesting leave to complain was known as a *petition of right*. The individual who felt wronged by the king could have his case heard and adjudicated only if he received prior permission to complain through the granting of a petition of right. Harry Street wrote that a standard procedure for requesting such petitions was established in England during the reign of Edward I, and no real procedural changes were made after the fourteenth century.[14] Any individual whose petition of right was not granted—leave to sue was not given—was totally remediless and had no legitimate avenues of redress open.

The petition of right process fell into disuse beginning in the fifteenth century because of its quite complicated procedural requirements, but it was revived in the nineteenth century. The 1800s witnessed a total transformation of English societal patterns and organizations, and, alongside this societal transformation, the perceived relationships between the state and the individual also changed. The nineteenth century brought the industrial revolution, economic growth and development, a modern warmaking capacity, governmental activity in fiscal and monetary policy, the development of the modern state structure and the rise of the bureaucracy, and the participation of the state in areas that previously were the sole preserve of the private sector. Specifically, the number and scope of governmental contracts with private individuals increased enormously, and, along with the contracts, came the inevitable disputes that the contractors attempted to settle by employing the traditional petition of right. The four hundred-year-old traditional rules of procedure governing the petitions of right were, however, no longer applicable to nineteenth-century conditions, and the process was altered.

The Petition of Right Act (1860) was passed in response to the changing relationship between the state and the individual. This act simplified and streamlined the procedure for requesting leave to sue compared to the fourteenth-century process, but, significantly, the 1860 act did *not* abolish the requirement of prior permission to sue, and if such permission were not granted, the individual still remained remediless. The petition of right could be granted only with the approval of the attorney-general (an agent of the king) and, as Street explained, the attorney-general had an unqualified discretion to grant or refuse the petition in individual cases, and such discretion was widely used.[15] The import of the 1860 act should not be minimized, however, This act gave statutory legislative recognition to the view that the state could be placed in the role of defendant and thus be liable for its actions. The classical doctrine of sovereign immunity was broached, for now there were recognizable areas of state misbehavior rather than the absolute claim that the king could do no wrong. This recognition was of and by itself a watershed, even though the individual still required—and often did not receive—the state's permission to sue. It would have been a quantum leap for the state to have moved in one step from total sovereign immunity to total liability. The 1860 Petition of Right Act was thus the intermediate stage in the development of the right to complain against the state.

The period 1860–1927 represented the next stage in the inevitable progress toward the state as defendant in the United Kingdom, and it demonstrated a major shortcoming of the 1860 act. Even in those circumstances where the attorney-general approved a petition of right, it was the individual civil servant or bureaucrat, and *not* the crown, who was the defendant in any complaints filed by an individual. Whatever the content of an award in favor of an individual, it was directed at the civil servant and not at the agency or at the government as a whole. The individual civil servant rarely had the financial resources to honor such a judgment, and thus whatever victory the individual might have won vis-à-vis the government was in reality without substance (a judgment that called for financial compensation but did not deliver such compensation brings very little redress to the individual). To remedy this situation, the lord chancellor in 1921 appointed a committee that presented its findings and proposals six years later in 1927. A draft bill was proposed to make the crown directly suable, as well as to abolish the requirements of the petition of right, but the bill was not passed.

A subterfuge was then employed for the next twenty years. This practice involved a suit against the individual civil servant, but the crown then paid any awarded damages (the crown itself was not sued). However, this practice necessitated the naming of fictitious civil servants to stand in for the government. All parties concerned were aware of the fictitious nature of the defendant, and the process worked reasonably well until after World War II. The House of Lords condemned the use of fictitious defendants in 1946, and in 1947 the court of appeal dismissed a case on the grounds that it had no jurisdiction over a fictitious defendant. The situation appeared to be at an impasse, and it was obvious that a new procedure was necessary.

The inability to sue fictitious or nominal defendants, the large number of accidents involving governmental vehicles during World War II, and the increased nationalization program of the postwar Labour government (which gave rise to the fear that more areas would be protected by sovereign immunity) all combined to resurrect the 1927 proposed bill. On February 13, 1947, the government introduced the Crown Proceedings Bill in Parliament. The bill was passed on July 31, 1947, and entered into force on January 1, 1948.[16] The 1947 Crown Proceedings Act abolished the necessity of the petition of right—prior permission was no longer required—and the act also made the crown directly suable without the need of having a fictitious civil servant as defendant.

The United Kingdom thus moved from classical sovereign immunity where the king could do no wrong to a situation where the state was suable, could be placed in the position of defendant, and was held accountable for its actions. Practically all of the limitations and responsibilities and liabilities that were incumbent on the private individual are now applied to the government, and the individual can bring suit in the courts for an alleged violation of a central personal liberty or for bureaucratic maladministration.

The situation in the United States regarding state liability has turned several full circles. Before the American Revolution, the colonies were operating under the English legislation described above (a cumbersome petition of right procedure). With the Constitution, however, the United States recognized governmental liability, although it was not stated explicitly. Article 3 (2) of the Constitution states that the federal courts' jurisdiction extends to ". . . controversies to which the United States shall be a party; . . . between two or more States, between a State and citizens of another State; . . . and foreign States, Citizens or Subjects." The controlling phrase in article 3 (2) is "between a State and citizens of another State," for this obviously intended that the state could be sued. In fact, this construction was upheld in 1793 when *Chisholm v. Georgia*[17] held that, indeed, a citizen of one state could sue another state. Thus the very earliest situation in the United States recognized that the state could err and sovereign immunity was not applicable.

This situation did not last long, however. The individual state governments were at that time on shallow financial grounds—many were heavily in debt—and the states immediately saw the financial implications of being liable for their actions in a court, with possible financial compensation as a judgment. Several states protested *Chisholm v. Georgia,* as well as against article 3 (2), to Congress, and one year after the *Chisholm* decision, Congress proposed the Eleventh Amendment. The Eleventh Amendment was ratified in 1798, and it effectively overruled *Chisholm* and qualified article 3 (2): "The Judicial power of the United States shall not be construed to extend to any suit in law or equity, commenced or prosecuted against one of the United States by Citizens of another State, or by Citizens or Subjects of any Foreign State." Various court decisions refined the Eleventh Admendment: a citizen of one state could not sue another state; a citizen could not sue his own state without its consent (the equivalent of the English petition of right); a state could not sue the United States; and a citizen could not sue the United States. The view that the king could do no wrong was resurrected, and the doctrine of sovereign immunity was reasserted.

We thus see a society that rebelled against royal prerogatives and sovereign immunity, and a society based upon the view that the "people" and not the government are sovereign, reestablish the English doctrine of sovereign immunity. A leading American constitutional scholar, Walter Gellhorn, offered an excellent explanation of why sovereign immunity—again, a doctrine of an absolute monarch against popular government—was invoked in the United States: "(I)ts survival in the United States after the Revolutionary War is attributable . . . to the financial instability of the infant American states rather than to the stability of the doctrine's theoretical foundations."[18] The doctrine's theoretical foundations were, in fact, hardly questioned until the late 1800s, but such justifications have a hollow sound when read in the latter twentieth century. Two such statements serve as illustration:

A sovereign is exempt from suit, not because of any formal conception or obsolete theory, but on the logical and practical ground that there can be no legal right as against the authority that makes the law on which the right depends.[19]

and

It would be inconsistent with the very idea of supreme executive power, and would endanger the performance of the public duties of the sovereign to subject him to repeated suits as a matter of right, at the will of any citizen, and to submit to the judicial tribunals the control and disposition of his public property, his instruments and means of carrying on the government in war and in peace, and the money in his treasury.[20]

But these judicial pronouncements did not satisfy public opinion in the United States, and, just as the states rebelled against article 3 (2), the people were not content with no real remedy against actions of the state. Individuals who felt wronged by the state were blocked from seeking redress in the courts, so they turned to Congress for compensation. If Congress accepted the petition—something that was not automatic—and judged that the individual had indeed been wronged, it would then pass a "private bill" to compensate the individual, payable from the Treasury. This process of petitioning Congress really did not do justice to the individual and was beginning to take up more and more of Congress' time and energies.[21] The complaints against this procedure led, in 1855, to the Court of Claims Act. This act created the Court of Claims, sitting in Washington, with three members appointed by the president to hear claims against the government—but not *tort* ("a wrong done to another person") claims—and submit the hearing record and their recommendation to Congress for a final decision. This did not effectively reduce congressional involvement, because the relevant congressional committee had to reread the record, and, if the committee decided in favor of the individual, a private bill still had to be pushed through both the House and Senate. In 1863 the Court of Claims was reorganized into a five-person tribunal with the ability to render judgments, and in 1868 the decisions of the court of claims were made appealable to the Supreme Court. This reduced Congress' role somewhat, but since the Court of Claims had jurisdiction only over contracts, all claims in tort were still subject to congressional acceptance and review.

It was not until the twentieth century that the United States increased the area of governmental liability. From about 1900 to World War II, various suits against the United States were allowed: patent infringement, maritime torts, and administrative settlement of claims such as federal employees' compensation, postal claims, and claims against various governmental public corporations. But the basic doctrine of sovereign immunity still remained with torts and Congress was once again, as it was in the 1800s, flooded with petitions for redress through private bills. Franklin D. Roosevelt's New Deal had a direct and immediate impact upon both the government's and public's view of sovereign immunity in the 1930s. The United States was now a society with welfare and social security as a stated goal, and more and more people came to believe that sovereign immunity should give way to sovereign responsibility.

As mentioned above, Congress was inundated with petitions of redress for actions in tort that could not be submitted to the Court of Claims. Street indicated, for example, that the 74th and 75th Congress each entertained more than twenty-three hundred petitions for private bills for compensation exceeding $100 million.[22] The changing nature of American society, the view that the government should be more responsible for its actions, the enormous number of incidences during World War II that did not lead to effective redress (accidents involving military vehicles), public disillusionment with the political favoritism involved in private bills, and congressional belief that they were spending more and more time on nonlegislative matters—all of these factors combined, and in 1946 the Federal Tort Claims Act was passed. The Federal Tort Claims Act, as Title IV of the Legislative Reorganization Act, renounced sovereign immunity over certain claims in tort against the United States. Jurisdiction over these claims were given to the federal district courts with the usual route of appeal. Of course, the Federal Tort Claims Act had several limitations—it did not represent a total abandonment of sovereign immunity—but it did give the individual in certain functional areas access to a system of redress via the federal court structure. Congress' role was severely minimized, and, in fact, the Tort Claims Act was introduced under the heading "More Efficient Use of Congressional Time." The United States government was now liable for its actions and could be placed in the role of defendant in the courts.[23]

The development of state liability in France roughly paralleled that in

Anglo-America, but it is much more significant because of the nature of the French sovereign. The feudal system with a divine right king at the apex was perhaps best illustrated in France, and the country totally denied any state responsibility, resting upon the twin notions of divine right of kings and sovereign immunity. The Revolution of 1789, however, started the slow erosion of state immunity. Statutes passed in 1789 and 1790 allowed individuals to sue public officials and bureaucrats for damages arising from the latter's activities. The agency or the state was not liable—only the civil servant in his individual capacity was—although this right was limited. The individual citizen required prior permission (a petition of right) from the *Conseil d'État* before suing an official. The *Conseil d'État* was for a long time under the direct control of the government; such permission was rarely granted and even then with difficulty. This prior permission to sue an individual was done away with in 1870, and from that time, French bureaucrats could be sued *without* the consent of the government for individual acts and only in a private capacity (*"fautes personnelles"*). A *faute personnelle* involves only the liability of the individual—not his agency or the government—and such cases are heard in the civil court structure.

The *Conseil d'État*, in 1872, had its area of juristiction extended to suits against the *départements* and the *communes*. The French recognized that "justice" was not the automatic output of governmental agencies, and it was not relevant whether a specific action could be traced to an individual bureaucrat. The *Conseil d'État* built up special rules concerning governmental liability, and several cases were decided on the doctrine of "bad administrative practice." The *Conseil d'Etat* also employed the view, when determining state liability, that the state may be liable for any damages caused a citizen even though there was no "legal" fault. The French *Conseil d'Etat*, discussed in greater detail in chapter 3, does provide an effective system of redress against the French government in its dealings with private citizens.

The classical Chinese concept of the mandate of heaven or, in modern Western terminology, the doctrines of *rex gratia dei* and sovereign immunity have been altered and tempered. Twentieth-century democracies no longer protect themselves behind feudal doctrines that originally meant to establish the absolute authority of the monarch over popular government, in some areas, over the claims of a universal church. Individual citizens in Western democracies who believe they have a legitimate claim against the state are no longer ignored or forced to rely upon the goodwill or innate sense of justice a society may, or may not have, regarding the relations between the state and the individual. A complex set of systems and procedures have been established to allow, and even encourage, the citizen to complain, to place the state in a position of defendant, and to seek redress for grievances.

The following six functional chapters present a public policy and non-juridical discussion of some of the major systems of redress available in

Western democracies. The presentation and discussion focuses on these processes' efficiency—efficiency in terms of time and expense. A procedure that entails high costs to the individual to pursue his or her complaint may make the process prohibitive for all but a small minority, but it is usually this affluent minority that is *not* abused by the bureaucracy. To be efficient and effective, a system of redress must be readily available to all economic levels, not just to those who can afford it. Also, if a certain avenue of redress requires inordinate time between the filing of a complaint and the final decision, a favorable decision for the individual, if offered years later, may only be a hollow or symbolic redress procedure. In other words, ponderous proceedings may be clothed in constitutional legalisms and safeguards, but such ponderous proceedings often do not work at the individual level. What is needed in many grievance situations is rapid response, not a drawn-out judicial process.

A second level of analysis is the degree to which the population accepts these procedures as right and proper—as legitimate conflict-management and conflict-resolution structures—and the degree of public esteem these institutionalized avenues enjoy. Are these bodies, and their resulting decisions, perceived as fair and impartial, or are they perceived simply as another instrument of state control and oppression or as window-dressing propaganda of a nonresponsive state?

Related to this question of public acceptance and esteem is the actual output of grievance proceedings: do they have any observable bias in the sense of ruling in favor of the state or does the individual have a reasonable expectation that the decision will be in his favor? A system of redress that always finds for the bureaucracy is most certainly suspect as a redress structure. The staffing policies—personnel, lines of authority and communication, responsibility— are relevant, since, depending upon such policies, there might be a built-in bias in favor of the bureaucracy. An individual charged with the responsibility of determining the validity of a complaint directed at his superior (a superior who controls the individual's working conditions and, perhaps, his very tenure in office) may simply not be able to operate in an effective manner. This problem is so obvious that it should be avoided but, as discussed below, too many redress systems unfortunately display this characteristic.

An additional area of discussion and evaluation concerns the "exportability" of various procedures to other cultures and societies. Since many of these grievance procedures and redress systems are intimately linked to a society's mores and value standards, it is frequently difficult to export them wholesale to a different environment. The imported model may exhibit the identical surface characteristics of the original, but its inner workings may be entirely different. Finally, the place of these redress systems in maintaining "good government" and individual rights is also discussed. These avenues of redress are posited to exist to strengthen individual dignity and consciousness, and it is these last points that are employed as the primary standard in evaluating the contribution of the relevant avenues of redress.

One of the institutionalized redress methods available is a society's regular hierarchial court structure. The United States and Great Britain emphasize this approach, although the courts are not the only avenue of redress available in these two countries, and, of course, the United States and Great Britain are not the only societies who prefer to rely on the regular court structures. Under certain circumstances, the courts can and do provide effective redress but, as beneficial as this process might be, a whole set of grievances also exists, especially in regard to the delivery of public services, that simply are not suitable to courtroom deliberations. Moreover, a country's regular court system often can be ponderous, time-consuming, and expensive for the individual seeking redress.

The example of Mr. Fitzgerald, a civilian employee of the U.S. Department of Defense, illustrates this problem of expense. Arbitrarily dismissed from his position for publicizing vast cost overruns in Defense procurement contracts, Fitzgerald had to pursue a lengthy court process before he was reinstated. He was left, however, with enormous attorneys' fees, incurred solely because he complained about his treatment by the bureaucracy. Attorneys are not expected to work for nothing, but such fees do militate against the effectiveness of the regular court structure. Although not directly linked to the courtroom process, for it is a characteristic more of the social system rather than of the process itself, one obstacle faced by an individual who wants to make use of the court system to lodge a complaint, particularly within the individual states in the United States, is that he must first overcome the doctrine of sovereign immunity. As mentioned above, the Federal Tort Claims Act applies only to federal activity, and it is not applicable to the states. Many states still invoke sovereign immunity, and an individual requires the state's permission or consent (petition of right) before filing the complaint. The contorted legal process in Ohio involved with the shootings at Kent State University by the Ohio National Guard illustrates this problem: Ohio's consent was necessary before the state could be sued, and years elapsed before the families of the dead students were able to seek effective redress.

A country's regular court system is not, however, as ineffective as the above comments may suggest. They are institutionalized, rigorous, and legitimate avenues of redress that in the long run, protect the individual from arbitrary and capricious bureaucratic behavior. The regular court hierarchy may not be the most ideal system, but it is an integral part of American and British societies, and the population is, on the whole, well-served by it.

A second method available to individuals seeking redress is a separate administrative court structure and/or specialized administrative tribunals. Many countries make extensive use of these specialized bodies (tax courts, for example), but the best example is the French *Conseil d'État*. The *Conseil d'État*, staffed by senior French civil servants, is designed, among other duties, to receive and act upon complaints from French citizens about bureaucratic insensitivities. The *Conseil* relies upon the French jurisprudential doctrine of *détournement de pouvoir* ("misuse of legitimate authority") in its decisions. The *Conseil* produces (usually) rapid but well-considered decisions with very little expense for the individual making the complaint. Even though the *Conseil* is staffed by civil servants, its decisions do not appear to show any bias in favor of the bureaucracy.

A third process is the ombudsman or "citizens' protector." The ombudsman is prevalent in Scandinavia, particularly Denmark and Sweden, although the office has been widely imitated throughout the world with mixed results. The New Zealand ombudsman, based upon the Danish model, is an effective element in that society's redress system, but several American municipalities exhibit a dismal attempt at the function (the "complaint department" at city hall), and many American universities have fared even worse with their misguided conception of the office. As the position generally functions in Scandinavia, the ombudsman serves as a problem solver, information conduit, and as Parliament's representative in the oversight function vis-à-vis bureaucratic behavior. The Scandinavian ombudsman has evolved into an institution that is perceived by the population at large to be *their* defender against bureaucratic arrogance and by the lower echelon civil servants as *their* defender against unjustified citizen complaints. The ombudsman usually produces fast decisions, acceptable to all parties, at practically no cost to the individual who requested the ombudsman's services. As described later, however, the ombudsman is a culturally based institution, and it simply cannot be exported wholesale to other societies, especially to American urban governments.

Most democratic societies also have redress available through parliamentary oversight procedures and through the legislative investigatory process, although the efficacy of this avenue varies widely. Illustrative of this method is the plethora of private bills introduced in the U.S. Congress to benefit a specific individual. Special investigatory committees have often entertained individual complaints against governmental activities, although, as is the case with a country's regular court system, this process is time-consuming and often deals with abstract political principles rather than with specific individual situations. Related to this domestic legislative oversight function, but much more difficult to evaluate the success of, is the situation where the legislature in one country attempts to employ its power and influence to protect citizens of another country from the latter's own government. The best example of this is perhaps the Vanik-Jackson Admendment to the bill granting the Soviet Union "most-favored-nation" status in its trade relations with the United States. The Vanik-Jackson Amendment requires the Soviet government to permit unhindered emigration before "most-favored-nation" status is granted. Here is an attempt by one legislature (the U.S. Congress) to protect individuals in another country (mostly the potential Russian Jewish emigres) from bureaucratic mistreatment by their own government (the denial of exit visas). The effectiveness of this system of redress for the Soviet citizen, however, still remains to be documented.

An additional avenue of redress is public international agencies and institutions—those organizations of a public, intergovernmental nature created and sustained by sovereign national states. These institutions usually have commissions, councils, and "courts" or tribunals to adjudicate a complaint from an individual against his or her government. Examples of these public international agencies of redress are the European Commission on Human Rights and the UN Commission on Human Rights. International procedures for protecting individual rights against one's government can take one of two forms. First, states may be, by international treaty obligations, "prohibited" from engaging in certain activities (protect the individual from the state), and the European Convention on Human Rights illustrates this form. Second, states may be "mandated" to act for certain groups with positive activity, and the UN Commission on Human Rights represents this second approach. Such international procedures can succeed *only* when states are already committed to protect the individual and to respect human dignity. If this prior commitment is not present, any recommendation from the international agency will be either subverted or simply ignored (that is, the Greek regime under the colonels and contemporary South Africa). But, as shown in chapter 6, the European system (European Commission and Court of Human Rights) is an effective, strong, and respected participant in providing an international avenue of redress to the citizens of the Council of Europe. It is unfortunate that the UN commission falls far short in its ability to protect an individual from the excesses of one's governmental bureaucracy.

Chapter 7 discusses what has perhaps become a very positive and successful way to achieve one's goals against a recalcitrant state. Since most, if not all, of the activities of public intergovernmental agencies are tinged with politics, many states ignore the actions of such institutions for they regard the activities as unwarranted and illegitimate political interference in their own domesitc policies. Low-key, nonpolitical, and quiet bargaining and negotiation by private, nongovernmental international agencies many times achieve results where the public "political" agencies have failed. Such private organizations—Amnesty International, the Red Cross, and HIAS (Hebrew Immigration Aid Society) are but three examples—cannot of or by themselves provide redress for the individual, but their "good offices" may aid in the path to an acceptable solution.

The final chapter in this book, "Concluding Essay," presents a brief summary of the various methods and offers comments on the future relationships between the state and the individual. Some areas of special contemporary concern are also discussed. The concluding chapter argues that any system of redress is doomed unless those people, agencies, and governments that establish redress procedures firmly believe in the desirability, need, and competence of the oversight agencies and readily submit to and honor any forthcoming decisions. Procedures, regardless of their outward attractiveness, that allow for the lodging of a complaint only with the permission of the state or that allow for execution only insofar as the content of the decision agrees with the state's prior position are hollow gestures and will not contribute to the protection of individuals from governmental and bureaucractic abuses of power.

NOTES

1. David H. Bayley, *Public Liberties in the New States* (Chicago: Rand McNally and Co., 1964), pp. 14–15.

2. Ibid., p. 15.

3. Sir Ernest Barker, *The Political Thought of Plato and Aristotle* (New York: Dover Publications, 1959), p. 1; Andrew Hacker, *Political Theory: Philosophy, Ideology, Science* (New York: The Macmillan Company, 1961), p. 23.

4. Some readers may have seen the film *One Million Years B.C.*, starring Racquel Welch and a motley collection of hideous animals. This film was a dramatization of what life might have been in the cave society: people did not converse but only grunted and gestured at one another; they ate the animals and vice versa; volcanoes erupted, and the rains came. The film is totally deficient as an art form, but as a commentary to the question at hand—the relationship between the "state" and the individual—*One Million Years B.C.* is relevant.

5. See Herrlee G. Creel, *Chinese Thought from Confucius to Mao Tse-tung* (Chicago: University of Chicago Press, 1953), especially chapter 3, "Confucius and the Struggle for Human Happiness," pp. 25–45. Creel presented an excellent discussion of the history of Chinese philosophy across three thousand years and showed how traditional attitudes have influenced contemporary China.

6. Ibid., chapter 8, "The Totalitarianism of the Legalists," pp. 135–58.

7. For what is perhaps the best brief introduction to the philosophical and political base of the Hindu caste system, see Taya Zinkin, *Caste Today* (London: Oxford University Press for the Institute of Race Relations, 1962), 69 pp.

8. D. Mackenzie Brown, *The White Umbrella: Indian Political Thought from Manu to Gandhi* (Berkeley and Los Angeles: University of California Press, 1964), p. 22.

9. Valery Chalidze, *To Defend These Rights: Human Rights and the Soviet Union*, trans. Guy Daniels (New York: Random House, 1974), chapter 1, "The Specifics of Soviet Law," pp. 3–41, esp. pp. 14–21.

10. "Fundamental Principles of Criminal Legislation," article 14, *Compilation of Laws*, vol. 2, p. 431. Cited by Chalidze, *To Defend These Rights*, p. 14.

11. For a chilling account of one man's experience with the Soviet Union's practice of incarcerating political dissenters in insane asylums, see Zhores and Roy Medvedev, *A Question of Madness*, trans. Ellen de Kadt (New York: Alfred A. Knopf, 1971). A more recent example of this can be seen with the case of General Pyotr Grigorenko. The general, one of the most famous and outspoken of the Soviet dissidents, was twice declared mentally "ill" and was committed to Soviet prison hospitals. On a visit to the United States, however, he sought another psychiatric examination, and the team of American psychiatrists "could find no evidence of mental illness in Grigorenko [or] evidence in Grigorenko's history consistent with mental illness in the past." See Walter Reich, "Grigorenko Gets a Second Opinion," *New York Times Magazine*, May 13, 1979, pp. 18, 39–46.

12. A painting in the Louvre Museum in Paris by David, *Studies for the Coronation of Napoleon*, has Napoleon seizing the emperor's crown from the pope and placing it upon his own head. Napoleon evidently did not want the pope to exercise authority on behalf of God. But *Studies* was not the official public painting of the coronation, for Napoleon did not want to display his lack of protocol publicly. The "official" painting of the event, also by David and in the Louvre, is *The Coronation of Napoleon*. *The Coronation* has Napoleon already crowned and leaves open the question of who—Napoleon or the pope—actually placed the crown. See Walter Friedlaender, *David to Delacroix*, trans. Robert Goldwater (Cambridge: Harvard University Press, 1964), pp. 29–30.

13. The discussion of the historical development of an individual's ability to sue the state rests upon Harry Street, *Governmental Liability: A Comparative Study* (Cambridge: Cambridge University Press, 1953), esp. chapter 1, "Historical Introduction," pp. 1–24.

14. Ibid., p. 1.

15. Ibid., p. 5.

16. Most of the members of the British Commonwealth of Nations generally follow Britain's lead in this area, although several countries enacted similar reforms before 1947. Australia, for example, in its Constitution Act of 1900 gave to its Parliament the ability to enact legislation regarding the right of individuals to sue the government, and in 1903 the Judiciary Act was passed. Part 9 of this act, "Suits by and against the Commonwealth and the States," gave the individual the right to sue the Commonwealth, both in contract and tort, *without* the necessity of a petition of right. The 1927 Canadian Petition of Right Act made the Canadian government liable, both in contract and in tort, for its actions and established a separate court—the Court of Exchequer—to hear such suits. A petition of right, however, was still required before gaining entry to the Court of Exchequer. New Zealand has closely followed the United Kingdom: the (New Zealand) Crown Proceedings Act of 1950 made the government liable for suit without a petition of right.

17. 2 Dall. 419 (U.S.).

18. Walter Gellhorn and C. N. Schenck, "Tort Actions against the Federal Government," *Columbia Law Review* 47 (1947): 722.

19. Justice Holmes in *Kawananakoa v. Polyblank*, 205 U.S. 349 at 353 (1907).

20. *Briggs v. Light Boats*, 11 Allen 157 at 162 (Mass., 1865).

21. W. A. Richardson, in "History, Jurisdiction and Practice of the Court of Claims of the United States," *Southern Law Review* 7 (1882): 782, gives an excellent description of the shortcomings of petitioning Congress: "Claimants, in fact, presented only *ex parte* cases, supported by affidavits and the influence of such friends as they could induce to appear before the committees in open session, or to see the members in private. No counsel appeared to watch and defend the interest of the government. Committees were, therefore, perplexed beyond measure with this case of business, and most frequently found it more convenient and more safe not to act at all upon those claims which called for much investigation, especially when the amounts involved seemed large. Moreover, when bills for relief in meritorious cases were reported, few of them were acted upon by either House, or, if passed by one, were not brought to a vote in the other House, and so fell at the final adjournment, and if ever revived, had to be begun again before a new Congress and a new committee, and so year after year and Congress after Congress."

22. Street, *Governmental Liability*, p. 12.

23. These comments refer only to federal activities and not to the individual state governments. The situation regarding individual state liability and sovereign immunity reflects almost all possible positions. Some states have constitutional prohibitions against suing the state; some allow suits only with the state's consent (petition of right); some allow suits for contract but not torts; some allow limited tort liability; still others give their citizens full right to sue both in contract and in tort.

THE REGULAR COURT SYSTEM:
Judicial Control over
United States Passport Policy

2

One of the more institutionalized and formal avenues of redress is a society's regular court structure. The United States and the United Kingdom make extensive use of these processes, and they emphasize the courts in the redress procedure. The courts are not, however, the only means of redress available to American and British citizens, nor are the United States and the United Kingdom the only countries that highlight the hierarchial court system. These courtroom proceedings are approached from the "adversary" process, and they are invariably ponderous, costly, and time-consuming. But even with these serious drawbacks, the courts can and do provide protection for the individual against administrative abuse and unwarranted restrictions on an individual's personal liberties, freedoms, and rights.

This chapter deals with the role of this institutionalized judicial process in the United States to permit and allow individual redress for alleged wrongs from the bureaucracy. The comments here refer only to activities of the federal government and federal agencies and not to the individual states, since the situation regarding individual state liability and sovereign immunity differs from state to state: some states have constitutional prohibitions against suing the state; some allow the pursuit of redress only with the state's prior consent (the petition of right); some allow suits for contract but not torts; some allow limited tort liability; others give their citizens full ability to seek redress both in contract and in tort.

As mentioned in chapter 1, the United States has turned a full circle regarding state liability and sovereign immunity. The Eleventh Amendment placed the individual state governments beyond suits by citizens of another state, and subsequent court decisions made the state's permission necessary before being sued by its own citizens (several have since given such permission). Court decisions also interpreted the Eleventh Amendment as preventing suits against the federal government. Sovereign immunity was lessened somewhat when the Court of Claims was given jurisdiction over contract controversies in 1863, but it was not until 1946 that sovereign immunity, with certain limited exceptions, was renounced by the United States government in two historic acts: the

Administrative Procedure Act and the Legislative Reorganization Act (especially Title IV, the Federal Tort Claims Act).[1]

THE ADMINISTRATIVE PROCEDURE ACT AND THE FEDERAL TORT CLAIMS ACT

The 1946 Administrative Procedure Act dealt primarily with the establishment, within each federal agency, of specific operating guidelines for the review of citizen complaints directed at the agencies' actions and decisions. This act, in short, put an end to administrative abuse of the individual and provided American citizens with the right to seek redress against bureaucratic mistreatment, first with the agency and then with the courts.

The Administrative Procedure Act, and its subsequent versions, requires most federal agencies to provide the public with all relevant information, rules, opinions, orders, records, organizational framework, personnel lists, rules of procedures, and rules of substance. Of course, this dissemination of agency records has some limitations: the Central Intelligence Agency (CIA) is not required to make public its list of covert personnel, nor is the military required to make available the specifications of its latest weapons. Each agency is required to publish in the *Federal Register* the information noted above, and the subsequent Freedom of Information Act (FOIA) requires each agency to respond within a reasonable time to individual requests for information and/or records. If an individual believes that a federal agency is not properly complying with a request for such information, he can seek redress through a United States district court.

The district court has the authority, if an individual complains, to force the agency to make available the desired information in general and/or to order the agency to provide the specific records improperly withheld from the complainant. This access to information serves the individual well in any complaint against the government: agency decisions must be based on public rules and reasons rather than some vague notion or arbitrary standards.

The act also requires each agency to establish an internal redress and appeal procedure so individuals can complain about specific agency actions and decisions. These internal procedures to adjudicate disputes between people and the agency are not courts of law, but due process of law must be observed. The individual petitioner must receive, along with the original decision, notice that he has the right to appeal, and this notice must contain all the relevant information on how to go about it (who and where to write, what records are needed, time allowed to file an appeal). If the individual wants to pursue his complaint, he can proceed to the internal review board.

The individual seeking redress has the right to have counsel and other "interested" parties with him in the pursuit of his complaint before the agency's review board. He must receive adequate notice about when and where the hearing will take place, and he has the right to receive full copies of the hearing's transcript. The individual before this board is, in effect, placing the state's agents in the position of defendant and is attempting to persuade them to change their original decision or, if not, to justify the original action. The final adjudication of this dispute is made by the agency's board—some agencies have hearing officers—and if the individual's complaint is dismissed, written reasons for the denial must be given. The transcript of this hearing or appeal then becomes the record for the next stage in the redress procedure if the individual so desires.

Establishing an internal agency review process does not mean automatically that all unjustified complaints will be dismissed and that all legitimate complaints will be redressed in favor of the individual. A built-in bias against the complaining individual may exist, and the review process may only be window dressing. The Administrative Procedure Act recognized this possibility, and the act provided for judicial review of the agency's appeal decision. An individual is required to exhaust the bureaucratic remedies before turning to the courts, but the agency does not have the final decision—the individual then enters the regular federal court structure to pursue his complaint.

One short but crucial paragraph in the act gives the courts authority to review administrative actions and decisions. Not only is this paragraph important because it gives the individual another avenue of redress against the government, but it also—in muted language—renounces sovereign immunity and accepts the view that the king can do wrong or authorize his agents to do wrong and that the sovereign nation-state can be placed in the role of defendant and be held accountable for its actions. The paragraph reads as follows:

A person suffering legal wrong because of agency action, or adversely affected or aggrieved by agency action . . . is entitled to judicial review thereof. An action in a court of the United States seeking relief other than money damages and stating a claim that an agency or an officer or employee thereof acted or failed to act in an official capacity or under color of legal authority shall not be dismissed nor relief therein be denied on the ground that it is against the United States.[2]

The federal courts have thus been made available to American citizens who want to pursue a complaint against a bureaucratic agency. The court, if it so wishes and if it thinks that "irreparable injury" may be done to the individual, can postpone the effective date of the agency's contemplated action and/or preserve the status of the individual, pending conclusion of the court's review proceedings. This ability of the court to "preserve the status of the individual" until the redress procedure has run its course is a major advantage to the court system. As discussed below in the chapters dealing with the ombudsman, parliamentary-legislative oversight, and public and private international agencies, whatever redress may be secured is after the fact. With these latter systems of redress, the individual suffers wrong until it is put right; with the courts, the individual is well protected and may not suffer at all. The process is time-consuming, however, and it is costly—the individual is well advised to be represented by counsel in court.

The court that has original jurisdiction in the complaint filed by an individual dissatisfied by the internal agency review is the United States district court for the district in which the individual resides. Any appeals from the district court follow the usual route: the court of appeals for that circuit and then the Supreme Court. The written record of the original decision and of the review decision becomes the basis of the court's review, although the court does have the ability to admit "new facts" into its record. In its review of agency behavior, the court can of course dismiss the individual's complaint and uphold the original decision as right, proper, and legitimate. The federal judges are by no means rubber stamps for every bureaucratic decision, but neither are they citizen advocates against the government. The "burden of proof" is on the individual to show that he was wronged by the administrative decision, and one's day in court does not automatically mean that the individual will receive satisfactory redress.

If the reviewing court finds that the individual has indeed been wronged, it can compel agency action that it believes was unlawfully withheld or unreasonably delayed, or it can hold agency action as unlawful and set it aside. The Administrative Procedure Act lists a series of reasons the court can use in cancelling agency actions: arbitrariness, capriciousness, or an abuse of discretion; action against the individual's constitutional rights, powers, privileges, or immunities; action in excess of statutory provisions; failure to observe due process of law; action unsupported by substantial evidence; or action unwarranted by the facts.[3]

The Administrative Procedure Act thus established the principle that the government was liable for administrative abuse, and a formal redress system was created, beginning with the specific agency itself and ending in the federal court hierarchy. The second historic act in 1946—the Federal Tort Claims Act—put the finishing touches on the end of sovereign immunity regarding torts. As mentioned in chapter 1, individuals had to seek redress from Congress for suits in tort but the Federal Tort Claims Act completely altered both the concept of sovereign immunity and the process of securing redress.

As was the case with the Administrative Procedure Act, the Federal Tort Claims Act renounced in a muted paragraph the historic claim to sovereign immunity regarding torts:

The United States shall be liable . . . [for tort claims] in the same manner and to the same extent as a private individual under like circumstances . . . [but] the United States shall not be liable for interest prior to judgment or punitive damages . . . except in wrongful death.[4]

The already-existing Court of Claims (this court had jurisdiction over contract claims) was reorganized, Congress was removed from the process, and the United States district courts entered the redress procedure for tort claims. The system as it now exists has the Court of Claims and the district courts having concurrent original jurisdiction over certain types of claims (for example, tax recovery and civil actions not exceeding $10,000) and each having separate original jurisdiction over other types of claims. All tort claims are first heard in the district court. The district court involved is the one located in the district in which the individual seeking redress resides. The United States has only one Court of Claims. It sits in Washington, D.C., with seven judges appointed by the president with the advice and consent of the Senate.

An individual who believes that he has suffered a tort at the hands of the government or from a governmental agency can thus turn to the federal courts for relief. This right to seek redress, however, has some limitations: the individual must have exhausted whatever agency remedies are available, the claim has to be made within two years, and certain areas of government activity are still protected by sovereign immunity (for example, military action). But assuming that these conditions have been met, the individual no longer has to plead hat-in-hand with the manor lord or with the king for redress. The United States has renounced almost all of its sovereign immunity—both in contract and in tort—and the individual seeking redress has access to the federal court structure.

The route of appeal for tort claims is different than it is for most other federal cases. Original jurisdiction in torts belongs with the district courts, but appeals from the district court are not made to the circuit court of appeals. The appeals are made to the Court of Claims in Washington, D.C., and then to the Supreme Court. The process can be ponderous and time-consuming, but the individual cannot benefit from the lengthy process. Under the Administrative Procedure Act, the courts can prevent an agency from applying their decision until the appeal has run its course. The individual, in many cases, has an interest in having the appeal stretch on and on. However, it is an entirely different situation with torts: the damage (if any) has already been done—the courts cannot enjoin a past event—and the lengthy redress procedure brings no benefit to the individual, especially if it takes years to resolve the claim.

Notwithstanding these disadvantages, the American citizen can complain about the treatment he receives from the king's agents, and, more important, he has a reasonable expectation that the complaint will be adjudicated in a fair and impartial way. The federal judges in the United States are independent, competent, and dedicated servants of the law, and they have not hesitated to employ their view of the law to protect a single individual from official mistreatment ever since the doctrine of sovereign immunity was renounced.

The Administrative Procedure Act and the Federal Tort Claims Act, both enacted in 1946, dealt with what is termed here *legal* questions: the interpretation of a contract; who was negligent in an accident; did the postman really trample the roses; would the government be liable if Skylab fell on a person's house. These are legal questions, and, although important, they do not touch on "political" questions: the right of every citizen to enjoy constitutional guarantees and not to have his central personal freedoms restricted. The involvement of the federal court structure in protecting the political rights of individuals far predates 1946—it is based on the tradition of the courts' ability of judicial review of the constitutionality of government actions and policies. The section below presents an extended discussion of the courts' protection of individuals in providing them redress based not on the 1946 acts but, rather, on political rights and freedoms contained in the Constitution. It is also based on the view that any governmental actions and decisions that are, in the view of the court, contrary to constitutional guarantees, are illegal, null, and void.

THE PROTECTION OF INDIVIDUAL RIGHTS:
INTERNATIONAL TRAVEL, PASSPORTS, AND FOREIGN POLICY[5]

The contribution of the United States federal court system in providing an effective avenue of redress for the individual against governmental and/or bureaucratic mistreatment is beyond question. First enunciated in *Marbury* v. *Madison*, the doctrine of judicial review has had a long and honorable history in protecting the individual from official transgressions concerning both due process of law (the application of public policy) and constitutional legality (the substance of the policy itself). Some of the best-known Supreme Court decisions have involved a single individual's complaint that the king's agents had wronged him and that the individual was entitled to redress. The example discussed in this section is far less dramatic or publicized than, say, *Brown* v. *Board of Education* or the *Baake* case, but it nonetheless illustrates the ability of United States citizens to be protected against their government. The Constitution places certain types of behavior beyond the reach of the government and the bureaucrats: the courts have allowed the individual to force the state into the position of defendant while protecting the individual.

The role of the courts is examined here by discussing their protection of the individual from government mistreatment in both the application and content of passport legislation, especially through the bureaucrats in the Department of State's Passport Division. This is an instructive example, for throughout the process, the government argued "sovereign immunity": passports were an integral part of "foreign policy," and thus the individual had no standing to complain about the treatment received. The courts did not accept this argument and have brought the entire area under close scrutiny to protect the individual from governmental mistreatment and to provide the individual with an effective avenue of redress against the state.

To write that the United States government can be held accountable by individuals in the formulation and execution of foreign policy is misleading, for, by virtue of its constitutional position, the executive branch has effective power in this functional area. The president and secretary of state usually enjoy unlimited discretion in the conduct of foreign affairs, and the courts will not interfere, for example, with the president's refusal to grant diplomatic recognition, nor will they comment on the use of American troops abroad or upon the "legality" of executive agreements. That a decision regarding passports is a "foreign policy" decision has long been advanced by the president and secretary of state, and, traditionally, it has been accepted that the issuance and regulation of passports is an integral part of the general conduct of American foreign relations.

If the control, and often the denial, of international travel by American citizens through passport regulations dealt solely with foreign policy, any individual who believed that he was mistreated would have no standing whatsoever to complain. Both the substantive content of the legislation and its application to specific individuals would be beyond accountability: the various legislation cited above retains "sovereign immunity" protection for "foreign policy" decisions, and, in addition, the 1946 Administrative Procedure Act specifically exempts foreign affairs from the requirements of due process.[6] The Passport Bureau within the Department of State, given this interpretation, would be totally free to act as it saw fit without being held accountable for its actions.

But passport decisions and the treatment individuals receive from the bureaucrats when requesting a passport have become open to judicial review and control, because, in the court's reasoning, basic constitutional issues are involved when the secretary of state and the Passport Bureau limit the right to travel by arbitrary means. The courts have simply not allowed the Department of State to mistreat American citizens under the guise of "national interest" or "foreign policy." The following comments trace the process by which the federal court structure has protected the individual by forcing the secretary of state—although an agent of the king—to be accountable for his acts. These comments are concerned only with the question of United States citizens leaving and entering the country; the welcome they may receive elsewhere is not relevant. The term *passport* refers to the normal passport issued to the ordinary traveler and not to the various types of special passports issued to the military, diplomatic corps, or to high-ranking government officials.

The Constitution is silent on the right to travel beyond United States borders, and as far as such travel was concerned, nothing was done before 1918 to restrain citizens from leaving the country. This excludes the 1799 Logan Act. This act has never been applied because it is unenforceable.[7] The freedom to travel was a dominant theme in United States policy before World War I: the war of 1812 and the War with the Barbary States were due, in part, to unwelcomed restrictions placed upon American traders; Japan was "opened up" in the name of freedom of access; China was subjected to "spheres of influence" via the Open Door Policy, for everyone, at least in the view of the Americans, had the right to travel and trade in China, and millions of immigrants were permitted entry into this country. This theme continued into the twentieth century: the United States has always maintained that everyone has the right to leave—and return to—his own country.

It was not until 1918 that this unlimited and unregulated right of American citizens to travel abroad was restricted. A passport became a legal prerequisite, but this restriction was lifted in 1921. In 1942, in the midst of World War II, limitations were once again placed upon travel. International travel was thus closely tied to passports because possession of the document was now required by law before such travel could take place. The Department of State created its Passport Bureau, and its bureaucrats then had the ability to grant— or deny—individual requests for passports.

Passports are not a new phenomenon. They have existed since ancient times, but their nature has changed since their first use. The term *passport* was, at its inception, applied to a document given to an enemy alien or to a departing foreign ambassador or emissary to allow the bearer to pass freely through the lines of the issuing power (a safe-conduct pass). Passports were slowly transformed, however, into a type of "letter of recommendation" issued by a government, or by various officials of a government, to selected private individuals for use abroad. The current usage is that a passport is a document issued only by a specific official of a government (usually the secretary of state or foreign minister or interior minister) and only to its citizens or nationals to identify the bearer when abroad. It is also a request to foreign governments to allow the bearer to pass without delay or hinderance and in case of need to give all lawful aid and protection.

The U.S. Supreme Court defined the nature of a passport in 1835 as:

> . . . a document which, from its nature and object is addressed to foreign powers; purporting only to be a request that the bearer of it may pass safely and freely; and it is to be considered rather in the character of a political document, by which the bearer is recognized in foreign countries as an American citizen, and which, by usage and the law of nations, is received as evidence of the fact. It is a mere *ex-parte* certificate; and if founded upon any evidence produced . . . establishing the fact of citizenship, that evidence . . . ought to be produced . . . as higher and better evidence of the fact.[8]

The old idea of a passport—that it was a privilege granted only to those in the good graces of a government official—was not harmful to liberty or to the rights of the individual because the document was not required for one to leave the country. But between 1918 and 1921, and from 1942 to the present, the possession of a passport was no longer a nicety but a legal requirement. Those who found themselves *not* in the good graces of a government official now could not leave the country. The possession of a passport is necessary for Americans to go to all countries except a few in the Western Hemisphere (Americans need not have a passport to travel, for example, to Canada, Mexico, and the Caribbean Islands). Through a long process beginning in 1902 to the present, authority was granted, in congressional acts and presidential proclamations, to the secretary of state (and the Passport Bureau) to issue passports—or to *refuse* to issue passports—in his capacity as chief officer for the conduct of American foreign policy.[9]

The logic behind the decision to give such authority to the Department of State rather than to some other office is clear: since the Department of State was concerned with foreign policy and since international travel was a function of that policy, the department should therefore have authority over passports to regulate travel. President Eisenhower emphasized this view in 1958:

> Since the earliest days of our Republic, the Secretary of State has had the authority to issue or deny passports. Historically this authority stems from the Secretary's basic responsibilities as the principal officer of the President concerned with the conduct of foreign relations . . . the Secretary should have clear statutory authority to prevent Americans from using passports for travel to areas where there is no means of protecting them, or where their presence would conflict with our foreign policy objectives or be inimical to the security of the United States.[10]

The 1950s and 1960s were the years of the most blatant mistreatment of individuals by the secretary of state and the Passport Bureau, all under the guise of foreign policy, and, as such, the department claimed sovereign immunity for its actions. Most of the passport denials were due to the hysteria of the Cold War and the Communist threat, but several denials appear to be a result of plain mean spiritedness on the part of the bureaucrats. The situation in the early 1950s was such that a passport request could be denied with no reasons given for the denial and with the individual having no redress avenue open to him.

Armed with the authority to regulate passports, the Passport Bureau began to deny passport applications in an arbitrary and capricious way: the affected persons' activities abroad would not be in the "best interests" of the United States. The passport of Beverly Hepburn was not renewed, for example, because she allegedly engaged in the internal political affairs of Guatemala (such activities, presumably, were the sole preserve of the Department of State). A department spokesman said that to renew the passport would not have been in the national interest.[11] Hepburn was not afforded the opportunity of a hearing, nor was she allowed to appeal the decision: a modern reenactment of the serf in front of the manor lord, but in place of *rex gratia dei* and sovereign immunity, "foreign policy" was the reason she could not complain about the treatment received or attempt to make the government accountable for its actions.

In another instance, Paul Robeson's passport was revoked because ". . . any trip that Robeson would make would not be in the interest of the United States." The *New York Times* reported that Robeson's activities in left-wing movements and his outspoken criticism of this country's international policies had much to do with the revocation.[12] One of the most tenuous arguments offered for revocation was put forth by the Justice Department in a brief filed before the District of Columbia District Court on behalf of the secretary of state. The government argued that ". . . if Robeson spoke abroad against colonialism he would be a meddler in matters within the exclusive jurisdiction of the Secretary of State."[13]

Although the two examples above appear tenuous, at least "reasons" were given for the action: the individual activities would not be in the "best interests" of the United States or the activities would impinge upon governmental prerogatives. But passport applications were denied without *any* reason given, for, it was thought, disclosure of the reasons would prejudice the conduct of United States foreign relations. John Foster Dulles consistently maintained that passport denials could be effected *in camera* ("in private chambers") under the guise of foreign policy, and that the individual had no standing to complain about the decision. Dulles commented.

I have reached this conclusion [denial of passport] on the basis of confidential information contained in the files of the Department of State, the disclosure of which might prejudice the conduct of U.S. foreign relations . . . and because the issuance of a passport [to Mr. Dayton] would be contrary to the national interest.[14]

Other passports were denied because the applicant wanted to travel to areas where the United States did not maintain the usual diplomatic civilities. The Department of State refused to issue passports because the prospective traveler could not be afforded protection, for it was believed that protection of citizens was in accord with the the "best interests" of the nation. It appeared that the department was slowly evolving the standard that a citizen could not travel to any country if he could not be afforded the usual protection offered American citizens and property abroad by the embassies and consulates. But this standard was not applied fairly or consistently, and, consequently, the result was no standard except the personal whims of mean-spirited people. A passport was revoked not because of the nonpresence of an ambassador, but, rather, because the ambassador did not like the prospective visitor, did not want to protect him, and did not want him in "his" country.

The passport of the Honorable Judge Clark, former chief justice of the United States High Commission's Court of Appeals in West Germany, was quickly invalidated for travel to Berlin after he had made some remarks protesting the arrest of some American citizens by German authorities. It was reported that the then United States ambassador to the German Federal Republic, James B. Conant, had strongly objected to Judge Clark's visit and did not want him granted reenty privileges. Judge Clark's comment on this bizarre affair was the extent to which he could complain: "It is preposterous to say that Conant can exercise some sort of censorship on persons whom he wishes or does not wish to come to the country to which he is accredited. This has never been held to be the function of an Ambassador."[15]

The arbitrary and capricious action described above was pursued on grounds that a passport decision was a pure foreign policy decision, and, therefore, the department had absolute power and discretion to take such action *without* any means of redress for those individuals who believed they were mistreated. The department's conception of the role passports had in the conduct of foreign relations illustrates the rationale underlying travel regulation and the absence of methods of redress:

> The Secretary's authority both to deny or restrict passports stems from his basic Constitutional powers in the conduct of foreign relations . . . [he] may deny passports [because] . . . the applicant's travel . . . is inimical to U.S. foreign policy or detrimental to the orderly conduct of U.S. foreign relations . . . I believe we have a responsibility to see to it that individual Americans are not allowed capriciously to disturb the delicate international situation by breaking restrictions which have been imposed for sound foreign policy reasons.
>
> When the Secretary issues a passport restricted for travel to certain areas, he is, in our view, making a determination that it is contrary to the foreign policy objectives of the U.S. to have American citizens traveling within those areas . . . *if this authority is used on grounds which are clearly based on foreign policy, the courts will not substitute their judgment for that of the Secretary.* . . . The Secretary of State's power to withdraw or withhold a citizen's passport is not designed to be a punishment. It is designed as an instrument of foreign policy.[16]

It *is* true that if the department's authority to make decisions (and mistreat individuals) were based clearly and solely on foreign policy issues, the courts would not substitute their judgment for that of the secretary. The department and Passport Bureau would then be totally free to dispense with due process of law (as provided for in the 1946 Federal Administrative Procedure Act) as well as substantive justice—the Passport Bureau could act as if it were the manor lord, dismissing petitioners for redress at will and at whim. But such decisions limiting international travel are *not* solely "foreign policy" concerns, for they affect basic constitutional rights and the way people are treated by the government. The courts, therefore, have maintained close scrutiny over the department's actions to insure that administrative discretion did not eliminate procedural or substantive justice. Although the government has pleaded that regulation of travel is within its preserve, the courts have appeared to be more impressed with individual rights, and the courts have held the government accountable.

The right to travel has been reaffirmed several times against various restrictions placed upon it. In 1900, Chief Justice Fuller stated ". . . [liberty] is deemed to embrace the right of the citizen to be free in the enjoyment of all his facilities; to live where he will. . . ."[17] More recently, in 1964, the Supreme

Court reaffirmed this right to travel. Justice Douglas, in a concurring opinion in *Aptheker v. Secretary of State*, stated:

> The right to move freely from state to state is a privilege and immunity of national citizenship. None can be barred from exercising it, though anyone who uses it as an occasion to commit a crime can of course be punished. But the right remains sacrosanct, only illegal conduct being punishable. Absent war, I see no way to keep a citizen from travel within or without the country *unless there is cause to detain him.*[18]

Comments such as those by Justice Douglas had little effect on the Department of State, for all the Passport Bureau had to do was to manufacture "cause." The department listed various criteria it had employed as "cause" to restrict travel from the very beginning of its activities regarding passports. Reasons given as "cause" were: fugitives from justice and persons under court restraining orders; persons repatriated at government expense, repayment not being made; persons likely to become public charges; criminals with long records and recent offenses; participants in political affairs abroad whose activities were deemed harmful to good relations, and persons whose previous conduct abroad has been such as to bring discredit on the United States and cause difficulty for other Americans; fraudulent applications; persons determined to be mentally ill; minor children whose travel is objected to by one or both parents; and persons whose activities abroad would violate the laws of the United States or the host country.[19]

Through a long legal process, the federal courts have intervened in the department's decision-making process regarding restraint of travel, and they have protected the status of the individual vis-à-vis the bureaucracy. For example, the passport of Ms. Bauer was cancelled for the sole reason that her assumed activities in the future would be contrary to the best interests of the United States. No opportunity whatsoever was afforded Bauer to appeal this "foreign policy" decision. Unable to secure redress from the bureaucratic agency, Bauer then turned to the courts for redress, and a federal district court reversed the cancellation. Even though the court recognized that the conduct of foreign affairs is a political matter and thus within the discretion of the executive branch, it held that such conduct must not be in conflict with any constitutional guarantees:

> This Court is not willing to subscribe to the view that the executive power includes any absolute discretion which may encroach on the individual's constitutional rights, or that the Congress has power to confer such absolute discretion. We hold that like other curtailments of personal liberty for the public good, the regulation of passports must be administered, not arbitrarily or capriciously, but fairly, applying the law equally to all citizens without discrimination, and with due process adopted to the exigencies of the situation.[20]

The utter lack of any procedure by which the aggrieved applicant could appeal the decision of the department was sufficient cause for the court to void Bauer's cancellation. The Department of State, consequently, established a Board of Passport Appeals[21] within the agency itself (the composition and lines of authority of this board, however, did not hold out much hope for the individual naive enough to appeal). But even with the establishment of this Board of Appeals, the individual applicant continued to have little effective redress, because the Department of State maintained that it could not violate the confidential character of the passport files by making them public information in the Board of Appeals. The department based this insistence of nonexposure on the grounds that the conduct of foreign relations would be jeopardized if the reasons for their actions were to be publicized.[22] This appeals board was an all-too-obvious window-dressing redress procedure, for no one was able effectively to rebut "evidence" that was not made known to them. The courts, however, in a series of cases,[23] refused to sanction the denial of passports based on confidential information in the possession of the secretary and that was not made available to the applicant—this was held to be unconstitutional as a denial of due process. Invariably, the department opted to issue the passport rather than make public its vital secrets.

The Department of State and the Passport Bureau also maintained that it was contrary to the national interest if Communists were allowed to travel abroad and engage in activities that would advance the Communist cause. Not known for its originality, the Department of State borrowed the "Attorney General's List," and any individual who belonged to one of the subversive organizations on the list became a Communist and thus ineligible for a passport. The court ruled, however, that this list was designed for screening government employees and could not be employed to determine who was or was not a Communist or to determine who could or could not travel abroad.[24]

A new method of determining who were Communists was thus needed by the department. It discovered a relatively simple procedure—ask the applicants! Anyone who refused to sign an affidavit denying membership in the Communist party was *ipso facto* a Communist and could not obtain a passport. The secretary refused to issue a passport to Rockwell Kent because he would not sign such an affidavit. Kent stated that "I am not a Communist and I have never been a Communist, but I'll be damned if I will sign one of those things."[25] Kent, having his application denied, then turned to the courts for redress against this governmental mistreatment. The process was time-consuming and Kent did not receive his passport in the meantime, but in 1958 the U.S. Supreme Court agreed that Kent had cause to complain.[26] The Supreme Court held that paragraph 215 of the Immigration and Nationality Act of 1952 and paragraph 1 of the Act of Congress of July 3, 1926, simply did not authorize the secretary of state to withhold a passport for noncompliance with the signing of an affidavit. The Court did not rule on the question whether it was constitutional to withhold a passport from a Communist, because Kent's passport was denied for not signing the affidavit, and it was, at that point, immaterial whether the applicant was, or was not, a Communist.

The above cases assumed that the secretary had broad discretion to deny passports, but the federal courts did not subscribe to the view that this discretion was absolute, and thus they provided the individual who complained about the treatment received with various procedural safeguards. But due process of law would mean very little if the secretary and the Passport Bureau could deny an individual's passport application on any substantive grounds deemed sufficient. That is, if the courts could not intervene with substantive issues, it would mean the Department of State could continue to refuse applications for practically any reason as long as due process was observed. Two main substantive issues were evident in the denial of passports: a Communist could not travel anywhere, and no one, including Communists, could go to certain countries.

The almost blanket refusal to grant passports to "known" Communists was based on the view that international travel by Communists would threaten the national security of the United States. Pursuant to the Internal Security Act of 1950, the secretary of state adopted the policy of refusing to issue passports—and thus preventing international travel—to those Americans who were allegedly going to work against the national interest (that is, Communists). This view is illustrated by the 1959 remarks of John Hanes, the then administrator of the department's Bureau of Security and Consular Affairs, when he stated that the possession of a United States passport ". . . clothes them [the Communists] abroad with all the dignity and protection that our government affords. And yet their dedicated purpose in life is to destroy our Government and our freedom."[27]

This practice of withholding passports from Communists was very similar to the preventive detention regulations in countries such as India and the Republic of South Africa. Preventive detention means a governmental official or bureaucrat has the wide discretion to prevent mobility of certain people if the official suspects the individual *might* do something in the future. Restriction on mobility could be jailing, house arrest, or the South African practice of *banning*—the individual is restricted to his residence and cannot speak with more than one other person at a time. In a sense, the denial of a passport to a Communist was *house arrest*: the affected individual could not travel abroad, and thus mobility was limited. But this restriction was *not* a consequence of something the individual did in the past; rather, it was a consequence of some bureaucrat's vague suspicion that he *might* do something in the future. The Department of State, of course, did not classify its treatment of such individuals as "preventive detention"—they described it as "protecting the national interest"—but the end result was identical to the South African situation.

Two interesting cases in 1964 dealt with paragraph 215 of the 1952 Immigration and Nationality Act (it is unlawful for a United States citizen to *leave* or *enter* the country without a valid passport).[28] These cases, *MacEwan v. Rusk* and *Worthy v. U.S.*, were decided in the lower federal courts and did not reach the Supreme Court and represent the latest interpretation of paragraph 215 of the 1952 act. The *MacEwan* decision held that it is consitutional, in times of war or (the ever-present) national emergency, to make it unlawful conduct for a United States citizen to leave the country without a valid passport. This restriction, of course, applied only to situations in which the individual had left the United States directly for another country, where, through bilateral international agreements with the United States, a valid passport was required both to depart the United States and to gain entry into the host country (for example, the Soviet Union). This restriction did not apply to situations where, through such bilateral agreements, valid passports were not required (for example, Canada and Mexico).

The provision in paragraph 215 making it unlawful for a citizen to *enter* the United States (from areas other than Canada and Mexico) without a valid passport was held to be unconstitutional in the *Worthy* case. The court believed that a citizen had an inherent right to return to his own country, and the simple nonpossession of a valid passport could not prevent him from exercising that right. The individual involved was William Worthy, a well-known journalist. His passport was not renewed upon expiration, because he refused to give the Department of State assurances that he would abide by its area restrictions (Cuba in this case). Worthy then went to Cuba and returned without a valid passport—he did not have, in fact, any passport. He was duly convicted in a federal district court of entering the United States without a valid passport.

Worthy appealed this decision and the court of appeals reversed the district court's findings. The court of appeals ruled in favor of the individual and his rights vis-à-vis administrative regulations and practices designed to restrict those rights. In reversing Worthy's conviction and in redressing his grievance—the government did not appeal the reversal to the Supreme Court—the court of appeals said that the enjoyment of a citizen's rights cannot be made conditional upon first requiring the individual to commit a criminal offense. In other words, an unlawful departure differs from an unlawful entry, because a citizen who does not leave the United States can continue to exercise all of his rights of citizenship, whereas someone in Worthy's situation could only regain a citizen's rights by committing a criminal offense (entering without a valid passport). The court also likened the situation to exile—a form of punishment that *cannot* be inflicted on American citizens. The court ruled that a citizen has an *inherent* right to return to his own country and to deny him that right (or to make it conditional upon first committing a criminal offense) is to deprive him of the liberty guaranteed by the Fifth Amendment.

Preventive detention of Communists, or the practice of withholding passports from Communists, did not reach the Supreme Court until 1964. In

Aptheker v. Secretary of State, due process was not at issue because Herbert Aptheker had his procedural rights observed by the department. Rather, the issue under review was the substantive question of whether the Department of State could refuse passports to members of Communist organizations (that Herbert Aptheker was a Communist was not disputed by anyone). The U.S. Supreme Court came to the rescue of the individual against what they thought to be governmental mistreatment of an American citizen, and Aptheker eventually received his passport. The Court held that the practice of denying passports to members of Communist organizations was unconstitutional, because it arbitrarily restricted the right to travel, thereby abridging the liberty guaranteed the individual by the First, Fifth, and Fourteenth Amendments. Justice Goldberg delivered the opinion of the Court:

> Since freedom of association is itself guaranteed by the 1st Amendment, restrictions imposed upon the right to travel cannot be dismissed by asserting that a citizen's right to travel could be fully exercised if the individual would first yield up his membership in a given association.[29]

Mr. Justice Black, in a concurring opinion, recognized the preventive detention nature of the Department of State's practice and stated:

> Under the due process clauses of the 5th and 14th Amendments, neither the Secretary of State nor any other governmental agent can deny people in the United States their liberty to do anything else except in accordance with the Federal Constitution and valid laws made pursuant to it. The entire Subversive Activities Control Act is unconstitutional as (1) a bill of attainder, (2) restricting liberty without the benefit of a trial according to due process, which requires a jury trial after indictment, and (3) denying the freedom of speech, press, and association.[30]

The *Aptheker* decision effectively eliminated the department's power to withhold passports from Communists. The courts, probably believing that those people who actually work toward the violent overthrow of the government want to remain in the country to perform their duties, forced the department to issue passports to all political persuasions. The individual applicant no longer would be faced with the situation of beir g restricted in international travel because some bureaucrat did not agree with the applicant's political beliefs or associations.

The Department of State's powers, prerogatives, and discretion in this "foreign policy" area were thus slowly being eroded by the courts in protecting the individual from being wronged by the state. The department found itself legally mandated to issue passports to practically every applicant, except, of course, to those with fraudulent applications or to fugitives from justice—quite a change from previous practice of denying passports at whim for "confidential" reasons without the right of appeal. The Passport Bureau found itself more in the role of a rote technician doing paper work rather than making substantive decisions on passport applications. The *Aptheker* case, however, did not touch upon the second substantive issue, namely, the long-term practice of the department of not validating *all* passports for travel to certain countries and thus prohibiting *any* American citizen—regardless of political belief—from these areas. This second question came to the Supreme Court in 1965 and 1967.

The Department of State denied the request of Louis Zemel to endorse his otherwise valid passport for travel to Cuba as a tourist. Zemel then instituted a suit in a federal district court against the secretary of state, arguing that the section of the Immigration and Nationality Act relating to travel control of American citizens during a national emergency and the section of the Passport Act authorizing the secretary of state to issue passports under rules prescribed by the president were unconstitutional. He also claimed that the secretary's regulations restricting travel to Cuba (the other countries prohibited at the time were North Vietnam, Albania, North Korea, and the People's Republic of China) were invalid.

The three-judge district court, in a 2-1 decision, ruled against Zemel. The court held that the secretary of state is not authorized to withhold or cancel passports of citizens because of their beliefs or associations. Such a standard could not be employed to restrain the citizen's right of free movement, and the government does not have the power or discretion to restrain travel of citizens with whose politics it disagrees (the *Aptheker* decision). But, the court continued, the government does have the power to forbid the travel of *all* citizens to particular geographical areas because of war or national emergency (every president since Franklin D. Roosevelt has extended the "national emergency" power first declared in 1942). Judge Blumenfield commented:

> This is a regulation that . . . designates certain parts of the world forbidden to all American travelers. This can hardly be regarded as arbitrary or capricious by this plaintiff.
>
> Congress has provided that the Executive should take all necessary steps short of an act of war to protect the rights and liberties of American citizens on foreign soil. . . .
>
> Certainly it is consistent with an overall policy that he should exercise that authority, granted by law, to prevent incidences occurring in those countries where normal diplomatic relations are non-existent.[31]

Obviously dissatisfied with the district court's ruling, Zemel appealed to the Supreme Court, but the Supreme Court affirmed the lower court's decision. In a 6-3 decision, the Court held: (1) the Passport Act of 1926 contains a grant of authority to the executive branch to impose area restrictions on the right to travel and thus to refuse to endorse valid passports of American citizens for travel to Cuba (and, by extension, to the other countries on the proscribed list), (2) the secretary's refusal violated neither due process of law nor the First

Amendment's guarantee of free speech, (3) the Passport Act contains suffi-
ciently definite standards for the formulation of travel controls by the executive
branch, and (4) area restrictions that apply to all citizens are foreign policy decisions. Chief Justice Warren delivered the majority opinion:

> In this case . . . the Secretary has refused to validate appellant's passport, not be-
> cause of any characteristic peculiar to appellant, but rather because of foreign policy
> considerations affecting all citizens.
>   . . . the fact that a liberty cannot be inhibited without due process of law does not mean
> that it can under no circumstances be inhibited . . . the Secretary has justifiably con-
> cluded that travel to Cuba by American citizens might involve the nation in dangerous
> international incidents, and that the Constitution does not require him to validate pass-
> ports for such travel.[32]

The Supreme Court thus declared in *Zemel v. Rusk* that the secretary of
state has the authority, emanating from his position as the chief officer concerned with the conduct of United States foreign relations, to declare certain
countries off limits to all citizens, and that otherwise valid passports need not
be endorsed for travel to such specific countries. In addition, the individual
seeking redress in such situations had no standing to complain, because area
restrictions are a bona fide "foreign policy" decision. But *Zemel v. Rusk* was
redefined only two years later in 1967. In retrospect, *Zemel v. Rusk* established *only* the principle that the secretary does not have to endorse an otherwise valid passport for certain countries, and the case did not touch upon the
question whether a United States citizen could or could not go to the banned
areas or be prosecuted if he did indeed visit the proscribed countries.

The secretary of state was not required to endorse a passport for travel to,
say, Cuba. But the passport had to be issued and validated for travel to other
countries not on the proscribed list. Since most foreign countries required a
valid and endorsed passport before allowing entry or travel visas, the area
travel ban was relatively successful—one could not go to Cuba without a passport specifically endorsed for Cuba. But, and this was the next crucial question, what would be the consequences if one or all of the proscribed countries
did not require an endorsed passport before granting entry and the traveler
visited such country in a round-about manner, that is, the traveler neither left
nor entered the United States directly from a proscribed country but, perhaps,
traveled via Toronto or Mexico City (one might even argue that in this situation, a passport is not required at all because the document is not necessary for
travel to Canada and Mexico). In any case, the traveler has conformed strictly
to the legal requirement of not *leaving* the United States without a valid passport (no one ever attempted to describe a trip between Mexico City and
Havana as "entering or leaving" the United States). But was such a traveler
liable for prosecution—up to five years imprisonment and/or a fine of
$5,000—under the regulations issued by the secretary of state for having

traveled in the proscribed area(s)? These latter questions came to the court in 1967.

In 1962 Helen Travis entered Cuba without a passport specifically endorsed for that country (Cuban officials appeared not to have been overly concerned). She did, however, have possession of an otherwise valid passport, and she did not leave the United States directly for Cuba, nor did she return directly. Upon her return, however, the government pursued prosecution, and she was convicted of traveling to a proscribed country (Cuba) in violation of section 1185(b) of the 1952 Immigration and Nationality Act. The conviction was affirmed by the court of appeals, and this decision was then appealed to the Supreme Court by Travis. In a parallel case, Messrs. Lee, Levi, and Laub were indicted in a district court in 1966 for conspiring to violate section 1185(b)—arranging travel to Cuba for persons whose passports were not endorsed for Cuba. The district court dismissed the indictment, but the government appealed the dismissal to the Supreme Court.

The two cases were heard together, and a unanimous Court reversed the *Travis* conviction and affirmed the *Lee, Levi,* and *Laub* dismissal.[33] The decisions were based on the Court's view that the statute under question was not violated, since area restrictions are not criminally enforceable (five years and/or $5,000) upon an otherwise valid passport. That is, the Justice Department could prosecute individuals for leaving the United States without a valid passport, but since the people who went to Cuba (or who were planning to go to Cuba) did have a valid passport when leaving and returning to the United States, *no* crime was committed. Justice Fortas gave the opinion of the Court:

... we agree with the District Court that the indictment herein does not allege a crime. If there is a gap in the law, the right and the duty, if any, to fill it do not devolve upon the courts. The area travel restriction, requiring special validation of passports for travel to Cuba, was a valid civil regulation . . . (*Zemel v. Rusk*). But it was not and was not intended or represented to be an exercise of authority . . . which provides the basis of the criminal charge in this case.[34]

In other words, the Department of State attempted to extend congressionally sanctioned criminal penalties for not having a valid passport when entering or leaving the United States to its *own* administrative regulations regarding travel in the proscribed areas. The Court, however, rightly ruled that the secretary of state *cannot* promulgate and enforce criminal prohibitions on his own initiative without the express delegation of such by the Congress. Congress has never made travel in the secretary's proscribed areas a crime, and thus the Supreme Court concluded that Travis was convicted of a violation, and Lee, Levi, and Laub were charged with the conspiracy to violate, a nonexistent criminal prohibition.

The *Travis* and *Lee, Levi, and Laub* decisions, in effect, required the Department of State to seek congressional passage of the necessary statutes to make it a criminal offense to travel to those areas banned by the secretary. It is a meaningless administrative regulation to ban certain areas if the prospective traveler can still visit them, assuming, of course, the traveler has an otherwise valid passport. Congress has been most hesitant to give the secretary this authority, and although sporadic attempts at such legislation have been made in Congress, such a bill has yet to be made into law. Faced with congressional hesitation and judicial opposition, the Department of State, in March 1968, announced that it would no longer continue its policy of punishing those individuals who violated the area travel ban. Apart from the *Travis* and *Lee, Levi, and Laub* cases, punishment usually had taken the form of passport revocations and denial of renewal applications.

The department also modified its ban by stating that certain classes of people would be able to receive endorsed passports for these countries: China, Cuba, North Korea, and North Vietnam but not Albania. People such as journalists, educators, physicians, and businessmen (but not "ordinary" individuals) who had a "legitimate" interest in traveling to the restricted countries would receive an almost automatic endorsement of their passports. The March 1968 announcement was not, however, endorsed by the Republican party and presidential candidate Nixon. Although by no means having a monopoly on restricting travel under the guise of foreign policy, the Republican party has traditionally taken a very dim view of the individual citizen's standing to complain about "foreign policy" passport decisions. One of the planks of the party's 1968 platform dealt specifically with these matters:

> The Republican Party abhors the activities of those who have violated passport regulations contrary to the best interests of our nation and also the present policy of reissuing passports to such violators. We pledge to tighten passport administration so as to ban such violators from passport privileges.[35]

It appeared that the Nixon administration was girding up once again for more controversy and restrictions but not criminal prosecutions—only Congress can declare travel in certain areas a criminal act, and it has refused to do so (it is also questionable, given the Court's past decisions, whether such legislation would be constitutional). In retrospect, however, the statement above was only campaign rhetoric: not only did the Nixon administration not tighten passport legislation, but it also began the almost total dismantling of any restrictions whatsoever on passports and international travel.

The Nixon administration began a process continued by Ford and Carter: the policies of detente with the Soviet Union and the normalization of relations with the People's Republic of China. Area restrictions seemed out of place in this atmosphere, and not one single court case has occurred since the *Travis* and *Lee, Levi, and Laub* cases dealing with the use or misuse of passports. The area restrictions have also disappeared: on a recent passport (issued in the summer of 1980 and valid until 1983) absolutely no restrictions are imposed about where the passport is valid. The individual citizen had thus secured redress, via the courts, against a governmental agency's abuse and mistreatment of individual rights.

One is unable to comment upon future events—Congress *may* legislate a travel ban; the department *may* resurrect their policy of revocation and denial—but the current position is that the Department of State has had its authority effectively eroded by the federal courts in the latter's defense of the individual. This is not because passports and travel do not deal with foreign policy, but rather because when dealing with individuals, the Department of State, even when acting from foreign policy considerations, has to be subservient to the U.S. Constitution, and the Constitution protects the individual from governmental and/or bureaucratic mistreatment.

In the late 1940s and throughout the 1950s, the individual citizen indeed had a difficult time in the passport field. The Department of State utterly disregarded the notion of due process in carrying out a function it claimed to be solely within its power. Individuals were mistreated by having their passport applications denied or by having their passports cancelled without notice, without the opportunity to be heard or complain, without the chance to confront witnesses, without the benefit of counsel, without the opportunity to appeal the decision, and, for a time, without the opportunity to see the information upon which the decision was based. Unable to secure any redress from the agency, the aggrieved individuals turned to the formal judicial process. The federal courts simply would not allow such practices to continue and finally convinced the Department of State that, even in foreign policy, the department must adhere to constitutional guarantees.

The courts also refused to sanction the usurpation of power by the Department of State not granted to it by either the Constitution or Congress. The Department of State attempted to determine who was or was not a Communist; to punish suspected future violators of United States law; to punish suspected future violators of foreign law; to determine the financial status of citizens; to engage in preventive detention; and to determine the "best interests" of the United States. None of these activities belonged to the Department of State's bureaucrats, and the courts prohibited the department from pursuing them in relation to passport administration.

Great progress was also made in substantive areas: basic individual rights were being abridged when the department refused to issue passports to alleged Communists and other people with whose politics it did not agree. The area travel ban has been so circumscribed that it has even disappeared, and it is no longer an effective tool upon which to base foreign policy decisions. Some future secretary of state may want to place the Bahamas on a resurrected restricted list, but, because of the complaints of mistreatment in the past, individual United States citizens can travel to any country that grants them entry without legitimate retribution being made against them by any governmental agency.

The federal courts have so protected the individual that passports have become just another document one files away. The passport *has* to be issued to *all* applicants, except for very narrowly defined reasons: fraudulent applications, fugitives from justice, people declared mentally ill, and the like. A passport is *not* required to leave the country directly for countries such as Canada, Mexico, and the Caribbean Islands. A passport is *not* required of United States citizens to enter the United States from any other country (the *Worthy* decision). A United States citizen is free to travel in *any* country that grants entry, passport or no passport. A passport's role now is only that it is required to leave the United States directly for a country that through bilateral agreement with the United States requires a passport (the European Community countries, for example). But a liberal reading of the Courts' decisions suggests that, assuming countries grant entry, a United States citizen can travel *anywhere* in the world via Canada or Mexico without a passport and return directly to the United States without violating any congressional legislation or administrative regulation.

Through a long and costly procedure, individuals complained about the treatment they received, and passports were so downgraded that now they serve some very mundane functions. Passport administration generates money for the Passport Bureau and provides employment for some bureaucrats; the document is a convenient piece of personal identification if one wants to use a charge card in London or cash some traveler's checks in Paris; the document is recognized in international law as evidence of citizenship. The history of United States passport policies demonstrates that a person who believes he has suffered a wrong from the king or from the king's agents is entitled to judicial review and protection from bureaucratic and administrative mistreatment and abuse.

SOME CONCLUDING COMMENTS

The regular court system in many societies is the primary bulwark in protecting the individual from administrative illegality or bureaucratic criminality. In societies such as the United States, where the courts have the ability for judicial review of legislation, the courts can also provide protection against encroachments on personal liberties and freedoms. Charged with the law adjudication function, the institutionalized court hierarchies mandate due process of law for the relationships between the bureaucrats and the people they are to serve. The formal judicial process, however, is lengthy and costly—it may take years after the original alleged mistreatment occurred before the individual is granted redress.

But however long this process may take, an independent judiciary in a society that believes the court's decision to be legitimate is an excellent and effective avenue of redress against governmental mistreatment of the individual. The bank guard has indeed turned upon the tellers on behalf of the customers.

NOTES

1. The Administrative Procedure Act was originally enacted on June 11, 1946. That act was repealed as part of a general revision by Public Law 89-554 (September 6, 1966), but most of the original provisions of the 1946 act were retained in Public Law 89-554. See Title 5, *United States Code*, Part 1, especially Sections 501ff. and 701ff. The Legislative Reorganization Act was enacted on August 2, 1946. Most relevant to this discussion is Title IV of that Act—the Federal Tort Claims Act. See Title 28, *United States Code*, various sections.

2. Public Law 89-554 (September 6, 1966), Title 5, *United States Code*, Section 702.

3. Ibid., Section 706.

4. Federal Tort Claims Act, Title 4, Legislative Reorganization Act of 1946; Title 28, *United States Code*, Section 2674.

5. An earlier version of this section was originally published as "Judicial Control Over Passport Policy," *Cleveland State Law Review* 20, no. 2 (May 1971): 271–85. Copyright ©, *Cleveland State Law Review*. Sections of that essay are reproduced here with the permission of the *Cleveland State Law Review*.

6. Title 5, *United States Code*, Sections 553 and 554.

7. The Logan Act, forbidding private citizens from negotiating with a foreign government, was directed at a member of the U.S. Senate who had persuaded Tallyrand to lift the Napoleonic embargo against the United States and who also hoped to persuade the British to stop the conduct that ultimately led to the War of 1812. See Charles E. Wyzanski, Jr., "Freedom to Travel," *Atlantic Monthly* 190, no. 4 (October 4, 1952): 67. The act reads: "Any citizen of the United States, wherever he may be, who, without authority from the United States, directly or indirectly commences or carries on any correspondence or intercourse with any foreign government . . . with intent to influence the measures or conduct of any foreign government . . . in relation to any disputes or controversies with the United States, or to defeat the measures of the United States, shall be fined not more than $5000 or imprisoned not more than three years, or both." Title 18, *United States Code*, Section 953. A literal interpretation of the Logan Act would make the person who sent a birthday card wishing long life to Fidel Castro liable for punishment.

8. *Urtetiqui* v. *d'Arcy*, 34 U.S. (9 Pet.) 692 at 699 (1835). The Department of State, however, believed the passport was evidence of citizenship and that lack of the document would prevent an individual from receiving the benefits of United States protection while abroad. See U.S. Department of State, "Department Policy on Issuance of Passports," *U.S. Department of State Bulletin*, June 9, 1952, p. 919. However, the right to United States protection derives from the fact of citizenship and not from the possession of a passport—a passport may facilitate such protection, but that is its only function.

9. For the relevant passport laws and regulations, see the following: Foreign Relations and Intercourse, 22 U.S.C. 212 (1902); 22 U.S.C. 213 (1917); 22 U.S.C. 211-a (1926); War and National Defense, 50 U.S.C. 785 (1954); Immigration and Nation-

ality Act, 8 U.S.C. 1185 (1952); Executive Order No. 7856, 22 C.F.R. 51.75 and 51.77 (1938); and Presidential Proclamation No. 3004, 18 F.R. 489 (1953).

10. Dwight D. Eisenhower, cited in "Administration Recommends New Passport Legislation," *U.S. Department of State Bulletin*, August 11, 1958, p. 250.

11. As reported in the *New York Times*, September 7, 1953, p. 8.

12. *New York Times*, August 4, 1950, p. 1.

13. Brief for Appellee, p. 20. *Robeson v. Acheson*, 198 F. 2nd 985 (D.C. Cir., 1952).

14. John Foster Dulles, "Appendix to Opinion of the Court Decision and Findings of the Secretary of State in the Case of Weldon Bruce Dayton," *Dayton v. Dulles*, 357 U.S. 144 at 153 (1958).

15. *New York Times*, July 9, 1955, p. 31.

16. Roderic L. O'Connor, "The State Department Defends," *Saturday Review*, January 11, 1958, pp. 11–12; emphasis supplied.

17. *Williams v. Fears*, 179 U.S. 270 at 274 (1900).

18. *Aptheker v. Secretary of State*, 378 U.S. 500 at 129 (1964); emphasis supplied.

19. These categories are based on answers given by the Department of State to the Senate Foreign Relations Committee, *Hearings Before the Senate Foreign Relations Committee on Department of State Passport Policies*, 85th Congress, 1st Session (1957), pp. 38–39, as cited by the Report of the Special Committee to Study Passport Procedures of the Association of the Bar of the City of New York, *Freedom to Travel* (New York: Dodd, Mead and Co., 1958), pp. 45–46. This report gave its approval to criteria (1), (2), (6), (7), and (8) as grounds upon which to deny a passport. For (3), the report believed that the Department of State had no authority to determine the financial status of an applicant except as relating to (2). As to (4), it is difficult to determine exactly what is a "long" record and what constitutes a "recent" offense. Besides, the report stated, a former criminal is free to travel as any other citizen once he has been punished (it is immaterial if foreign countries refuse entry). The report, and the courts, did not agree that (5) was sufficient cause to deny passports. The last criterion, (9), should not be employed because the policing of criminal activities, within or without the United States, is not a function of the Department of State.

20. *Bauer v. Acheson*, 106 F. Supp. 445 (D.C. Cir., 1952).

21. Rules of the Board of Passport Appeals, 22 C.F.R. 51.151–51.170 (January 9, 1954), 19 F.R. 161.

22. The department commented: "The very nature of foreign negotiations requires caution and secrecy, and the premature revelation of the President's acts, or his motives, may ruin in an hour the results of laborious diplomacy. . . . [C]ourts ought not risk the exposure of reasons for passport cancellation when such exposure will inevitably in some cases put in jeopardy delicate foreign relations." Defendant's Memorandum, *Foreman v. Dulles*, Civil No. 4924–54 (D.D.C., 1955), at 2–3.

23. *Clark v. Dulles*, 129 F. Supp. 950 (D.D.C., 1955); *Kamen v. Dulles*, Civil No. 1121–55 (D.D.C., 1955);. *Nathan v. Dulles*, 129 F. Supp. 951 (D.D.C., 1955).

24. *Shachtman v. Dulles*, 225 F. 2nd 938 (D.C. Cir., 1955).

25. As reported in the *New York Times*, July 9, 1955, p. 31.

26. *Kent et Briehl v. Dulles*, 357 U.S. 116 (1958).

27. *U.S. Department of State Bulletin*, May 18, 1959, p. 724.

28. *MacEwan v. Rusk*, 228 F. Supp. 306 (D.C. Pa., 1964), affirmed (C.A.3), 344 F. 2nd 963; *Worthy v. U.S.*, 328 F. 2nd 386 (C.A.5 Fla., 1964).

29. *Aptheker v. Secretary of State*, 387 U.S. 500 (1964).

30. Ibid.

31. *Zemel v. Rusk*, 228 F. Supp. 65 (D.C. Conn., 1964).

32. *Zemel v. Rusk*, 381 U.S. 1 (1965). Justice Black dissented on the grounds that the Passport Act violated the provision in Article 1 of the Constitution granting all legislative power to Congress. Justice Douglas, joined by Justice Goldberg, dissented on the grounds that restrictions on the right to travel in times of peace are not valid unless there is some clear countervailing national interest.

33. *Travis v. U.S.*, 385 U.S. 491 at 131 (1967); *U.S. v. Lee, Levi, Laub*, 475.

34. *U.S. v. Lee, Levi, Laub*, 17 L. ed. 2nd, at 533–34 (1967). Justice Fortas also wrote that it appeared that the government's actions were arbitrary, for "although Department records show that approximately 600 persons have violated area travel restrictions since the enactment of Paragraph 215(b) of the Immigration and Nationality Act, the present prosecutions are the only attempts to convict persons for alleged area transgressions." This "active misleading" by the government was, for Justice Fortas, another reason to dismiss the cases, especially when Justice Fortas cited department statements made in 1950 (regarding the then travel ban on Eastern Europe) that area restrictions only exist to warn the traveler about the lack of United States protection, and that they do not prevent the individual from actually entering the restricted countries.

35. Cited from *The Congressional Quarterly Almanac*, 90th Congress, 2nd Series, Vol. 24 (Washington, D.C.: Congressional Quarterly Service, 1968), p. 993. The regulations referred to by the Republicans were the administrative regulations issued by the secretary, not those provided for by Congress.

SPECIALIZED ADMINISTRATIVE COURTS: The French *Conseil d'État*

3

A second approach to the protection of individuals from bureaucratic mistreatment and governmental abuse relies upon the use of specialized administrative tribunals or courts as an avenue of redress against the state. Similar in many respects to a country's regular court structure, such administrative tribunals are quasi-judicial proceedings, and they are only marginally less institutionalized or formalized than the regular hierarchial court system. But the underlying concept to, and role of, these tribunals are identical to those employed by the regular courts' use of judicial review and rulings of unconstitutionality; they are also identical to those processes discussed in subsequent chapters. Given the proper political environment and organizational framework, these specialized administrative tribunals can serve as a society's major bulwark in protecting the individual's legal and human rights from governmental limitation, encroachment, or abuse.

The specialized administrative tribunals approach the relationships and authority patterns between the individual and the state in the more "modern" sense of sovereign immunity. As discussed in chapter 1, the modern view of sovereign immunity does not regard the concept as sacrosanct; the king can err and can authorize others to do wrong in his service or in the administration of public policy; the government and its agents are liable for their actions; the state can be placed in the role of defendant. Depending upon the particular society in which these tribunals operate, and depending upon the jurisprudential principles of the society, administrative tribunals can protect the individual and provide redress on various grounds for negative state action or for bureaucratic mistreatment.

The ability to supervise the administration of public policy rests upon diverse judicial principles. Some of these administrative tribunals can employ the doctrine of judicial review and from this constitutional authority declare certain bureaucratic decisions and activities unconstitutional. Others can negate and punish administrative behavior as being contrary to generally accepted principles of law; still others can employ the doctrine of abuse of legitimate power (*détournement de pouvoir*). But regardless of the specific juridical principle invoked, these specialized tribunals have a strand of common agreement cutting across all of them: the legislative grant of discretionary authority to the administration does *not* mean the bureaucrats have arbitrary power to do as they see fit. If arbitrary power is alleged—and this does not have to encompass illegality—the individual then has an avenue available to adjudicate the grievance by competent, impartial, and independent proceedings.

Specialized administrative tribunals and courts are the logical extensions of a somewhat different conception that continental Europe has of the law, courts, and the judging function compared to the conception prevalent in Anglo-American judicial cultures. This is not to imply that such administrative courts do not have a role in Anglo-American societies—on the contrary, they most assuredly do as seen below—but these institutions are much more widespread on the European continent, with the French *Conseil d'Etat* as the pristine example. In order to have a clearer view of the role these tribunals play in the redress process, it is first necessary to present a brief discussion of the law and second to show how the countries who make extensive use of administrative tribunals relate them to the law and to other domestic court hierarchies.

The "law" in any organization or society is simply a statement—in codified written terms for developed societies or in verbal common-law or traditional forms for primitive societies—of that particular society's value system, containing precepts on behavior. The law identifies the kind of behavior allowed and the behavior rejected by the dominant value system, and it contains various levels of punishment for those violating these stated values. In addition, the legal code defines the relationships among individuals, giving each person certain rights and extracting certain obligations vis-à-vis other people. The legal system in any society thus fulfills two primary functions necessary to the stability and reproduction of the social system: socialization and integration.[1]

The law serves as a socializing agent, for it makes explicit rules of behavior that a community regards as legitimate as well as illegitimate; the law thus socializes all members of the organization into the dominant value system. The law also has an integrative function. By identifying the rights and obligations of people to each other, the law plays an important role in conflict mediation, management, and resolution. This integrates a society into a coherent whole by providing institutionalized avenues of settling disputes.

Since it reflects the political culture, value system, environment, and level of economic development, the actual content of the law will of course differ from society to society and over time. The legal code of the traditional Eskimo society may place heavy emphasis on how the seal catch is to be distributed; the traditional Taureg society in North Africa may emphasize the common accessibility to wells and fresh water. The content of the *United States Code*, for example, deals with entirely different values and standards of behavior than the Koran-based pronouncements of the ayatollahs in Iran. The content of the law may thus differ, but the types of law are common practically to every society. These types or categories of law are *private law* (generally, "the civil code describing the relationships between and among private individuals") and *public law* (generally, "the criminal code describing the relationships between the individual and the society at-large or the state").

With the private law or civil code, the state is passive and participates only as the referee or arbitrator to the private dispute. That is, if an individual believes that his legal rights were infringed upon by another individual, it is for the aggrieved person to take the initiative. One may engage an attorney and pursue the complaint or go to a local small claims court. The dominant values of the society are not violated, but, rather, only the specific legal rights of the individual (contract disputes, wills, property claims, faulty merchandise, guarantees, insurance claims, and so on). The law, courts, and judges are of course involved, but only as the referee to settle the private dispute in a peaceful manner. The state provides its good offices to settle the conflict, but it will not take the initiative or intervene if the private individual declines to pursue the complaint.

The second category or type of law is "public"—the criminal code—and this defines the relationships among individuals in terms of society's dominant value system as well as the relationship of the private individual vis-à-vis the state itself. Here the individual has violated the norms of society—murder, treason, theft, sabotage, rape—and the state itself is now a party to the action. The state will initiate the proceedings by pursuing prosecution and punishment; the aggrieved individual does not have the option of not "pressing charges" in, say, a murder. In this general category, the aggrieved individual is only a bystander because the state's public judicial enforcement agencies are the prosecutor. One of the major characteristics of a modern legal system, as compared to the legal system in a traditional society, is that the state has taken over the punishment of people who have violated society's norms.[2] Rather than leaving such punishment to the private devices of revengeful people, the state has assumed the monopoly of violence, and the violator is punished by the collective entity.

In general, then, private law defines the arena of conflict resolution between individuals with the state as referee; public law defines the relationships between individuals and society's value system with the state as prosecutor. But there exists a third possible combination or option: the individual wants to bring an action against the state or its agents. With this situation, the private individual is the prosecutor-plaintiff, and the state is neither referee nor prosecutor but the defendant. The civil and criminal codes sometimes—again, this depends upon the particular country—cannot deal adequately with these situations. Several societies, particularly on the European continent, have developed a third category of law: administrative law (for example, the *droit administratif* of French jurisprudence).

Administrative law recognizes, at least in the societies reviewed here, that the state can err, that the people also have sovereign immunity, and that the population has the right to complain about alleged bureaucratic mistreatment. This type of law defines how the government should act in relation to the people and outlines the redress process. Redress here does not include criminal activity—the criminal code has adequate jurisdiction over a bureaucrat who engages in official criminal activity—but, rather, it deals with situations of alleged bureaucratic abuse of power or arrogant behavior. Specialized administrative tribunals interpret and adjudicate complaints by individuals on how they are treated by the bureaucracy; these tribunals are *not* involved with disputes between two private individuals or with criminal trials.

Western democracies have responded to these categories of law in various ways. In the United States, the regular federal court system is not differentiated about the substance of the case—criminal, civil, or administrative—and the federal courts have jurisdiction in practically any controversy. The United States court system reaches its apex with the Supreme Court, which has final general supervision, including administrative law questions originally adjudicated in lower tribunals. Great Britain has made more extensive use of specialized administrative tribunals and consumer councils (in relationship to the nationalized industries) than has the United States, but in Britain, too, the regular court hierarchy is not differentiated.

Some European countries, however, have established judicial boundaries among the types of law and have created separate court hierarchies to adjudicate the different controversies. In France the structure of the courts is divided into three distinct hierarchies: criminal, civil, and administrative.[3] Within the administrative law court structure, the *Conseil d'Etat* supervises the administration of public policy. The Federal Republic of Germany has moved even further.[4] In Germany the court structure is divided into six separate hierarchies, each with its own court of appeals. The six parallel systems deal with civil law, criminal law, administrative law, social security questions, labor relations, and financial questions.

It is with these specialized administrative tribunals and courts that this chapter is concerned. They are not "constitutional" courts with unlimited authority to nullify state public policy. Rather, they are some cultures' response to the problem of bringing some measure of justice and sensitivity to public administration and to insure that people are treated with respect by the bureaucrats.

EUROPEAN ADMINISTRATIVE LAW

Control of the administrative function and judicial remedies against bureaucratic abuse of power take various forms across the European continent, both East and West, and employ a variety of institutional frameworks.[5] The five forms discussed briefly in this section are (1) hierarchical review within the administration itself or "internal control"; (2) specialized commisions with popular participation; (3) administrative tribunals; (4) regular court structures; and (5) the central focus of this chapter, review and control by separate administrative courts.

The first procedure, termed *internal control*, is the usual first line of attack for any individual who wants to complain against the bureaucracy. In some Eastern European countries, especially the Soviet Union and Rumania, individual complaints are made to the administrative unit just above the one responsible for the alleged infraction or mistreatment. "Control committees" are attached to each administrative unit, and the majority of individual complaints are settled (although not necessarily in favor of the complaining individual) at this level. The Soviet control committees may impose a variety of sanctions upon the specific civil servant if gross dereliction of duty is discovered. If a crime is involved, the control committee will forward the entire matter to the Procurator's Office for resolution.[6]

All Western Europe administrative law systems allow redress to be made directly to the involved bureaucrat himself. This personalized avenue of redress (*recours gracieux* in French law), however, seldom results in satisfaction for the individual who believes he was mistreated. *Recours gracieux* is not an effective remedy because of the built-in (and understandable) bias the specific bureaucrat brings to the complaint. The bureaucrat concerned, having made his decision, is not likely to alter his original course of action solely because someone complains. Of course, in some instances the original decision was altered in favor of the individual citizen, but for the majority, *recours gracieux* does not provide satisfaction.

When *recours gracieux* does not provide satisfaction to the individual, request for redress is then made to a higher level within the same administrative unit (*recours hiérarchique*). But this, too, is usually ineffective, since this "higher authority" may not want to annul or change the original decision made by the lower unit, especially since the higher authority is usually the person responsible for the general guidelines or instructions in accordance with which the original decision was made.

The limitations to *recours gracieux* and *recours hiérarchique* are recognized by those countries where these avenues exist. Belgium, France, Greece, and Cyprus (to name but a few) permit the individual who has complained to the internal processes to bring the matter to a separate administrative court or tribunal if the original complaint is not replied to within a specific time (four months in France, thirty days in Cyprus) or if the individual is not satisfied with the decision of the internal review procedure. The internal review process is not very effective: it is not an impartial independent process, and with *recours gracieux*, application is made to the same person who is being complained against. But internal control procedures do have one advantage: they can serve to decrease time-consuming and expensive court-tribunal cases or hearings. Some complaints can be weeded out at this decentralized level without overloading the dockets or the more institutionalized and formalized administrative avenues of redress.

The second form, specialized commissions, is widespread (especially in France and Belgium), but these commissions play only a marginal role in the redress of grievances. Their major function is to involve private individuals in the process of government and public administration. Some element of public control exists over the administration, if the public representatives on these commissions have some input in the determination of public policy, and a few of them do adjudicate complaints. Examples of specialized commissions in France are the Commission for the Aged, Commission on Investments of Local Communities, and (still in existence but with a decreasing work load) a commission to deal with war damages and compensation.[7] These commissions are not judicial bodies or courts and, although sometimes able to provide relief in certain specific and limited situations, are not a major participant in the redress process.

The third process, administrative tribunals, frequently has the trappings of a judicial body, but decisions of these redress avenues are not final. That is—and this distinguishes administrative "tribunals" from administrative "courts"— tribunal decisions can be appealed to a higher authority. Depending on the particular country, this higher authority can be the regular court hierarchy (Denmark and the United Kingdom, for example) or a separate administrative court (the French *Conseil d'État*). A large number of these specialized administrative tribunals have been established across Europe. One such example in France is the *Conseil Général des Bâtiments de France*, which deals with the control and adjudication of property transactions within public contracts.

The United Kingdom has established a number of administrative tribunals. The extent and variety of its tribunals, which now serve approximately one hundred and thirty thousand people annually, are a logical extension of the British welfare state. They are informal and independent adjudication agencies, with a special relationship with both the relevant ministry and the judiciary.[8] In general, the individual who lodges a complaint with one of these tribunals has the right of appeal to the regular British court structure.[9]

Both the theory and practice of administrative tribunals in the United Kingdom were drastically altered in the 1950s as a result of the "Crichel Down" episode.[10] This incident, involving a property claim, revealed an unacceptable lack of safeguards or protection for an individual vis-à-vis the administration (it was only because of the personal intervention of the minister—and *not* because of any prescribed procedure—that an inquiry was held). As a result of much public concern over how this one individual was (mis)treated by the administration, a committee was established in 1955. The committee, known as the Franks Committee after its chairperson, Sir Oliver Franks, was charged by Parliament to examine the then-current chaotic administrative tribunal system and redress procedures and to make recommendations on administrative adjudication of grievances against the state.

The Franks Report was delivered in 1957, and most of its proposals eventually found their way into public policy through the Tribunals and Enquiries Act (1958).[11] Sifting through the multiplicity of tribunals, the Franks Committee classified the various tribunals into five main groups according to the matters they dealt with: (1) land and property tribunals (local valuation courts, agricultural land tribunals, the rent tribunal); (2) social service tribunals (national insurance tribunals and industrial injury tribunals); (3) health service tribunals (medical practices committees); (4) transport tribunals (licensing authorities for public service vehicles); and (5) various miscellaneous bodies (the independent schools tribunal). The Tribunals and Enquiries Act also established a National Council on Tribunals that has since coordinated the workings of the tribunals and thus has reduced the diversity in their operating procedures.

This National Council on Tribunals supervises the workings of the entire system, and it advises the various tribunals on rules of procedure and appointments. The council, however, has little influence over personnel, since the chairperson of each of the tribunals is appointed by the lord chancellor and the other members are appointed by the relevant government department or ministry. These tribunals are thus staffed by personnel appointed by the very bureaucratic agency that the tribunal is expected to supervise. This presents some question about the tribunals' bias or fairness, and this problem is discussed below. The Council of Tribunals also supervises many "internal control" procedures—the inquiries held by government departments before the minister's decision. The council has given a quasi-judicial atmosphere to these in-house inquiries or hearings—rules of procedure have been established, and the individual who brings a complaint is entitled to a full transcript and report of the inquiry—and these developments have reduced somewhat the minister's discretion, for he must limit himself to the open facts in reaching his decision.

The efforts of the National Council on Tribunals notwithstanding, a great deal of variation still exists among the procedures and activities of the different tribunals.[12] Some tribunals are quasi-judicial bodies: the individual making the complaint or seeking redress can have legal counsel at the hearing, complete written records of the proceedings are kept, and the individual can appeal to a regular court on the basis of this record if he is not satisfied by the tribunal's decision. Other tribunals have a much less formalized procedure and operate on a more ad hoc basis. The rent tribunal, for example, which is supposed to determine "fair" rents for some properties, appears to be only the outward extension of the ministry: the minister of housing appoints the tribunal, and no records are kept of its deliberations. On the other hand, the land tribunal (adjudicates disputes over property valuation) is appointed by the lord chancellor rather than the departmental minister. This particular tribunal sits in public and travels in circuit around the country; its public written decisions explain the reasons for whatever final decision it may reach.

The British experiment with these administrative tribunals reflects the difficulty of balancing administrative effectiveness with judicial fairness, for, as R. M. Punnett wrote, often an inverse relationship is found between maximum administrative effectiveness and maximum judicial fairness.[13] One real advantage to the use of administrative tribunals as a means of individual redress vis-à-vis the state is that they are able to weed out many disputes and thus reduce the load on the regular courts. In addition, they are cheap, speedy, less constricted by formalized legal rules, very accessible to the public, and usually composed of people who are experts in the subject matter. But these "experts" undermine the judicial fairness of the tribunals, for no matter how fair the system may be, it *appears* to be unfair. The system that allows the concerned minister to appoint the members of the tribunal runs contrary to the honored principle that no party should adjudicate a case in which it is itself involved. The tribunals *are* open to the charge (if not the guilt) of not being impartial, because their real master is the government bureaucracy and the minister rather than the search for an equitable solution. To have all of the tribunals operating under hidebound rules of procedure with independent judges would increase the appearance of fairness but would, in turn, reduce their speed and cheapness. But since the administrative tribunals in Great Britain are subject to review by the regular court structure, whatever built-in bias that may exist is excusable on grounds of their ready accessibility to the population.

The many consumer and consultative councils established in the United Kingdom play a very limited role in the redress procedure.[14] These consumer and consultative councils operate in reference to the nationalized industries and public corporations, and they are intended to protect the interests of the consumer in the face of the monopolistic character of nationalized industries. The British law courts provide the consumer with adequate protection against the public corporation for breach of contract, negligence, and other tort actions. But the courts do not control price levels, adequacy of service, facilities, or how employees of the nationalized industries and public corporations treat the public. These latter questions are usually determined by the public corporation itself.

William A. Robson wrote that efforts were made since the end of World War II to "remedy the extremely weak position in which the consumer was placed in relation to the earlier generation of public corporations set up prior to 1939."[15] A series of agencies was set up with the "duty" of safeguarding consumer interests: these include two separate coal consumers' councils (one for residential consumers and one for industrial users); one central and several regional transport consultative committees; fourteen consultative councils for electricity supply and twelve for gas; and the Air Transport Advisory Council; the British Broadcasting Corporation also has a whole series of advisory councils.

These consumer and consultative committees and councils are not monolithic in terms of composition, functions, or powers, but all of them are expected to deal with citizen complaints about the treatment received from the nationalized industries. Robson concluded, however, that these councils are not an effective avenue of redress, and he wrote that

> . . . there is a need for administrative tribunals to take over from the consumer and consultative councils a task they [the councils] are unable to perform effectively; namely, inquiring into complaints by individual consumers or members of the public against the public corporations in matters other than those which can properly form the subject matter of a legal action or criminal proceedings in the ordinary courts.[16]

The above remarks were written in 1960, but, twenty-one years later, such a transfer of jurisdiction and authority has yet to take place. The consumer councils may be well suited to deal with questions of broad public policy (for example, the availability of electricity in rural areas or the closing of branch railway lines), but they really cannot handle individual complaints on an individual basis. They are too big (twenty to thirty members), too pressed for time (most members have full-time jobs), and, as is the situation with the administrative tribunals, include representatives from the same public corporation that is the subject of the complaint or grievance. Robson concluded that it is difficult for these councils to participate in the redress process, and, regardless of whatever shortcomings the administrative tribunals may have, the tribunals are at least geared for the redress process and should receive competence over the nationalized industries and public corporations.

The fourth process mentioned above is the regular court structure. As discussed in chapter 2, the regular court system is a primary participant in maintaining legality, constitutionality, and in protecting human rights and the status of the individual in the administration of public policy. The example of court activity in this area concerned the passport policy of the U.S. Department of State and how the federal court hierarchy employed judicial review to protect people from abuse by the petty bureaucrats in the Bureau of Passports and Consular Affairs. But the United States is not the only society that assigns to the regular and unified court hierarchy the tasks of applying administrative law and adjudicating complaints by people against the actions of the bureaucrats, especially when it concerns the use of discretionary power.

The above discussion of the administrative tribunals in Great Britain notwithstanding, these tribunals are not independent of the ordinary courts as, for example, are the administrative courts in France. The regular British court structures can receive appeals from these tribunals, and the courts have the power to annul or alter the decisions made by the tribunals. A similar situation also exists in Denmark and Norway: the regular court systems in Denmark and Norway have the authority to review administrative acts, and they have the ability to declare acts of the administration unconstitutional.

A strong role is even played by the ordinary courts in those countries possessing a system of administrative courts. In Austria, the Constitutional Court has the final authority over the constitutionality of legislation and administrative actions, including those controversies where the individual has alleged a violation of central personal liberties and individual human rights. In Belgium, the ordinary courts apply criminal law against administrative officials, and these courts also have the ability to levy fines against bureaucrats under civil law provisions. In Italy, article 113 of the constitution specifies that the ordinary courts are to guarantee individual rights against the acts of the bureaucracy, and, finally, in Germany, article 19 of the Federal Republic's constitution specifies that any person whose rights are violated by the administration may appeal to the ordinary courts. Superior to all of the courts in the Federal Republic, including the administrative courts, is the Federal Constitutional Court. This court enforces the protection of human rights as provided for in the constitution and thus has the final decision regarding administrative abuse of human rights.

The fifth and final process mentioned above, a separate administrative court system, deals with the disputes between individuals and the administration. The French *Conseil d'État* is the best example of this separate hierarchy, and the *Conseil* is discussed in somewhat more detail below. The French *Conseil d'État* has, however, its parallel in a number of European countries and, not surprisingly, in a number of former French colonies in Africa. A *conseil* along the French lines exists in Greece, Turkey, Cyprus, Belgium, Austria, Germany, Finland, Spain, and the Netherlands. These of course vary in terms of personnel and jurisprudential theory, but they are similar to the French *Conseil*, and the following discussion of the French *Conseil d'État* also describes many of the operating characteristics of these other administrative redress agencies.

THE FRENCH *CONSEIL D'ÉTAT*

Specialized independent administrative courts, separated from the regular judicial structure, are best illustrated by the French *Conseil d'État*. This institution is almost two hundred years old, but its functions and powers have changed over the years as a result of the evolution of French society and the changing nature of the political environment. As it now operates, the *Conseil* has the power to advise the government on the constitutionality of proposed legislation and to adjudicate complaints lodged against the administration by individual French citizens. The *Conseil* may annul the enabling legislation under which the bureaucrat acted or annul the specific action itself without touching the enabling legislation. The *Conseil* can also provide redress (compensation) for the individual who has been mistreated by the king's agents.

History[17]

The official date given to the *Conseil's* establishment is in article 52 of the Constitution of the Year VIII (1799), although Napoleon did not create it from nothing—the *Conseil's* origins and roots can be traced to the *Ancien Régime*. The *Conseil* is linked to other institutions that, in previous centuries, aided the French kings in various tasks. In pre-Revolutionary France under the Louis and the Bourbons, the *Conseil du Roi* (King's Council), sitting in Paris, advised the king on political, legal, and administrative matters. This *Conseil* was basically a political body, managing conflict and resolving disputes among the nobility and the powerful regional dukes. Twelve regional royal courts (*parlements*) formed the basis of the French judicial process, but these *parlements* appeared to be more interested in their own power and authority than their function as an institution in the adjudication process. The *parlements* constantly interfered in the operation of the executive government from Paris and sabotaged various reforms the king wanted to introduce. Wanting to maintain a monopoly on the legal process, the *parlements* would prevent a subject's appeal for justice to the *Conseil du Roi*. The individual would go hat-in-hand to the *parlements*, but most requests for redress would be rebuffed—only a very small number of complaints got through to the *Conseil du Roi* in Paris.

The 1789 French Revolution was a radical break with tradition in practically every area, and the *parlements* were not untouched. The power of these *parlements* was shattered soon after 1789 by the famous (and still in force) law of August 16-24, 1790. Article 12 of this law reads:

Les fonctions judiciares sont distinctes et demeureront séparées des fonctions administratives. Les juges ne pourront à peine de forfaiture troubler de quelque manière que ce soit les opérations des corps administratifs ni citer devant eux les administrateurs en raison de leurs fonctions.[18]

This absolute separation between the judicial and administrative functions gave total liberty to the administration: the *parlements* (courts) could not judge the bureaucrats, the power of the king was reduced, and the *Conseil du Roi* was abolished. The situation for some time, therefore, was that absolutely no avenues of redress were in operation, and the individual had no process of appeal for protection against bureaucratic abuse or mistreatment. Laws passed in September and October 1790 gave to each government minister in Paris the power to review his ministry's actions. This had no real effect on the redress process since Paris was a long way off for many people, and very seldom did the minister second-guess his own original decision.

Napoleon recognized the faults of this type of system and as part of his far-reaching administrative reforms, established the *Conseil d'État* in 1799.[19] The *Conseil d'État* had some linkages with the defunct *Conseil du Roi*: to advise the executive on administrative matters. The *Conseil d'État* was not a totally independent redress agency in 1799, but its foundation was in place. Napoleon as first consul, and then as emperor, was the head of the *Conseil d'État*, and the institution's first task was to draft new laws and administrative regulations and to resolve difficulties that occurred in the administration of public policy.

The power of the embryonic *Conseil* was limited, for it was an arm of Napoleon's imperial government, but it did provide an avenue of redress. The law of 1790 prevented people from using the ordinary courts for complaints against the state, and the *Conseil* filled this gap. Various decrees in 1799 marked out the *Conseil's* powers: it could hear complaints against the state only on appeal from the concerned minister's decision. The individual, after pleading with the minister for redress and still not satisfied, could then appeal to the *Conseil*. The *Conseil*, however, could not adjudicate the complaint—it could only advise the head of state on what action to take—and the real effective power to set aside improper administrative acts remained with the head of state.

This situation—the minister first having to hear the complaint and then the *Conseil* having only advisory functions—lasted until the Third Republic. The beginning of the *Conseil's* existence as a truly independent administrative court is in the law of May 24, 1872. This law empowered the *Conseil* to reach decisions in suits against the state in its own name; that is, the *Conseil* received the legal authority to render binding decisions without having to advise the head of state on what to do. Thus the *Conseil* could deliver judgments in the name of the French people rather than in the name of the head of state. The *Conseil* was no longer merely an advisory body to the executive but a true court. However, its jurisdiction was not altered in 1872—complaints still had to be brought before the relevant minister, and the *Conseil* could hear only cases on appeal from the minister's decisions.

Some problems arose over which court—the regular (civil, criminal) court hierarchy or the *Conseil*—had jurisdiction in particular cases. It was the head of state who, upon advice from the *Conseil*, decided where the case should be heard. This practice became unworkable, because the *Conseil* usually claimed for itself any conflicts of jurisdiction and, also in 1872, a special court was established, the *Tribunal des Conflits*, to resolve jurisdictional disputes. The *Tribunal des Conflits* has nine members: the minister of justice (its chairperson), four members drawn from the *Conseil d'État*, and four members from the *Cour de Cassation* (the Court of Cassation is at the apex of the regular court system). The *Tribunal des Conflits* does not decide cases: it is not a court of appeal and it is not constantly in session. Only if there is a dispute regarding jurisdiction competency is the *tribunal* called into session to decide which branch of the judiciary—administrative or regular—will hear the case.[20]

The requirement of first having to plead with the minister before coming to the *Conseil* was abolished in 1889.[21] The *Conseil* was given original jurisdiction on all complaints against the administration, and the individual seeking redress had ready access to this redress avenue. This organization lasted until 1953 when a severe backlog prompted a reorganization. The *Conseil* in Paris was years behind in its docket, and to speed up the process, twenty regional *Conseils* were created. These regional *Conseils* (called *tribunaux administratifs*) are now the courts of first instance for most cases, and the Paris *Conseil* serves as the appeal body for decisions coming from the *tribunaux administratifs*. The reorganization reduced the backlog, and the system provides relatively quick decisions.

The *Conseil d'État*, originally an arm of Napoleon's imperial government, has over the past one hundred and eighty years evolved into an effective and independent institution with control over how the king's agents treat the population. The scope of state activity has increased dramatically in France in the twentieth century—a logical result of its planned economy and welfare provisions—and the *Conseil* was already in place to protect the individual from state abuse or bureaucratic mistreatment. As mentioned above, the French experience was the model for other countries in Europe.

Powers and Jurisprudential Principles[22]

The *Conseil d'État* has two functions. The first function is to serve, as did the *Conseil du Roi*, as the principle expert adviser to the government. The *Conseil* gives advice on the drafting of various bills and decrees concerning their constitutionality, and some specific types of legislation must be submitted to the *Conseil* before the legislation can enter into force. The *Conseil* also advises the government ministries and departments regarding administrative problems and the interpretation of specific ordinances and regulations.[23] The *Conseil* has the ability to propose administrative reforms, but these must be approved and implemented by the usual parliamentary process.

The *Conseil's* second function is judicial, and it is with this function that this discussion is most concerned. The *Conseil d'État* deals with disputes between and among the different governmental departments and, more importantly, with cases where individual French citizens believe they have been (or will be) wronged by state actions or that they have been mistreated by the bureaucracy. French society clearly recognizes that the king can do wrong or authorize others to err: the *Conseil d'État* places the state in a position of defendant and provides redress for individual grievances. Specific actions by specific bureaucrats, as well as the enabling legislation behind the specific actions, can be challenged by the individual on various grounds: power had been exceeded by the administration, the mandated procedure was not followed, or powers not used for the purposes originally envisaged.

Two types of complaints are made to the *Conseil*: a *recours de pleine juri-*

diction and a *recours pour excès de pouvoir*. The first type, *recours de pleine juridiction*, is used by an individual seeking damages against the administration and does not concern general legislation: contract disputes, automobile accidents involving the police or postal service, and so on. Complaints of this nature, however, first must be directed at the relevant ministry for compensation and damages. If the government department does not grant compensation or if the individual thinks damages that are awarded are too small or if the ministry does not respond within a certain time (usually four months), the individual then has two months to seek redress in the administrative courts (the regional *tribunaux administratifs* and then the *Conseil d'État* in Paris). If the *Conseil* decides in favor of the individual, it can, with force of law, direct the government department to compensate the individual.

It is an entirely different situation if an individual believes he was harmed, or likely to be harmed, by a regulation issued by a public official (public officials in France include practically anyone on the state payroll from the mayor of a small commune through the administrative hierarchy to a far-reaching governmental decree). In such situations, the individual does not seek damages or compensation or does not "sue" anyone—the individual wants the decision or regulation annuled or quashed. Here the individual places the state in the position of defendant with a *recours pour excès de pouvoir*—he is complaining about a general regulation and its alleged harm to himself and other people. This type of complaint must be filed within two months from the time the regulation was first published.

As F. F. Ridley and Jean Blondel write,[24] it is the *recours pour excès de pouvoir* that has allowed the *Conseil d'État* to be an effective avenue of redress for the individual and to protect people from administrative abuse. The *Conseil* would have remained as a very formal and uninteresting process if it had limited itself to formal illegality: the annulment of acts and decisions because prescribed procedure was not followed or if the authority making the decision was not legally authorized to do so (*ultra vires*). The *Conseil* has moved beyond *ultra vires* and has employed the doctrine of *détournement de pouvoir* in setting aside administrative regulations. *Détournement de pouvoir* is the use of legal powers in a distorted manner or for purposes not originally contemplated by the enabling legislation.

The use of *détournement de pouvoir* by the *Conseil* as the grounds upon which to annul bureaucratic decisions allows the *Conseil* to probe beyond the surface of the decision that, on a superficial level of analysis, is entirely justified and legal. Through this doctrine, the *Conseil* can consider the motives behind the decision and whether these motives are in the public interest. The *Conseil* has been especially careful to protect the public interest when faced with apparently legal restrictions on individual human rights and public liberties. One of the most famous cases decided by the *Conseil*—the *Barel et al.*

case—involved this protection of individual human rights against state abuse.[25]

In 1953 five students tried to gain entry into the *Ecole Nationale d'Administration* (the ENA is the prestigious in-service training institution for the senior grades of the French civil service) but were refused permission to sit for the entrance examination by the state secretary acting on behalf of the prime minister. The refusal was based on the ground that the students were thought to be members of the French Communist party (it was against public policy at that time to allow Communists to occupy high-level administrative positions—positions that are almost automatic upon completion of ENA studies). The students appealed to the *Conseil* for redress, but the state secretary refused to provide an explanation for his decision. The secretary simply stated that he had full legal authority to determine who could, or could not, sit for the examination, and in this particular case, Barel *et al.* could not. The *Conseil* promptly annuled the decision and the students were afforded the opportunity to take ENA's entrance examination.

The exercise of administrative discretion in this case had absolutely no legal limitation—the secretary *did* have the statutory authority to determine eligibility criteria—but the *Conseil* saw this as *détournement de pouvoir*. Barel *et al.* were mistreated, and their basic human rights—the right of political belief—were abused. The *Conseil* held that the original decision denied equal rights of access to French government service on the grounds of political belief and, as such, was contrary to the general principles of French law as contained in the Declaration of the Rights of Man. The *Conseil* also has not hesitated to deliver unfavorable opinions to the strong de Gaulle regime: the *Conseil* refused to sanction General de Gaulle's special court established under article 16 of the Constitution of the Fifth Republic (emergency powers), and it declared, in 1962, that de Gaulle's proposed use of a referendum to change the method of electing the French president was unconstitutional. This latter decision, however, had no effect for it was one of the rare occasions when the head of state ignored the *Conseil*: de Gaulle appealed to the people, and the referendum passed by an overwhelming margin. The *Conseil* has had very little conflict with those—Georges Pompidou and Valéry Giscard d'Estaing—who have followed de Gaulle.

The power to review and possibly annul governmental decisions is not unlimited, however. The French make a clear distinction between *actes de gouvernement* and *actes d'administration*. The former is beyond the reach of the *Conseil* and includes purely "political" acts (sending bills to parliament, dissolution of parliament) and acts of sovereignty (international relations, treaties, use of French military troops abroad, recognition of other countries, decisions taken by diplomats). These *actes de gouvernement* are unchallengeable, but their scope is both limited and well defined.

Finally, the *Conseil* decides cases as an arbitrator rather than as a judge. It is not bound in all circumstances by existing legislation nor is *stare decisis* ("precedent") always followed. Each individual case is examined on its merits, and the *Conseil* represents a radical departure from the usual French theory of judging by not automatically applying codified law to each case.

Procedure

Procedure in the *Conseil d'État* is different from that employed in the regular courts, and this difference works well for the individual who is seeking redress. The procedure is really an investigation by the *Conseil* on behalf of the individual to discover whether the complaining individual's allegations against the state are justified. This method has several advantages for the individual, and they illustrate the effectiveness of this avenue of redress.

First, about the only thing the individual has to do to get his case heard is formally to file a motion against the public authority in the administrative courts. This simple motion is used for both the *recours de pleine juridiction* ("seeking compensation") and the *recours pour excès de pouvoir* ("seeking an annulment of a decision"). The small filing fee does not prevent people from using the *Conseil*. An individual may retain legal counsel (and thus pay his fees) to present the case, but a lawyer is not required to pursue a complaint. Since the *Conseil* itself investigates the problem, one really does not require legal counsel to prepare the "facts"—the notice to sue or complain is sufficient to start the process.

Another advantage to the individual is with the *Conseil's* investigation. A member of the *Conseil* (an *auditeur* or a *maître des requêtes*) investigates the complaint and may find facts, arguments, or interpretations that the individual had overlooked or could not discover himself. The *Conseil* has access to the administrative files—access that is denied to the individual making the complaint—and thus all relevant information is no doubt made available. The action of the *Conseil* here resembles the action of the Scandinavian ombudsman—the redress agency itself takes the initiative and aids the individual against the state rather than forcing the quite powerless individual to "prove" the complaint in the face of the absence of all relevant information.

The *auditeurs* and *maîtres des requêtes* may spend months investigating specific cases. Their report and conclusions are then given to those who actually decide the case, the *conseillers*. The report's function is to clarify the issues—issues both of law and fact—for the benefit of the judges. The complaining individual need not have legal counsel throughout the entire process (although a recent tendency is for more and more people to engage an attorney), but the defendant—the public authority or bureaucratic department—must have legal counsel. The latter is the defendant and may not be unrepresented in the administrative courts.

The process is inexpensive, relatively quick, and provides advantages to the individual. The French have recognized that private individuals have little power vis-à-vis a governmental department, and the procedure employed in the *Conseil* is an attempt to make these power relationships more symmetrical or equal. This does not mean the state is considered "guilty" before the process begins; on the contrary, it only means that the state's overwhelming power is neutralized by the *Conseil*.

Organization and Staffing

The *Conseil* has five sections, with four of them belonging to the administrative side and the fifth, the judicial section.[26] The four administrative sections—concerned with the constitutionality of proposed legislation and requests for advice from government ministries—have separate subject matters: finance, interior, public works, and social affairs. Each of the administrative sections has a president and from six to ten *conseillers*. The judicial section—concerned with the *recours de pleine juridiction* and the *recours pour excès de pouvoir*—is much larger. It has a president, two vice-presidents, and a number of *conseillers* equal to the total number in the four administrative sections. The judicial section is divided into nine subsections, and judgments are made by these subsections. In important cases, several of these subsections come together to decide a case, but the entire judicial section does not sit together to hear a case.

The distinction between the administrative and judicial sections is concerned with functions only. The *conseillers* may move from one section to another, and several specific committees within the *Conseil* are made up of both sets of *conseillers*. The working conditions, salary, and so on are the same across all sections. The *auditeurs* and *maîtres des requêtes* are more heavily represented in the judicial section for obvious reasons, but they, too, may move from section to section. The usual line of promotion begins with the entry level position of *auditeur*, about age twenty-five to twenty-six, to a *maître des requêtes*, about age thirty-five, and, depending upon competency and personnel needs, the *Conseillers d'État* are drawn from the *maîtres*, about age fifty. No lateral entry exists, and most make a career with the *Conseil d'État*.

The personnel are drawn from the intellectual elite of French society. The *Conseil d'État* is a *grands corps* in French civil service, and its members are now recruited directly from the prestigious *Ecole Nationale d'Administration*. A law degree is not required, although many do have such training. As high-ranking civil servants, these people have all the guarantees of other high-ranking French civil servants: they can be dismissed only for cause, they cannot be transferred out of the *Conseil* against their will, the prestige of the office is high, and salary levels are adequate even accounting for the high cost of living in Paris.

The *Conseillers d'État* are civil servants sitting in judgment over other civil servants, but seldom has a hint of favoritism for the government position been evident in complaints brought before them. Their decisions are as likely to be against the government as they are to be for it, and the legitimacy of their decisions is not questioned. The *conseillers* are experts in administrative matters, and they are well equipped to deal with administrative problems.[27] The *Conseil d'État* is congruent with French culture and values and works well for the individual in the redress process.

SOME CONCLUDING COMMENTS

The French *Conseil d'État* represents a fair balance between the needs of a modern, efficient, and technological administrative apparatus, on the one hand, and the principles of legality, on the other. These principles are not limited to the impersonal French code but extend to general principles of law, including the precepts of the Revolution and the Declaration of the Rights of Man. The *Conseil* attempts to respect administrative action without curbing it with a hidebound formalism. It is not a watch-dog agency, ready to swoop down at a moment's notice, but neither does it hesitate to protect the individual from bureaucratic abuse or mistreatment.

The French philosophy on the role of the state in society allows a much greater positive role for the state compared to other societies. But linked to this view of the powers of the state is the view that the state also has obligations to its people. The state is responsible for its actions and thus can be held liable for illegality and/or for misuse of legal power. The delegation of authority from Parliament to the administration is not by itself sufficient to defend against a charge that this power was used unjustly. The actions of the bureaucrats must not only be within the letter of French laws but also within their spirit.

The *Conseil d'État* has survived and has gained influence and prestige, because it is a low-key institution. Its powers were really not detailed in the constitutions, and thus it has escaped the usual flows of authority over the past one hundred and eighty years with the changing French systems. It has survived empires, monarchies, Vichy, and five republics, doing its job quietly, efficiently and competently. The French population is well served by the *Conseil d'État*, for it does place the state in a position of defendant, and it does provide redress for individual grievances.

However, the *Conseil* system as an avenue of redress has one major shortcoming. The *Conseil* may be an excellent check or curb on past unacceptable behavior, but it contributes little to encourage or spur good future behavior. It is an *ex post* institution, reacting to individual complaints. This lack of positive education for the future behavior of the administration compares very unfavorably with that of the ombudsman. One of the major—if not *the* major—task of the ombudsman is not to punish past behavior but, rather, to encourage future good behavior. The *Conseil* is silent in this regard, but, as is discussed in the following chapter, the classical Scandinavian ombudsman is future oriented.

NOTES

1. Stanley Rothman has an excellent discussion of the legal system's functions in his *European Society and Politics* (Indianapolis and New York: The Bobbs-Merrill Co., 1970), esp. chapter 20, "Law, Society, and Politics in Western Europe," pp. 609–62.

2. Ibid., pp. 609–14.

3. See F. F. Ridley and Jean Blondel, *Public Administration in France* (New York: Barnes & Noble, 1965), esp. chapter 5, "The Administration of Justice," pp. 125–59.

4. Arnold J. Heidenheimer, *The Governments of Germany*, 2nd ed. (New York: Thomas Y. Crowell Co., 1966), esp. chapter 7, "The Judicial System and the Constitutional Court," pp. 156–71; Elmer Plischke, *Contemporary Governments of Germany*, 2nd ed. (Boston: Houghton Mifflin Co., 1969), esp. chapter 7, "The Judiciary," pp. 120–38.

5. The discussion of these five institutional frameworks rests upon "The 1962 Seminar on Judicial and Other Remedies Against the Abuse of Administrative Authority with Special Emphasis on the Role of Parliamentary Instructions," Stockholm, Sweden, June 12–25, 1962 (New York: United Nations, 1962), 34 pp.

6. The procuracy in the Soviet Union, among other activities, exercises "general supervision" over public authorities to guard against abuses of law. See Walter Gellhorn, *Ombudsmen and Others: Citizens' Protectors in Nine Countries* (Cambridge: Harvard University Press, 1966), esp. chapter 8, "The Soviet Union," pp. 336–71. However, as Gellhorn wrote (p. 346), the function of general supervision sometimes takes a subordinate place: "procurators devoted themselves to zealous enforcement of criminal laws while carefully failing to observe their fellow officials' abuses. Infringements of personal rights tended to be ignored, attention was concentrated on protecting the State's supposed interests."

7. Ridley and Blondel, *Public Administration in France*, p. 149.

8. For an excellent examination of the origin and development of these tribunals, their membership and organization, and their supervision by Parliament, the courts, and the Council on Tribunals, see R. E. Wraith and R. G. Hutchesson, *Administrative Tribunals* (London: Allen & Unwin, Ltd., 1973).

9. An important exception to this right of appeal to the regular courts is in cases dealing with national insurance; here the ultimate appeal is to the national insurance commissioner.

10. Crichel Down was an area of land in Dorset that had been requisitioned by the Air Ministry in 1940 as a bombing range. It was agreed, when the land was originally acquired, that the original owner would have the opportunity of taking over the land when the Air Ministry was finished with it. But after the war, when the Air Ministry no longer had any use for the land, instead of being returned to the previous owner, it was offered to other departments. The Ministry of Agriculture took it over, and when the

original owner claimed the land, the Ministry of Agriculture ignored the complaint and would not release the land. See R. D. Brown, *The Battle of Crichel Down* (London: Bodley Head, 1955).

11. Geoffrey Marshall, "The Franks Report on Administrative Tribunals and En-quiries," *Public Administration* 35 (Winter 1957): 347–58; William A. Robson, "Administrative Justice and Injustice: A Commentary on the Franks Report," *Public Law* (Spring 1958): 12–31.

12. R. M. Punnett, *British Government and Politics* (New York: W. W. Norton & Co., 1968), p. 338.

13. Ibid., p. 336.

14. The classic and definitive work in the area of nationalized industries and public ownership is by William A. Robson, *Nationalized Industry and Public Ownership*, rev. 2nd ed. (London: Allen & Unwin, Ltd., 1962). Robson's chapter 10, "Con-sumers' and Consultative Councils" (pp. 243–77) details the organizational frame-work of these councils.

15. Ibid., p. 244.

16. Ibid., pp. 271–72.

17. The discussion of the historical evolution of the *Conseil d'État* is based upon L. Brown and J. Garner, *French Administrative Law* (London: Butterworth Law Pub-lishers, Ltd., 1967), pp. 18–21; Mauro Cappelleti and William Cohen, *Comparative Constitutional Law* (Indianapolis and New York: The Bobbs-Merrill Co., 1979), pp. 29–33; and upon what is perhaps the best book on the *Conseil*, Marie-Christine Kessler, *Le Conseil d'État*, Cahiers de la foundation nationale des sciences politiques (No. 167) and published with the cooperation of Centre nationale de recherche scientifique (Paris: Armand Colin, 1968), pp. 29–52.

18. Cited in Kessler, *Le Conseil d'État*, p. 28. The English translation is as follows: "Judicial functions are distinct and will always remain separate from administrative functions. Judges [in the civil courts] may not, under penalty of loss of office, concern themselves in any manner whatsoever with the operation of the administration nor shall they call administrators to account before them regarding the exercise of their official duties.'

19. Kessler (p. 28) reproduces some of Napoleon's remarks: "Je veux instituer un corps demi-administratif, demi-judiciaire qui reflète l'emploi de cette portion d'arbi-traire nécessaire dans l'administration de l'État. On ne peut laisser cet arbitraire entre les mains du prince parce qu'il l'exerce mal ou négligé de l'exercer." Originally in Pelet de la Lozère, *Opinion de Napoleon Ier sur divers sujets de politique et d'administra-tion recueillis par un membre du Conseil d'État; et récit de quelques évenements de l'époque* (Paris: Firmin-Didot, 1833), p. 190.

20. Ridley and Blondel, *Public Administration in France*, pp. 154–55, also remark that the *Tribunal des Conflits* has the power to assign a case to a particular jurisdiction if the individual's request for redress was not heard in any court because of an alleged lack of jurisdiction.

21. It was the *Cadot* case that marked this stage in the *Conseil's* evolution. Individ-uals still could go to the minister if they wanted before appealing to the *Conseil*, but such a first step was no longer a legal requirement. See Cappelleti and Cohen, *Com-parative Constitutional Law*, p. 32.

22. This section is based upon Ridley and Blondel, *Public Administration in France*, pp. 156–58.

23. One such example of a request to the *Conseil* for advice is given by Kessler, *Le Conseil d'État*, p. 400. The *Conseil* was told by the minister of health that a commune, after building a new hospital for the general population, wanted to use the old hospital solely for the care of the area's elderly priests. The advice sought concerned whether this was acceptable in light of the general French principle that public hospitals were open to anyone who required care.

24. Ridley and Blondel, *Public Administration in France*, p. 157.

25. The *Barel* case is from Andrew Shonfield, *Modern Capitalism: The Changing Balance of Public and Private Power* (New York and London: Oxford University Press, 1965), pp. 414–15.

26. The regional *tribunaux administratifs* are organizationally separate from the *Conseil* with their own recruitment function. The typical *tribunal* has four or five judges, with no separation into administrative or judicial sections.

27. The personnel of the *Conseil*, to increase their expertise, are permitted (and encouraged) to take leaves of absence for several years. The leaves can be spent with an administrative department or in the private sector. The philosophy underlying this is that the people will, upon return to the *Conseil*, have a better understanding of the administrative function both from the view of the bureaucrats and from the population's perspective. The idea that this could lead to possible conflict of interests is dismissed by the French.

THE OMBUDSMAN OR CITIZENS' PROTECTOR:
The Scandinavian Model and Attempts at Cloning

4

The ponderous, lengthy, costly, and formal legal procedures described in chapter 2 and the somewhat more streamlined procedures outlined in chapter 3 may in the long run be able to provide avenues of redress and afford the individual with protection against administrative abuse. These formal legal institutions and proceedings are excellent in regard to outright acts of illegality or criminality by the bureaucracy and in regard to administrative abuse of existing legislation. As discussed in chapter 2, the intervention of the American federal court hierarchy most certainly did terminate abuse of existing passport legislation by the U.S. Passport Office within the Department of State. For certain types of complaints or grievances, the courts, tribunals, law, and the formal judicial process are ideally suited to protect the individual's status vis-à-vis the state.

But this book is dealing with the atypical societies, and their sacrosanct legal procedures and institutions are in reality ill suited for many of the grievances people may have concerning the bureaucratic apparatus. We are dealing here with a set of Western democracies that, with few individual exceptions, have a civil service and administrative personnel and agents of the king who are competent, dedicated, and honest people who show very little "official criminality" in their dealings with the public. Although widely publicized and rightfully deplorable and inexcusable, the Ohio National Guard's killing of the students at Kent State University was an aberration: the overwhelming majority of the king's agents in the United States and Western Europe do not engage in similar behavior in the twentieth century. If the grievance is of the magnitude of Kent State, however, the best possible system of redress is to retain a competent attorney and seek satisfaction in the courts.

Most of the grievances in contemporary Western democracies do *not* entail the demand to sue, to exact a financial penalty from the bureaucrat or the bureaucratic agency, or to lock up the miscreant. Rather, many of the grievances in our technocratic and computerized urban society are only—but not merely or unimportantly—concerned with the individual's desire to be treated with respect and to expect efficient, courteous, and humane service from the state, especially in the area dealing with the delivery of public services or in the receipt of government benefits. For the most part, such grievances involve requests for information and explanations, services one believes one is entitled to, and sometimes an apology and a few outright demands for a revamped application of bureaucratic operating procedures—seldom is there the demand to sue or to put anyone behind bars. In other words, it is the daily frustration of having to deal with the administrative apparatus that gives rise to citizen complaints rather than any alleged blatant illegality of the bureaucrats themselves.

An example illustrates this essential difference about the nature of complaints that do not belong in the courts but nonetheless should be resolved in the interests of legitimacy, system support, and individual satisfaction. Several years ago, I had an unfortunate and frustrating experience while renewing a driver's license. The then current procedure was to fill in a standard form, sign it, pay the renewal fee, surrender the expiring license, and receive the renewal. This could not be done through the mail, and one was required to appear at the local bureau. Accordingly, I went to the local bureau and received my renewal quickly and painlessly. While at the counter, I inquired about my wife's renewal: "Would it be possible," I asked the clerk, "for me to take a blank form home, have my wife fill it in and sign it, and then for me to return it and receive her renewal?" The clerk assured me that as long as all of the forms were properly completed and I surrendered the expiring license, I could indeed receive the renewal, and my wife's presence at the bureau would not be necessary.

I returned a few weeks later with all of the required forms, signatures, checks, and documents. Unfortunately, there was a long line, and the wait was approximately thirty minutes before reaching the clerk at the counter. Expecting fast and courteous service once I reached the counter, I was in for a rude shock. The clerk looked at the form, brusquely announced that red ink was not acceptable (my wife had used red ink), tore up and discarded the form, and called for the next person in line. There I was: no renewal, thirty-one minutes and bus fare wasted, and, most important, the prospect of another thirty-minute wait to get another blank form (only the clerk would dispense the forms—they were not on a table with free access). The uniformed (and armed) security guard at the bureau informed me that line cutting was frowned upon, and he recommended that I not try to push to the front of the line, even if it were only to request a new form.

The additional thirty minutes in the line provided ample opportunity for reflection on redress procedures: I had what I considered to be a valid complaint about the treatment received, but what avenues were available to me and for what ends? To have used the formal court procedure with a lawyer and judge and jury would have been ludicrous, an exercise in overkill, and, in all probability, not at all applicable to my complaint. Whom could I possibly charge as "defendant"—the clerk? Her supervisor? The person whose turn it was next? The security guard? The head of the motor vehicle bureau in the state capital? The Governor? My wife? What "charge" would I allege, and what "damages" could I possibly seek—lock up the clerk? Seek reimbursement for my bus fare (20¢)? Require the state to issue my wife's renewal without the necessary signed form? Have the governor apologize for the actions of a state bureaucrat? Would any attorney even consider this "case"? I was convinced that, buried somewhere in the relevant manual for bureau clerks, the ink color was probably specified and that the clerk was correct in rejecting the form. I did not want to sue anyone, and the entire situation was free of illegality or criminality. The ponderous judicial process was ill suited to my complaint, especially since my wife's license was about to expire, and she needed the renewal, grievance or no grievance.

My unvoiced and nonpursued complaint concerned a psychological need to have my frustration alleviated and a political need to express my dissatisfaction; my complaint did not involve a desire to have someone put in jail. I would have liked to have the clerk told by her supervisor that if similar situations were to happen again, the form should at least be ripped up and discarded with a smile and not with a sneer; that perhaps signs ("Black Ink Only") should be posted so other people would not have to stand in a line that leads nowhere; that perhaps the bureau's operating procedures might be altered to accept any color ink and/or have the forms available at a table so there would be no line merely to get a form; or, in the best of all possible worlds, to have the entire process of license renewals automated and completed through the mails (the procedure described above has indeed been revised, but since photographs are now taken for renewals, the lines and waiting time are larger and longer than ever).

My complaint was not pursued, because no satisfactory avenues were available for that particular situation. It is precisely for situations like the one described above that the ombudsman would be extremely useful. The ombudsman, if one existed, might have recognized the merits of my complaint and might have been able to prevent similar well-meaning but unsuspecting people from falling into the identical situation. The ombudsman might have done his best to put a human and humane face on public administration and educate the clerks—and their supervisors—about the needs and feelings of the individual whom they are to serve.

The ombudsman would not have punished anyone—not only was I not seeking revenge but also the ombudsman normally does not have the power or authority to "punish"—but, perhaps, the ombudsman's intercession might have led to an official apology from the bureau for not informing me in advance about the correct procedure. Such a letter would have thoroughly and completely redressed my grievance without ponderous proceedings. The ombudsman is ill suited for a Kent State type of situation but is ideally suited for mundane and everyday citizen complaints. If I had been a Dane or a Swede or a New Zealander, I might have received that letter; being in Ohio, all I could do was grumble and tell my wife to get her own renewal.

THE CLASSICAL MODEL

The office of ombudsman is not new. It originated in Sweden in 1809, but it was not until Denmark established its ombudsman in 1955 that awareness of, and interest in, the institution spread beyond Scandinavia. The term itself is of Swedish origin, and the closest English rendition of ombudsman would be "citizens' protector," although it is usually not translated, and the term *ombudsman* has found its way into current English usage. The descriptive term *ombudsman* has received wide acceptance, but it is applied to a whole set of differing processes, and, outside of Scandinavia, the same term can now mean different things in relation to its specific cultural and organizational setting. The term *ombudsman*, when employed without any descriptive adjective, refers to the classical Scandinavian model; the qualifiers *quasi*, *executive*, or *specialized* describe an ombudsman who has some characteristics similar to the classical model but who is different in several significant areas. The following comments differentiate these types and provide an introduction to the classical Scandinavian model.

Several definitions have been put forth in the literature to describe the classical Scandinavian model, but only a few of these are presented here. A 1974 resolution by the International Bar Association's Ombudsman Committee defined the ombudsman as follows:

An office provided for by the Constitution or by action of the legislature or parliament and headed by an independent, high-level official who is responsible to the legislature or parliament, who receives complaints from aggrieved persons against government agencies, officials, and employees or who acts on his own motion, and who has the power to investigate, recommend corrective action, and issue reports.[1]

Stanley Anderson listed five characteristics that he considered essential to the office: the ombudsman should be "(1) independent, (2) impartial, (3) expert in government, (4) universally accessible, and (5) empowered only to recommend and to publicize."[2] Three essential characteristics were identified by Donald C. Rowat: "(1) the Ombudsman is an independent and non-partisan officer of the legislature, usually provided for in the constitution, who supervises the administration; (2) he deals with specific complaints from the public against administrative injustice and maladministration; and (3) he has the power to investigate, criticize and publicize, but not to reverse, administrative action."[3]

Another description was offered by Larry Hill: the classical ombudsman is "(1) legally established, (2) functionally autonomous, (3) external to the administration; (4) operationally independent of both the legislature and the executive; (5) specialist; (6) expert; (7) nonpartisan; (8) normatively universalistic; (9) client-centered but not anti-administration; and (10) both popularly accessible and visible."[4] Hill continued his description of the classical model:

The institution's mission is to generate complaints against government administration, to use its extensive powers of investigation in performing a postdecision administrative audit, to form judgments which criticize or vindicate administrators, and to report publicly its findings and recommendations but *not* to change administrative decisions.[5]

In summary, then, the classical Scandinavian model is a competent nonpartisan individual, chosen by Parliament and responsible only to Parliament, who is charged with receiving complaints from individual citizens about the treatment they receive from the bureaucracy. The ombudsman has full access to files and documents; he can attempt to achieve a "friendly settlement" in cases where he sees merit on both sides to the controversy; he can recommend future changes in administrative practice (that is, his role to "educate" the bureaucracy to prevent reoccurrences rather than a role of "punishing" people for past behavior). The ombudsman cannot normally levy a fine against anyone, nor can he normally institute judicial proceedings against an individual bureaucrat or against an administrative agency. He cannot deal with complaints concerning parliamentary acts—such acts are public policy and thus "political" decisions—but only with complaints concerning the implementation or application of such decisions by the administration. The ombudsman can usually handle complaints against practically anyone on the state payroll but not against private entities (that is, a department store, a private corporation).

It should be obvious that, at least in those societies that have created a functioning classical ombudsman, the doctrine of sovereign immunity has been severely diluted. Although the inability of the ombudsman to handle grievances or complaints against parliamentary actions—the political decisions—may retain the view that the king can do no wrong, the very legislation that establishes a classical ombudsman recognizes that the king (parliament) *can* authorize others to do wrong in the implementation of these political decisions. The classical ombudsman has evolved into an effective avenue of redress for those individuals who believe themselves wronged by the king's agents. However, of all of the hundreds of institutions and people categorized as an ombudsman, only a small minority can truly be termed a classical organization as described above. The majority of such positions are quasi or executive or specialized ombudsmen, or more unfortunately, merely glorified complaint officers with the more politically pleasing title of ombudsman.

This second type of ombudsman—the quasi or executive ombudsman—has one or more of the above essential characteristics missing. The most significant and crucial characteristic lacking is the one of independence and autonomy, for without real independence, such an ombudsman is severely limited in whatever else he may be able to accomplish. This lack of independence is usually due to the sometimes deliberate blurring of the appointing entity and the group the ombudsman is expected to evaluate. The classical model has no such blurring: parliament appoints the ombudsman to receive complaints against the administration and the ombudsman is responsible to parliament—the ombudsman cannot receive or investigate complaints against parliamentary decisions or against members of parliament, and he is not responsible to the administration. The quasi or executive ombudsman, on the other hand, is usually an in-house official who somehow is expected impartially to investigate complaints against the very agency or personnel who have appointed him and to whom he is responsible.

Examples of such nonautonomous ombudsmen are internal police review boards, university ombudsmen, municipal complaint departments, and most specialized ombudsmen whose area of competence is restricted to certain functional groups (for example, prison and hospital ombudsmen). Of all of the institutions and positions that carry the title ombudsman and that reproduce some of its characteristics, only about fifty can be categorized as falling within the classical Scandinavian model. The remainder are those quasi-ombudsmen found in universities, asylums, city hall complaint bureaus, and so on. These fifty classical ombudsmen are not limited to Scandinavia as they once were. The office is receiving more and more worldwide attention, and the New Zealand ombudsman, for example, established in 1962, has all of the essential characteristics listed above and is an excellent reproduction of the Danish or Swedish model.

Larry B. Hill identified the locations of many of these classical ombudsmen.[6] Scandinavia has about nine (six in Sweden and one each in Finland, Denmark, and Norway); the British Commonwealth has about twenty with one each in New Zealand, Fiji, Mauritius, and India (Maharashtra); Australia has five (Victoria, South Australia, Western Australia, Queensland, and New South Wales); the United Kingdom has four (Northern Ireland, the British parliamentary commissioner, and the commissioners for local administration in Scotland and Wales); and, still within the Commonwealth, Canada has eight (one each in Alberta, Quebec, Manitoba, Nova Scotia, Ontario, and Newfoundland and two in Saskatchewan). France has one; Switzerland (Zurich) has one; Italy (Tuscany) has one; and Israel has three (the commissioner for complaints from the public and one each in Jerusalem and Haifa). Finally, the United States has approximately ten classical ombudsmen: Hawaii, Iowa, Nebraska, Alaska, Montgomery County/Dayton (Ohio), King County/Seattle (Washington), Jackson County/Kansas City (Missouri), Atlanta, Detroit, and Wichita.

Space does not allow for a full discussion of all of these classical ombudsmen, nor does it even permit a comparison of two positions.[7] The section below deals, therefore, with the common strands found in the classical Scandinavian model. That is, the following discussion does not attempt to describe any one specific institution but, rather, to present a composite view. Each specific office will, of course, vary somewhat from this composite picture but not significantly. The areas discussed are: the origins and history of the office; its functions; administrative details such as appointment procedures, salary, staff, qualifications, costs, time, and accessibility to the public and accessibility to government files; its powers and the limitations to which these powers are subjected; the image or perception that the public, bureaucracy, press, and ombudsmen themselves have of the office; some summary case loads; and its exportability to other cultures.

The ombudsman originated in Sweden in 1809 (the *Justitieombudsmand*) under the philosophy that the governing bureaucracy should be controlled in its dealings with the population. The office was to serve the interest of Parliament—he was chosen by and responsible to Parliament—as a counterpart to the attorney-general (*Justitiekansler*) who was a "domestic official . . . empowered to supervise the application of the law by judges and other officials [but] whose office had long been a part of the royal administration."[8] The parliamentary ombudsman would not be the king's agent but, rather, the people's agent, and he enjoyed the ability to institute proceedings against government officials and judges. Such proceedings, however, would be heard by the general court structures and not by Parliament. The Swedish ombudsman had a long and honorable history, but it received very little attention beyond Sweden. It was not until almost one hundred and fifty years later, when Denmark established the office, that people beyond Scandinavia became aware of and interested in the institution.[9]

The Danes took almost ten years to establish their ombudsman. The Constitutional Commission of 1946, in a report in 1953, recommended the introduction of a system based on the Swedish *Justitieombudsmand*. The 1953 Danish constitution provided for Parliament to appoint one or two people to supervise the civil and military administrations. Parliament passed the enabling legislation in 1954, and the supervisory powers were vested in a single person. The office formally began activity in 1955.

The typical Scandinavian ombudsman is chosen by, and responsible to, the legislative body, for example, the national Parliament. In democratic theory, Parliament embodies and represents the people's will, and, therefore, the ombudsman is the people's representative vis-à-vis the bureaucracy. The ombudsman is usually appointed by an all-party consensus, with a unanimous vote, without having several candidates publicly vying for the position. The office would suffer an extreme disservice if several candidates were seeking the position, each exaggerating their grandiose schemes and promises "if elected." This is not to say, however, that no competition for the office ever occurs. In some systems, the majority party or ruling coalition in Parliament may nominate one person, the minority may nominate another, and, obviously, the majority's nominee wins the parliamentary vote. Even if only one name is submitted to Parliament, heated discussion and debate in party caucuses may still result before agreement on the nominee is reached.

Any "political" considerations that enter the selection process are usually dealt with before the vote in Parliament, and, from one perspective, the selection of the ombudsman is not a "political" decision. Past experience has shown that the Scandinavian ombudsmen—whomever he may be and however he may be chosen—have generally been free of previous partisan political activity and party affiliations. Larry B. Hill found, in fact, that the classical Scandinavian ombudsman is wary of past political activity.[10] A full 100 percent of Hill's Scandinavian respondents believed offices such as theirs should not be filled by former politicians, and only 25 percent thought that having and cultivating close political connections, and having them generally known, could increase the effectiveness of their office.[11] The ombudsman must have an astute political sense to function, but the Scandinavians have not seen the office as a reward for former politicians or party hacks.

Although past political visibility would seem to disqualify a person from becoming an ombudsman in Scandinavia, a heavy emphasis is placed upon a legal background. Most systems specify that the ombudsman be "trained in the law" (lawyers, judges, law professors, and so on), although the possession of a formal law degree is not a specific requirement. Most ombudsmen do not enter a court of law as ombudsman, but a heavy portion of their work *is* legally relevant. They must be fully conversant with the administrative process and the entire structure and functioning of government, and the position entails constant analyses of the various statutes and laws. But this does not mean that the ombudsman is only another ossified cog in the application of impersonal legal codes and administrative procedures: several ombudsmen have encouraged a more personal and individualized application of "rules" (fit the rule to the person rather than fitting the person to the rule).[12] Many cases and opinions of the ombudsmen have contained the recommendation that "rules can be bent" in individual cases where hardship is present, and that each individual situation should be considered fully by the bureaucrat before applying the relevant policy.

The ombudsman's term of office is limited—either for a specified number of years or for the life of the parliament that appointed him. They thus do not have life tenure as do federal judges in the United States. The ombudsman can be removed by Parliament—this has not yet happened—and they can be reappointed—this has happened frequently. The position carries a relatively high salary in relation to the economic values of their societies, and the amount is usually pegged to those of the very highest levels in the civil service or cabinet positions. No hint of corruption about the ombudsman's office has arisen, and this is primarily because of the caliber of the people selected. The salary level, however, does play a role here: the ombudsman is paid a high enough salary so he is likely to be above kickbacks and bribes. In addition, the practice of selecting people who have already achieved a measure of success in life and thus are nearing the end of their career has militated against having the ombudsman attempting to employ the office only as way-station or a stepping stone to bigger and better things. The situation so prevalent in the United States with the federal regulatory agencies' commissioners receiving employment with those industries that they were formerly "regulating" simply is not duplicated with the Scandinavian ombudsmen. The ombudsmen also enjoy relatively full freedom over their own staff (hiring, working conditions, firing), and, in some societies, an appointment to the ombudsman's staff is an excellent way of gaining the expertise and understanding needed for a successful career.

The ombudsman is generally empowered to receive complaints from individuals and organizations, directed at those on the public payroll (in some systems, this extends to the military and the courts). But in no system with a classical ombudsman is the ombudsman empowered to handle complaints directed at parliament—complaints directed at the public policy decisions generated by the political process. This prohibition is well founded, and it aids in maintaining the ombudsman's autonomy vis-à-vis parliament. It is an agreed-upon precept that parliament represents the people, and the ombudsman should not be empowered to substitute one man's philosophy for parliament's collective wisdom, whether or not such collective wisdom is wise or silly, just or unjust. In addition, in those systems where parliamentary public policy can be reviewed, it is for the courts and the judicial process to so decide and not for the ombudsman. The population at-large also can review public policy through the electoral process, and the ombudsman is *not* seen as a one-person Supreme Court striking down legislative acts.

This total lack of competence vis-à-vis parliament also strengthens the ombudsman's autonomy. He is not placed in the untenable position of having to "investigate" those to whom he is responsible—a situation that unfortunately exists in most quasi-ombudsmen systems—and thus the ombudsman is not hindered by power relationships and authority patterns vis-à-vis those he is empowered to deal with. Linked to this is the dictum, however, that parliament can neither forbid nor mandate any specific action by the ombudsman. The office is dependent upon parliament, but it is also autonomous: the ombudsman is parliament's "watchdog" over the bureaucracy in the latter's administration and application of public policy.

Most ombudsmen have a wide discretion in terms of deciding which grievances and complaints warrant attention and which are to be summarily dismissed. Of course, several types of complaints must be declined by the ombudsman according to statutory limitations: anonymous ones; ones that have not yet exhausted other avenues of redress or are still under review by another agency; ones that relate to matters older than a specified time (New Zealand's limit is one year); or ones that are directed at agencies beyond the ombudsman's jurisdiction. In addition, most ombudsmen have the ability to dismiss any grievance that they believe is trivial, frivolous, vexatious, not made in good faith, or those in which the ombudsman believes the individual has little personal interest. These latter categories ("frivolous" or "vexatious") are not defined by statute, and thus the ombudsman's personal preferences and interests play a major role in determining which grievances will be investigated.

The process is relatively straightforward for the majority of complaints received by ombudsman. Most are from individuals (although the proportion of grievances filed by organizations and attorneys on behalf of a client is increasing), and a simple letter is all that is necessary. The Scandinavian ombudsmen have no filing fee, and this avenue of free redress—the ombudsman's office is responsible for all the costs involved with an investigation—has led to an increased use of the office by those in the bottom social-economic strata (especially prisoners complaining about prison conditions). New Zealand had a filing fee (approximately $2) when its ombudsman was established to discourage "frivolous" complaints. This fee was abolished in 1975, however, for it was thought that the fee was preventing some people from writing to the ombudsman. The frivolous complaints usually increase when it does not cost anything, but this is a small, and acceptable, burden if the office becomes available to all economic segments of society.

In fact, as both Larry B. Hill and Kent M. Weeks remarked, a major contribution of the ombudsman is to involve the poor and previously inarticulate segment of the population in the redress process and thus increase the levels of political efficacy, participation, and legitimacy. Most of the Scandinavian ombudsmen perceive their clients to be mainly the poor[13] who would not ordinarily pursue a grievance, and the ombudsmen have been able to extract meaning from obscurely—and often illiterately—described dissatisfactions. One does *not* require an attorney and a legal brief to pursue redress with the ombudsman, and this is another major contribution of the process.

An analysis of several ombudsmen's case loads shows that, after discounting those complaints that are summarily dismissed, approximately 50 percent of those investigated are "resolved" within about two weeks. This is an extremely fast redress process, but it also shows that little alleged criminality or malfeasance exists. Typically, the ombudsman's staff makes a simple phone call to the agency concerned, receives the relevant information and explanation, and then responds to the complaining individual (and, in most cases, the individual is satisfied with the ombudsman's response). Other complaints obviously take longer, especially if the investigation is complex and/or if the agency does not cooperate fully with the ombudsman, but the ombudsman usually produces fast resolution.

The ombudsman has access to information: the documents, the files, the memos. Very few agencies will "stonewall" an ombudsman's request for information, for they do not regard the ombudsman as a witchhunter. The ombudsman does not have to publicize every little detail—he can change the names to protect the innocent—and the bureaucrats know that he will not publicize every slight lapse from absolute perfection. This almost unhindered access to official information and documentary evidence—as well as physical access to agencies, for most ombudsmen have the ability to institute an investigation on their own and "inspect" facilities—insures that whatever the ombudsman may eventually decide is based on complete information. The population is aware of this, which helps to explain why the ombudsman's decisions are readily accepted: he is perceived as an impartial observer with all relevant information, and, therefore, his decision must be correct.

This acceptance of the ombudsman can be seen in the numerous situations in which the complaining individual receives an almost verbatim decision from the ombudsman that the individual originally received from the agency being complained against. But since the reasons were given by the ombudsman, who is not seen as a defender of the agency, rather than by the agency itself, the individual feels satisfied (that is, it is the source of the decision that is important, not its specific content). The ombudsman enjoys a high level of acceptance and trust among the population as well as from among the bureaucracy: many are in the fortunate position of being perceived by the population at-large to their defender against bureaucratic insensitivity *but* at the same time being perceived by the bureaucracy as their defender against unjustified citizen complaints.

The ombudsmen's case loads vary (some receive more than two thousand complaints a year but others receive less than one thousand), although the number of complaints per capita is similar among the Scandinavian ombudsmen. Of all of the grievances received, however, only 7 to 9 percent at most are eventually resolved in favor of the individual. This is a small percentage, and it is good evidence that, assuming the ombudsman is not just window dressing, the bureaucracies of these systems are honest, capable, and sensitive agents of the king. But these figures are also evidence that the ombudsman who discovers something wrong *will* act and protect the individual. As mentioned above, most cases do not involve alleged criminality: they are requests and complaints from individuals concerning inefficiency by the bureaucrats or what they perceive to be an unjust denial of government services and benefits.

Two brief examples of specific cases handled by a classical ombudsman illustrate the usual type of citizen grievances.[14] In one case, the state's Social Security Commission changed a long-standing practice that allowed some welfare recipients to receive (and cash) the voucher up to seven days before payment was actually due—the new regulation specified that vouchers could not be issued until the date when payment was due. A person came to the appropriate office one day to collect her voucher, but she was told she would have to return the next day. She thought this was unreasonable and complained to the ombudsman: "I left the office feeling near to tears and knowing that these civil servants regarded me as a nuisance for daring to question departmental red tape. Goodness knows life is frustrating enough trying to bring up four youngsters to be decent citizens without these petty restrictions. . . ." The ombudsman thought her complaint had merit, and the eventual result was that she received an apology from the commission's chairman and the chairman also instructed the entire staff "not to enforce the new procedure with unthinking rigidity in the early stages before people knew and understood it."

The second example concerned a foreign student whose financial support was cut off by the host country's Department of External Affairs. This student failed six of ten courses, but he wrote that the failures were due to personal problems that no longer existed. He believed that his problems should have been "more sympathetically considered" and that he should be given a second chance. The ombudsman investigated to ascertain whether these "problems" were, in fact, taken into account by the committee who decided to terminate the financial support. The ombudsman, satisfied that the committee did take these factors into account, held the complaint to be unjustified. This is an example of the ombudsman *not* attempting to substitute his judgment for that of the agency authorized to make such decisions.

The two cases above did not allege criminality or misfeasance: they dealt with individuals who wanted to be treated as individuals by the bureaucratic apparatus. But instances occur where the ombudsman may uncover such behavior and, if so, prosecution may be warranted. In some systems, the ombudsman can order a prosecution (Denmark) but in others, he can only recommend prosecution (Norway). The number of such cases, however, is low, and the findings of the ombudsmen show that the king's agents are generally honest people who perhaps only need some sensitivity training.

The ombudsman's greatest contribution is in the educational field—he can exert his good offices to prevent future occurrences of certain behavior and very rarely is past behavior punished. As Walter Gellhorn wrote, he is effective in cases that involve departures from accepted norms and not in cases where there is a clash of values. The Scandinavian societies are homogeneous cultures with such accepted norms of behavior already in place. The ombudsman cannot create the norms nor can he alter them. The classical ombudsman in the Scandinavian countries (and in New Zealand) have served the population well as an avenue of redress, but the classical model appears to have difficulty when another society attempts to import it.

SOME ATTEMPTS AT CLONING

The office of ombudsman and its place in society as an avenue of redress described above, with particular reference to the Scandinavian model, has generated a great deal of publicity and interest in the years since the Danish ombudsman was established (1955). This increased international awareness and prestige of the Scandinavian version of the institution was primarily a result of the operating procedures and individual personality characteristics of Stephan Hurwitz, the first Danish ombudsman.[15] Hurwitz was an indefatigable publicist and spokesperson for the office; he had an incredibly astute political sense; he knew the limits of his office but did not shy away from reaching those limits; he established excellent relationships with other governmental bureaus and the press. In short, it was by his efforts that the level of awareness, understanding, and respect for the office was raised, first in the consciousness of the Danish population—information about the ombudsman is now a standard part of the Danish school curriculum—and then beyond Denmark's frontiers. International interest was heightened as other cultures and societies recognized the merits of the institution, and the entire concept of the ombudsman was well served by Stephan Hurwitz.

The merits of the ombudsman, to emphasize an earlier point, do *not* involve the replacement of the specific society's judicial functions and institutions. The ombudsman cannot substitute for the law, courts, judges, tribunals, or attorneys, nor does the ombudsman replace or stifle the initiative of any public official who wants to exercise the legislative or parliamentary oversight function. In addition, the ombudsman does not supplant or even comment on any international obligations a country may have entailed by virtue of treaty arrangements. Moreover, the ombudsman does not substitute his judgment for that of the bureaucracy, and he does not overrule or invalidate administrative decisions. In fact, almost all of the systems with an effective classical ombudsman require that lower level redress procedures be employed and exhausted before resorting to the ombudsman. The ombudsman is thus an adjunct to and supplements the political process, and he is not seen as a competitor to the political process.

The British ombudsman or parliamentary commissioner for administration (PAC), for example, is most definitely an adjunct to the traditional British political process and administrative law system rather than a competitor. Finally established in 1967[16] after a long debate lasting for almost ten years, the parliamentary commissioner was seen by its supporters as necessary: many individual complaints were not admissible in the various tribunals, and, as Parliament found less and less time available for its increasing activities, redress through legislative oversight was becoming more and more difficult. The first draft of the legislation, however, ran into severe and heavy opposition from the members of Parliament, especially the back-benchers of both major parties. The members of Parliament (MPs) believed that the office as originally conceived would dilute their traditional role in the political process with the subsequent decrease in their authority. An argument was also made against the PAC in the sense that what might have functioned well in a Scandinavian country would not necessarily function in Great Britain with a population about eight-fold of Sweden's.

The final version of the parliamentary commissioner was thus a compromise: the institution's supporters were able to establish the office, but the MPs retained their traditional authority. The British PAC is an "officer" of Parliament, and he cannot receive complaints or grievances directly from the population. Any petitions that eventually reach his desk *must* be referred to him by an individual MP. The back-bencher has thus not ceded any responsibility or authority to the PAC since he can investigate only those grievances passed on by Parliament, and he has no real independent authority. The individual MP continues to be the gatekeeper, and most petititions that are referred to the PAC are those that either cannot provide any political mileage for the MP or are too "uninteresting" or "unimportant" for the MP's attention. This dependent role of the PAC is compounded by the fact that even when the PAC is authorized to investigate a complaint, the government ministers are not required to furnish him with any requested information or document. This organizational format and restrictions detract from the British parliamentary commissioner's overall effectiveness in the redress procedure, but they illustrate its role as an adjunct to the British political system, for the PAC was not designed to supplant the political process.

The essential merit and contribution of the classical Scandinavian-type ombudsman is that it is ideally suited to deal with what has been seen (through an analysis of several ombudsmen's case loads) to be the substance of the majority of individual complaints and petitions and grievances in Western democracies. These redress petitions do not allege criminal behavior; they do not involve a demand for financial compensation; they do not question the wisdom of public policy political decisions. The ombudsman (usually) deals with the complaints involved in everyday life in a postindustrial society—these complaints are predominantly concerned with the delivery of public services or the receipt of government benefits. The office of ombudsman does bring some measure of individual treatment and concern to the relationships between the bureaucracy and the public.

Many of the classical but non-Scandinavian ombudsmen have been successful, particularly the New Zealand ombudsman. The New Zealanders have perceived the nature of the classical Scandinavian model, and they have, with a few minor variations to suit their own culture and traditions, transplanted and effectively applied the institution. Established in 1962, New Zealand's ombudsman has been the object of intense international interest and study. One such analysis was performed by Kent M. Weeks in a study dealing with the role of the New Zealand MP and the opposition after the ombudsman was created.[17] Weeks investigated a whole series of questions, the most important being the following: Has the ombudsman preempted the traditional MP role in service to the constituent? Has the ombudsman affected the traditional relationship between the MP and his constituents by providing an alternative avenue of redress? Has the ombudsman altered the role of the political opposition by preempting the latter's traditional task of criticizing the government? Has the ombudsman hindered parliamentary supervision of the administration?

Weeks concluded that all four questions must be answered in the negative. The data show that the individual New Zealander MP's case load has not diminished subsequent to 1962, nor have the traditional relationships between the MP and the voters been altered. In addition, the ombudsman has neither aided nor hindered the opposition in the latter's criticism of the government, and Parliament as a whole still maintains general supervision of the bureaucracy. When interviewed about their reasons for having an ombudsman, the New Zealand MPs overwhelmingly responded that, in descending order, the office was an impartial umpire to review complaints, to provide the "little man" with the opportunity to have his complaint reviewed, and to have a low cost process of redress. Very few MPs thought the ombudsman's role was to relieve the MPs in handling complaints, to relieve the bureacracy itself in the complaint procedure, or, and this last point is discussed below, to prevent graft in public service.

The New Zealand political system functions in its traditional pattern, and Weeks concluded that the main benefit of the ombudsman system is "assuring the citizen complainant that legislation is implemented in a way that is efficient, fair, and consistent with the values of society."[18] Weeks wrote that the ombudsman functions as an *additional* access point, and he receives complaints from those people who, before 1962, had a low sense of efficacy and who did not participate in the system. Grievances from these people would have remained unvoiced had the ombudsman not existed. This process is crucial in maintaining system support and legitimacy and in reducing feelings of alienation among the less vocal segments of the population. The New Zealand ombudsman has earned the respect and suport of the political actors—especially the MPs—for the office has not upset the traditional grievance procedure but, rather, has supplemented the process.

New Zealand's ombudsman is not, of course, the only successful clone, but it is perhaps the best known beyond the boundaries of Scandinavia. Unfortunately, the institution's title and external trappings of respectability—independence, competence, neutrality—have been borrowed by other systems and cultures, but most of these display a deficient understanding of the function. Numerous structures have been established with the admirable title of "ombudsman" but without its essence. This unfortunate state of affairs has occurred for two basic reasons: those people responsible for establishing the position may have only the best and most altruistic intentions but either do not adequately understand the ombudsman's role in a redress system or do not really understand what is necessary for a functioning ombudsman (for example, calling an ordinary complaint department, which has only the ability to refer the individual grievance to another office, an "ombudsman"); or those people responsible may have "perfect" information on the ombudsman's function but whose intentions are suspect (for example, creating, at least on the surface, a mirror image of the classical model but then not providing it with the essential authority necessary to function properly).

More than a few "ombudsmen" have been established for "political" or public relations goals totally removed from their real function as an avenue of redress for the population against the bureaucracy. In the environment and rhetoric that characterize American political campaigns at practically all levels of elective office, it is good political strategy to announce a proposed ombudsman as part of the candidate's platform.[19] Such ombudsmen, if ever actually established, are usually subverted from functioning in an effective manner. Both types of clones—those established through blissful ignorance as well as those purposely subverted—are beginning to give the process a "bad press." The average American citizen has very scanty information about the classical Scandinavian model, and his knowledge and understanding of the office is usually limited to whatever local variety exists, and these examples should not be employed to represent the Danish or New Zealand model. Such local institutions, masquerading as ombudsmen, are poor and misleading attempts to reproduce the real thing and very seldom do they play an effective role in the redress process.

These clones do not provide adequate service to the clientele they are supposed to serve. Such "ombudsmen" are not limited to public political entities (state, county, or local municipalities), for there are numerous functional areas in the United States where one can find an ombudsman. The following is an annotated list of these functional areas, and each can produce an "ombudsman" on demand: hospitals (both public and private), universities, police and fire departments (that is, police civilian review boards), municipal services (water, sewage, trash collection, road repair, recreation, snow removal), transportation agencies, school boards, health maintenance organizations (HMOs), city hall complaint departments, prisons, asylums, public housing authorities, the military, newspapers, professional societies and organizations, and major private corporations and businesses.

Space does not permit a full discussion of all of these clones, but they share the same defective characteristic: these institutions do not give full independence or autonomy to the ombudsman, and the office is expected to handle complaints against the very agency that established the position. This lack of independence is the major drawback to an effective ombudsman, for it implicitly affects and pervades the entire process. Whereas in the classical Scandinavian model Parliament appoints the ombudsman to handle complaints against the bureaucracy but *not* complaints directed at the actions and decisions of Parliament itself, these clones are somehow expected to receive, investigate, and dispose of complaints directed at the appointing entity. The lines of authority and autonomy are blurred, and the ombudsman—regardless of his or her individual competence and personal dedication to the office[20]—simply cannot function according to the tenets of the classical Scandinavian model.

A UNIVERSITY OMBUDSMAN

One type of clone is the so-called office of ombudsman so pervasive at American colleges and universities. Such positions are relatively recent, for it was not until the late 1960s and early 1970s that they began to appear in increasing numbers. The first campus ombudsman in the United States was appointed in the fall of 1966 at Eastern Montana College in Billings. Approximately seventy more were in operation by spring 1971, and by the beginning of the 1975–76 academic year, over one hundred colleges and universities could publicize the fact that they, too, had an ombudsman. The reason behind this almost geometric increase in the number of ombudsmen on the campus was that the office was basically a result of a series of diverse social, political, and economic factors that had the universities as a common meeting point.

In the late 1960s and early 1970s, American universities were not ivory towers removed from the real world or insulated enclaves—they were centers of unrest, activism, politicalization, "confrontation" politics, and violence. Those were the years of the Vietnam War and Lyndon Johnson; of the 1968 Democratic Convention in Chicago and confrontation politics; of the urban riots from Newark to Oakland; of students being characterized as "bums" by Nixon and faculty being called "effete snobs" by Agnew; of university administrations' secret liaisons with CIA activities. The violence at Kent State, Columbia, and Berkeley—to name but three examples—characterized the university environment. Whatever the current level of student activism may be now, it is quiescent and almost idyllic compared to a decade ago.

Students were no longer content to sit hat-in-hand in the classroom and swallow whatever was served to them by their professors, as if the students were medieval serfs in abject submission before the manor lord; students were no longer content to let arbitrary policies from authoritarian and nonresponsive administrative officials remain unchallenged; statements found in most university catalogues to the effect that "the student could be expelled or suspended at any time for any reason" were seen as blatant violations of their individual rights.[21] The universities had a severe communication and credibility problem, and although it took some time, they eventually realized that they had to be more responsive and accountable to the people they purported to serve.

The universities, although not sovereign states or political units, nonetheless were (and still are) similar to a feudal organization with the trappings of *rex gratia dei* and sovereign immunity. Boards of trustees and their agents—the university president or chancellor—could not be "tried" in their own "court," and the serfs had no real right of redress against the manor lord's activities or decisions. The universities, moreover, were large bureaucratic organizations with all the shortcomings of such organizations. Rules, procedures, lines of command, hierarchial structures, and rewards and penalties all exist within the campus boundaries, and very few of these things were open for review by an external agency (a judge, for example, will not substitute his evaluation for a professor's in grading the content of a student's essay or exam). Some of the rewards and penalties meted out by the university had enormous impact for the student in the late 1960s: to flunk out of school invariably meant the loss of one's II-S draft classification, and failure to have a deferment was a one-way ticket to Vietnam.

The faculty themselves were not untouched by these events, and many became politicized and employed the classroom and the professional societies as a soapbox for their views.[22] But many younger faculty members without tenure were placed in an almost untenuous position. Institutions in the late 1960s also witnessed the beginning of the severe constriction in available teaching positions—the constriction has continued and even worsened in the 1970s—and many younger faculty members were hesitant to question the traditional procedures, policies, and decisions of the university's administrative hierarchy. It was becoming more and more difficult to secure another teaching position—especially if the prospective candidate had been denied tenure at one institution for "lack of maturity"—and few faculty members voiced their grievances against the administration. Again, the university president was not *ceasar gratia dei*, but effective avenues of redress against his decisions were few and far apart and were the exception to the rule.

Many faculty members, however, were not unresponsive to the students' situation. Fully aware of the consequences of failing grades, it was seen by many to be an act of symbolic protest—however futile—against the war in Vietnam and the government's policies not to fail students and thus keep them beyond the reach of draft boards. It was thus the faculty who were originally responsible for the widespread and blatant grade inflation (a D became a B, a C became an A), which, even though its original reason for existence has since disappeared, continues unabated throughout the United States.[23]

The office of ombudsman appeared as a panacea for most of these ills. The students would have an independent and impartial agent to "protect" them from administrative arbitrariness and a place where grievances could be lodged—a place other than with the person or office against whom redress is being sought. The ombudsman could lend his good offices to unravel the inevitable red tape and delays within the bureaucratic university (refunds, course scheduling, parking, and so on) and, hopefully, put an end to the usual response to a student seeking information (that is, "this is not the office you want—go see Ms. X in the other office [on the other side of campus]"). The ombudsman could also protect students from mistreatment by the faculty: discrimination on account of race, sex, ethnic origin, or religion is not entirely unknown within the university environment, and sexual harrassment, while not a common pattern, does occur from time to time. The ombudsman's office would also provide an impartial third party to a grade dispute between a student and the professor. The process of grade inflation did not, unfortunately, reduce such disputes—it increased them. The theory of rising expectations became operative: the D who received a B now demanded an A, and complaints over grades were fueled by higher grades.

The faculty themselves also saw some benefits with an effective ombudsman's office on campus. We would now have an independent and impartial agent to protect us from unfounded student allegations (student harrassment of faculty members is also an unfortunate campus characteristic), and, possibly, the ombudsman could employ his good offices and intervene in faculty complaints against the administration concerning questions such as tenure, promotion, course load, salary, and office space.[24] Finally, the administration could point to the ombudsman as evidence of good faith, of responsiveness, of admission that indeed grievances did exist within the university community and that henceforth, these grievances would be heard and acted upon without prejudice. By establishing an ombudsman, the university recognized that sovereign immunity no longer applied and that grievances and complaints should have an impartial "hearing" by someone *other* than the one being complained against.

The office of ombudsman was thus seen to be so ideally suited to the university environment that many were rapidly established. The opposition of numbers was not relevant here: if the United Kingdom could establish a PAC for approximately 55 million people (although without any direct access for these millions) and if Sweden's ombudsman could reach about 7 million people, then surely a university ombudsman—whose clientele numbered only in the thousands—would be an effective and accessible institution. Unfortunately, many of these university ombudsmen bear little resemblance, other than their title, to the classical Scandinavian model. Among the many reasons for this, one pervading reason (also applicable to all of the quasi-ombudsmen in the various functional areas listed above) concerns the problem of definition—definition in that, in the university environment, it is not a simple matter to determine exactly which entity is "parliament," the "administration and bureaucracy," and the "people." Such distinctions are self-evident in a national political entity but are blurred within the university, given the convoluted relationships and overlapping decision-making authority among the board of trustees, president, administrative officers, faculty and students.

Another general reason why the university ombudsman differs from the classical model concerns the claimed professional expertise of some of the actors within the university, which does not easily allow review by an external critic. Related to this is the twin problem of academic freedom and individual privacy, both of which are protected by law. A faculty member *is* the manor lord in his classroom and, with certain limitations of course, can determine who may enter that classroom during a lecture (this may apply to the ombudsman's request to "observe" the classroom situation). Compounding this lack of "access" is the real impact of the Buckley Amendment to the 1974 Family Educational Rights and Privacy Act: students' records are protected and the ombudsman does *not* have unhindered access to records of students who do not permit him access (it is difficult to evaluate a complaint of mistreatment if the ombudsman cannot ascertain how other students were treated in the same classroom).

The deceptively simple question of lines of authority that are not blurred in the classical model—parliament appoints the ombudsman to handle complaints from the population at-large directed at the bureaucracy with almost total accessibility to information—is yet to be resolved in any satisfactory way at most universities. The appointing group is invariably the object of complaints, and one can only surmise the degree of independence and autonomy if a university ombudsman must "investigate" the same administrative office that can remove him at will.

The office of university ombudsman has been described in some detail in the literature,[25] but almost all of these reports present either the surface characteristics of the office or self-images of the ombudsman's role. Seldom does the published literature contain the actual empirical behavior patterns or political limitations of the office. The discussion below is limited to one clone where I have information beyond the surface characteristics listed in the official publications. Although not necessarily a perfect image of all university ombudsmen, this one ombudsman in a large midwestern urban university generally has patterns and characteristics relative of the type.

This office of ombudsman was first established in 1970 upon the initiative of the student council, although the administration facilitated the procedure. The student council interviewed about twenty faulty members who expressed an interest in the position, and an associate professor (with tenure) from a department within arts and sciences was selected. The ombudsman was "paid" through the student council, but the money came from his department: his regular academic salary continued, but his course load was reduced and the administration graciously provided the funds necessary to enable the department to replace, on a part-time basis, the dropped courses. The position was not full time—only one-third of the individual's time was to be spent as ombudsman and he still spent two-thirds of his time in his own department— and no formal length of time was specified for the position. The office was abolished by the student council a short ten months later in the spring 1971 for two reasons: the student council thought the ombudsman was ineffectual, and they wanted to use the money for activities with higher student priorities (the money belonged to the administration, however).

Two fatal deficiencies were evident in this first attempt to establish an ombudsman: an almost total lack of publicity and authority. Compared to Hurwitz's constant efforts to publicize the office to the Danish population, this particular university's ombudsman was a well-kept secret—few faculty were aware that the ombudsman existed and even fewer students knew about the office. The office simply was not advertised through the campus newspaper, wall posters, or announcements in class by the faculty. The only publicity was through word of mouth, but this was ineffective, especially when most of the students had never before even heard the term *ombudsman* and thus had no conception or understanding of what they might have heard. The situation soon degenerated into one of having the ombudsman sitting in his academic office (he did not have a separate ombudsman office or phone listing) waiting for complaints from a population that was not aware of his existence or location.

The second fatal flaw involved an almost total lack of authority for the ombudsman in those few cases where he did receive a student complaint (faculty did not use the ombudsman, for he was a "student" advocate). The office was too blatantly linked to student interests and thus was seen as an opponent by most faculty and administrative officials. That is, the students simply could not give the ombudsman the legitimate authority to request faculty and/or administration files, and most requests for information were simply ignored. The ombudsman's first year of operation accomplished little other than to develop some public relations and a community image for the university, and the office did not achieve its true purpose of dealing with complaints.

Although the student council abolished the office after one year, a few months later, in the fall 1971, the position was reestablished from an entirely different framework. The dean of the College of Arts and Sciences "appointed" a different professor to serve as ombudsman but only for the College of Arts and Sciences. No student or faculty input went into this selection process, for none was solicited by the dean: the ombudsman was simply presented as the dean's creation and thus responsible to the dean. The ombudsman's teaching load was cut by 50 percent and the dean's office thus paid one-half of his salary. Shortly thereafter, the president insisted that the ombudsman serve the entire university community—and not just the College of Arts and Sciences—and the office was shifted to the academic vice-president. The academic vice-president now funded the office and the ombudsman was responsible to him. The office of this particular ombudsman has since been chosen by, responsible to, and funded by the academic vice-president with authority to act as a university-wide ombudsman. The released time has slowly increased, and now the ombudsman spends approximately 80 percent of his time as ombudsman and only 20 percent of his time within his academic department.

The amount of publicity about the office has vastly increased. Subsequent ombudsmen have placed notices and articles in the student newspaper; the office is noted in the official university publications (catalogues and the *Student Handbook*); most faculty are aware of the office and are expected to publicize it in class. This increased publicity has led to an increased use of the office by students (complaints about grades, refunds, parking tickets, alleged discrimination, and so on), and it appears that the ombudsman is almost at full capacity. No longer does one have the strange situation of having the ombudsman waiting in his office for calls that never come. The position now has the outward characteristics of an effective office, and recent ombudsmen have been respected professors, known for their fairness and understanding of the university environment. But has the office been a real, effective avenue of redress when its actual operation is scrutinized?

This particular university ombudsman process is not very effective when approached from the perspective of both the students and the faculty (it is perhaps more effective if approached from the university administration's perspective). This office is *not* independent from the administration, and this is the major obstacle to its effectiveness. Crucial to any system of redress, the ombudsman included, is the need to be free from any control by the agencies the system is supposed to oversee: an external critic must be, in fact as well as in name, "external" to those against whom complaints are directed. The classical Scandinavian model is explicit on this point: it is Parliament that "controls" the ombudsman, but the ombudsman is expressly prohibited from entertaining grievances directed at Parliament.

This particular university ombudsman, however—as well as most other university ombudsmen—is expected to handle grievances that concern the controlling agency and this is an untenable position. Many grievances within the university are ultimately directed at the academic vice-president's office, but it is the vice-president himself who appoints and pays the ombudsman. The final result is that the ombudsman serves as the university's "point man"; that is, he deflects criticism away from the administration and dilutes it rather than functions as a truly independent external critic. The academic vice-president makes and applies policies that affect the faculty in an immediate sense: promotions, decisions on tenure, the budget, are all filtered through his office. A faculty member who might have a grievance over a particular decision on, for example, tenure has little chance for the ombudsman to "investigate" the complaint vigorously.

The major problem within the university environment, then, as well as with most other quasi-ombudsmen, is that the separation between "parliament" and "administration" has become blurred, and such ombudsmen are severely constricted with their scope of activity. This problem can be solved, although universities are not ready to establish an external critic and then believe in that critic's importance. The solution lies in the redefinition of which groups within the university are the surrogate for parliament, the bureaucracy, and the population. The board of trustees *must* be the parliament that creates the ombudsman, but the trustees' policy decisions must be immune from review by the ombudsman. Everyone on the university's payroll—from the president to the groundskeepers—now becomes the administration and bureaucracy whose actions are open to review by the ombudsman. The population, those who can complain to the ombudsman, would include anyone affected by a decision or action from the "bureaucracy"—students, faculty, staff, and administration officials. With this separation, the university administration would be held accountable for its actions rather than employing a so-called ombudsman to deflect criticism.

What is required is for the board of trustees to appoint, pay, and control an "outside" person as ombudsman. This person thus would be responsible to the board of trustees—not to the president or other administrative officials—and therefore would be autonomous in his dealings with the university. The ombudsman, although fully aware of the university environment and processes, should be an "outsider" to avoid the inevitable conflict of interest problems that arise when the ombudsman is a faculty member.[26] Such a person would not be seen as a student advocate or administrative point man: he would be an impartial external critic within the university community, responsible to the board of trustees and charged with the oversight of the application and administration of the trustee's policies. Existing university redress procedures would not be affected, for, as in most of the classical systems, the individual would first have to exhaust existing review processes (faculty committees and so on) before having recourse to the ombudsman.

The above discussion of a university ombudsman can, within limits, be used as an example of almost all of the quasi-ombudsmen in the United States. Some are well meaning, and others are purposely subverted, but few of them offer the population an effective external critic to whatever "bureaucracy" may be concerned. The office of ombudsman *must* be independent of those it is supposed to evaluate.

SOME CONCLUDING COMMENTS

The above discussion of the ombudsman is generally favorable to the classical Scandinavian model, both in terms of the philosophy behind the institution as well as its real-life behavior. The quasi-ombudsmen, so prevalent in the United States, fall far short regarding the desired characteristics found in the Scandinavian model. We need not belabor the deficiencies of these quasi-ombudsmen any further: they are attempted clones who do not reproduce the original very well, and thus they do not adequately serve either the concept of the ombudsman or the people they are somehow supposed to "defend." These concluding comments, therefore, refer to the classical Scandinavian model and its role in a redress of grievances system.

The major and most crucial point to digest with any ombudsman is that the institution has several built-in limitations, and it would be a disservice to the office to expect it to function or achieve results beyond its ability and these built-in limitations. Whatever effectiveness the office may have will be impaired or lost if it tries to do too much. What, then, should the office not be expected to do?

First, and most important, the ombudsman is a creation of the political process, and it must stay within the limits established by political realities. The ombudsman cannot operate as a party partisan, uncovering "dirt" about the ruling party or coalition or hindering the opposition party or parties in their legitimate role of providing criticism of the government. The ombudsman must be totally and completely nonpartisan and "nonpolitical," for, if it is not, the office will be regarded as politics as usual and its effectiveness will diminish. This does not mean, however, that the ombudsman must be a political eunuch; on the contrary, the ombudsman must have an astute political sense to find his way among the corridors of power within the bureaucracy and to know when he has reached the office's political limits.

The office is not a panacea for society's ills, and it will not sweep out corrupt politicians or transform a corrupt political system. The ombudsman's ability to root out dishonest politicians ranges from very limited to nonexistent, and the office should not be expected to be the man on horseback. Those who have this goal in mind for an ombudsman will be severely disappointed—political witchhunts are incompatible with the redress of individual complaints or grievances against the bureaucracy. A much more powerful institution than the ombudsman is required to clean up the political system—a special prosecutor á la Archibald Cox and Leon Jaworski—and the ombudsman must shy away from such activities.

The ombudsman also should not be expected to deal with public policy as contained in parliamentary legislation. He cannot comment on whether these policies are wise or silly, just or unjust. The ombudsman must not be expected to substitute his individual judgment for that of parliament's collective wisdom. The office can deal only with the application of such policies to insure that they are administered fairly, humanely, and with sensitivity and concern for each individual. The wisdom or acceptability of the society's public policy should be questioned, of course, but the questioning must be reserved for the political processes, be they a court that can rule certain acts unconstitutional, a vote of nonconfidence in parliament, or a total change of the political decision makers due to the use of the vote by the population.

In addition, the ombudsman must not be seen solely as an advocate of one side or the other (the people or the bureaucrats). He must be an impartial broker to whom each party in the grievance process can look with trust and confidence. To find fault with *every* bureaucratic lapse from perfection will soon render the office as a petty nuisance, and the bureaucracy will ignore whatever the ombudsman may recommend. Finally, the office must not be expected to do everything, for, if it tries to, it will be so overwhelmed that it will do nothing. The ombudsman must not be mandated to investigate every letter of complaint that might reach his desk—an effective ombudsman must have the ability to refuse to act if he so desires. This will permit the ombudsman to deal with situations that are more likely to have an impact beyond the immediate case and thus fulfill his role of educating the population about what to expect of the bureaucracy as well as educating the bureaucracy on how to deal with the people.

The above are limitations to the ombudsman, but they are limitations that enhance its effectiveness rather than dilute it. The classical Scandinavian ombudsman does not engage in any, to use the more descriptive French term, *chasse aux sorcières*, and he is not out to affix blame in every situation. The ombudsman has excellent relations with those he is expected to oversee, and it is not an adversary process. It is a cooperative effort among those concerned with the same goal—a sensitive and polite bureaucratic apparatus. The ombudsman does not punish past behavior—the law, courts, and the judicial process punish criminal behavior—but, rather, he serves to prevent future occurrences by educating the bureaucracy.

An effective classical ombudsman does not stifle innovation within the civil service and public administration. The bureaucrats need not fear that the ombudsman is looking over their shoulder at every minute, waiting to swoop down at the smallest detail. In fact, the ombudsman has more often than not been a catalyst for innovation to a hidebound administrative agency: he can isolate those anomalies and aberrations in the bureaucracy and thus employ his good offices to help the agencies free themselves of the "but we have always done it this way" mentality.

The ombudsman can also play a role in increasing and strengthening the feelings of legitimacy in the system, to maintain stability, and to reduce alienation by raising personal efficacy. He can involve the poor and the inarticulate, the nonparticipating segments, and demonstrate that the political system is responsive, that it is liable for its errors, and that the final goal of the entire political and social enterprise is the well being and protection of the individual.

Perhaps the most important factor behind an effective ombudsman is the attitude of those who create the institution. As Gellhorn wrote, "those who select an external critic must themselves fully believe in the critic's importance and must wish him to succeed as a citizen's protector."[27] The ombudsman can function and be effective only in a society where the government, politicians, bureaucrats, *and* the people are already fully committed to good government and to the protection of the individual. In such societies, the ombudsman can point out the aberrations—he cannot force his own ideals and philosophy upon a recalcitrant society. But if the above conditions are present, and if everyone recognizes the ombudsman's limitations, the ombudsman can then be an excellent avenue of redress by being a citizen's protector against bureaucratic insensitivity.

NOTES

1. Cited by Bernard Frank, "The Ombudsman—Revisited," *International Bar Journal*, May 1975, p. 50.

2. Stanley V. Anderson, *Ombudsman Papers: American Experience and Proposals* (Berkeley: Institute of Governmental Studies, University of California Press, 1969), p. 3.

3. Donald C. Rowat, Preface to *The Ombudsman: Citizens' Defender*, 2nd ed., ed. Donald C. Rowat (Toronto: University of Toronto Press, 1968), p. xxiv.

4. Larry B. Hill, "Institutionalization, the Ombudsman, and Bureaucracy," *American Political Science Review* 68, no. 3 (September 1974): 1077.

5. Ibid. Emphasis supplied.

6. Larry B. Hill, "Defining the Ombudsman: A Comparative Analysis" (Paper delivered at the Annual Meeting of the Midwest Political Science Association, Chicago, April 21–23, 1977), n. 6, p. 45. The ombudsmen listed here do not necessarily represent the universe of classical ombudsmen but, rather, only those Hill decided to employ in his study. Others did not respond to Hill's written questionnaire, responded but were not included in the analysis, or were not even sent the questionnaire but nonetheless are "classical" types (for example, Canada's commissioner of official languages and the military ombudsmen in Norway and West Germany).

7. The literature in this area is voluminous and is increasing at a rapid rate. For an overview of five classical ombudsmen (Denmark, Finland, New Zealand, Norway, Sweden) and four quasi-ombudsmen (Yugoslavia, Poland, Soviet Union, Japan) in what is perhaps the best survey, see Walter Gellhorn, *Ombudsmen and Others: Citizens' Protectors in Nine Countries* (Cambridge: Harvard University Press, 1966). For a detailed discussion of the British parliamentary commissioner, see Roy Gregory and Peter Hutchesson, *The Parliamentary Ombudsman* (London: Allen & Unwin, Ltd., 1977). For New Zealand, see Larry B. Hill, *The Model Ombudsman: Institutionalizing New Zealand's Democratic Experiment* (Princeton: Princeton University Press, 1976).

8. Stig Jägerskiöld, "The Swedish Ombudsman," *University of Pennsylvania Law Review* 109 (June 1961): 1078.

9. Finland's ombudsman was established in 1919, but, as was the case with Sweden, the office generated little international attention. Norway created its ombudsman in 1962.

10. See Hill, "Defining the Ombudsman, table 10, "Ombudsmen's Orientations Toward Political Autonomy," p. 43.

11. The responses from the Scandinavian ombudsmen are different from the American ones (classical as well as quasi-ombudsmen), and this illustrates a major difference (and deficiency) of the American clones. Approximately 45 percent of the American ombudsmen surveyed said that they saw nothing wrong with former politicians becoming ombudsmen, and approximately 48 percent thought past political connections could increase the effectiveness of their office. Ibid.

12. Gellhorn cited a memorandum from a permanent head of a New Zealand cabinet department to his section chiefs: "Several months ago the Ombudsman spoke in public about the 'cold, impartial and often implacable application of the rules.' Thinking of the public service generally and of this department in particular I believe that there are some grounds for this comment. I wish to ensure that in future we as a department do not offend in this respect." Cited in Gellhorn, *Ombudsmen and Others*, p. 144.

13. Hill, "Defining the Ombudsman," table 4, "Ombudsmen's Perceptions of their Clients' Class Origins," p. 39.

14. Both cases are from New Zealand and are reported in Gellhorn, *Ombudsmen and Others*, pp. 135 and 130.

15. An academic lawyer, Stephan Hurwitz was born in 1901 and educated at the University of Copenhagen. He become a professor of law at the university in 1935 and vice-chancellor in 1953. He was also chief of the Danish Refugee Organization in Sweden in 1943; a member of the Danish Military Commission in London in 1944–45; and he was the Danish representative on the UN War Crimes Commission in 1945. He has written numerous books and articles on various legal subjects, and he has been awarded honorary degrees from the Universities of Stockholm, Oslo, Helsinki, and Reykjavik.

16. Sir Edmund Compton was the United Kingdom's first parliamentary commissioner for administration. For a discussion of the PAC, see Gregory and Hutchesson, *The Parliamentary Ombudsman*, and R. M. Punnett, *British Government and Politics* (New York: W. W. Norton and Co., 1968), pp. 339–41.

17. See Kent M. Weeks, "Members of Parliament and the New Zealand Ombudsman System," *Midwest Journal of Political Science* (present title: *American Journal of Political Science*) 14, no. 4 (November 1970): 673–86.

18. Ibid., p. 686.

19. Some time ago, I was a consultant to a candidate running for an elective office. I strongly argued for a press release on such a proposal to generate some free media coverage. It made no difference at the time if the voters didn't understand the concept—except that it was some foreign term that sounded good—or if the office were never established. The proposal for an ombudsman would show a candidate who cared for the "little man" (that is, voter) against the bureaucracy.

20. I have had several lengthy conversations with a few quasi-ombudsmen, including those within a university environment and in a private but large and world-famous teaching and research hospital. These ombudsmen are dedicated to the office, but some lack real independence and this restricts their effectiveness.

21. Even heterosexual activities between consenting adult (over twenty-one) students were at some places cause for disciplinary action or suspension—including those colleges not known for their fundamentalist morality—and the fact that such activities took place at an off-campus location was not relevant. The point is that most American colleges and universities were simply out of touch with their students.

22. Faculty activism within the political science discipline reached its peak in the late 1960s-early 1970s with the creation of the Caucus for a New Political Science. The caucus attempted to force the American Political Science Association into engaging in politics—something the association hadn't done for years—but the caucus was short lived. For a discussion of this episode, see Leon Hurwitz, *Introduction to*

Politics (Chicago: Nelson-Hall Co., 1979), esp. chapter 5, "Contemporary Challenges to Behavioralism," pp. 234–42.

23. Grade inflation has increased to the extent that, even in an ivy league school, most grades are either pass-fail (or satisfactory-unsatisfactory). In addition, the ability of students in many universities to withdraw from a course up to a very late date invariably means that no F's or D's are given out: these students drop the course and try again the following term.

24. These questions would best be handled through a collective-bargaining agreement between the administration and the faculty grouping, and thus the ombudsman would not be expected to intervene. But university administrations have traditionally employed all means possible to prevent the faculty from organizing and using collective bargaining.

25. A good example of the literature on university ombudsmen's perceptions and role models—but not the real behavior patterns and lines of authority—is by Kenneth L. Stewart, "What a University Ombudsman Does: A Sociological Study of Everyday Conduct," *Journal of Higher Education* 49, no. 1 (1978): 1–22.

26. An associate (or even assistant) professor is put in an untenable position if, as ombudsman, he is expected to "investigate" a complaint against the very people (his chairperson, dean, or vice-president) who have an important and almost controlling influence over his future promotions.

27. Gellhorn, *Ombudsmen and Others*, p. 438.

PARLIAMENTARY POLITICAL ACTIVITY: City Councilmen, the Question Period, and Extra-Constituency Activity

5

The procedures described in chapters 2 through 4 relate to a society's more institutionalized avenues of redress available to the individual vis-à-vis the state. Although effective, the regular court system is the ponderous judicial process where the law and the judge are paramount. The formal judicial process does not, however, *guarantee* the rule of law and the protection of the individual from state abuse. The institutionalized courtroom procedure is frequently used as the very means by which individuals are mistreated by the state.[1] The quasi-judicial administrative tribunals, as evidenced by the French *Conseil d'État*, are somewhat more streamlined, but they, too, are formalized and institutionalized avenues of redress. The ombudsman as an institution is much more free flowing and informal, but the ombudsman is nontheless a specialized agency with distinct operational limits and set boundaries to its activities. Of course, the courts, tribunals, and ombudsmen are "political" and participate fully in the political process. But these institutionalized procedures are specific and goal oriented, and as such, they cannot enter the real political thicket.

Activity in the redress process by legislative or parliamentary bodies contributes an entirely different perspective to a system of redress and to the protection of individuals. Activity coming from these entities are blatantly and unabashedly "political" rather than "legal" or "administrative." Some of this political redress may be as institutionalized and formalized as a court of law (the Question Period in the British Parliament, for example); other activity is more ad hoc, which ebbs and flows according to the political realities of the day, and which is attuned to the contemporary political atmosphere (such as President Carter's linkage of human rights to American foreign policy).

The participation of legislative and parliamentary bodies in a system of redress can operate at several levels. An individual member of a legislative group may employ whatever power or influence his position carries on behalf of a specific individual; in other areas, parliament as a whole can attempt to rely on national power and sovereignty to protect an entire class of individuals. In some situations, the legislative body itself can provide redress to an individual who has a valid complaint against the state, but under other circumstances, parliament cannot deliver satisfaction and serves instead as a preliminary step to other measures.

It must be emphasized that the redress activity of parliamentary and legislative bodies is performed by politicians and not by judges, administrative conseillers, or ombudsmen. These politicians are elected, at least in the countries reviewed, by the democratic process through universal suffrage. They are thus responsible to the electorate who, with varying degrees of ease, can vote them out of office. What are some possible reasons that might explain these political avenues of redress? Why do these politicians intervene on behalf of individuals against the very state the politicians embody? Three distinct but related reasons or motives are called, for lack of more descriptive terms, the politics of representation, the politics of opposition, and the politics of belief.

As a motive for providing redress to an individual, the "politics of representation" rationale has both positive and negative aspects. In a positive sense, the elected representative often sees such activity as an integral and necessary part of the job. Service to one's constituents—whether it is a response to a simple request for information or whether it involves putting pressure on a recalcitrant bureaucrat—has always been seen, especially in the localized political culture in the United States, as a prime component of the job. Such constituent service pervades all levels of elective office from a local city councilman to a member of Congress.

Some negative overtones, however, occur with this politics of representation and constituent service. Politicians may supply "special" service to individuals for more venal reasons: campaign contributions usually serve as the *quid* for the politician's *quo*. Much of constituent service may thus derive less from the desire to aid the individual and more from the desire to aid the politician. The process of reelection is a recurring theme in our democratic systems, and to be reelected, the politician cannot ignore requests for his services.

The "politics of opposition" rationale or motive for legislative activity in the redress process may ultimately aid the individual, but the individual's situation is not normally the major focus of concern. The major issue here is the future political fortune of the politician and/or his party, usually at the expense of the majority party currently in power. Alleged governmental mistreatment of an individual or official insensitivity are seized by the opposition as a weapon to bludgeon the majority in the always-present forthcoming election. The redress of individual grievances *may* be achieved within the politics of opposition but only as a side effect or as a spillover from the main prize—the political embarrassment of the government and additional votes at the next election.

The "politics of belief" rationale is on an entirely different level from the above two motives. This view holds that politicians are honorable people who are sincerely and honestly concerned with the human condition. Activities at this level are not seen as merely part of the job or the dues to pay to get reelected or political machinations designed to do in the opposition party. The politicians here have come to the realization that *political* actions may be the only way to protect certain individuals from governmental mistreatment, and thus they employ the power and influence of the legislative body to protect the individual or groups of individuals. The status of the individual is the central issue here—being reelected or hassling the opposition is only a secondary concern or may be completely absent.

Parliamentary activity in a system of redress is most effective when operating in the same constituency. That is, the legislator and/or the legislature maintains maximum advantage, influence, and flexibility within their own electoral boundaries or political system. The local city councilman often can be effective when dealing with complaints about the nondelivery of city services; a member of Congress or the British Parliament can be effective when dealing with cabinet-level departments or ministries. Parliamentary political activity in a redress system is, however, much more difficult to achieve and to evaluate if the terms of reference lie outside the particular constituency (extra-constituency behavior). The attempt by a parliamentary body to employ its power to protect individuals in another country from those individuals' own governmental apparatus is becoming widespread, but the effectiveness of such intervention has yet to be fully documented.

This chapter discusses and evaluates several parliamentary attempts to provide political redress for individuals. The evaluative comments offered here are from the perception of the individual who requires redress or needs an avenue to complain—has this person been helped by political intervention or not? The question of whether the politicians themselves have also been helped must be answered by them. The three general areas discussed include constituent service, the Question Period, and extra-constituency activity.

The intervention of the legislator in the redress system within the politics of representation sees the individual politician as a quasi-ombudsman. The local city councilman is the ward's conduit to city hall, and urban councilmen in the United States are perceiving their role more as ombudsmen and less as "lawmakers." The politics of opposition is discussed through the Question Period at Westminister. The Question Period is a traditional British parliamentary procedure where, among other things, the government of the day is expected to defend its actions and justify the bureaucrats' treatment of the population. The politics of belief activity focuses on some extra-constituency attempts by the United States Congress to protect citizens of other countries from the latter's own governments. This last example concerns the linkage of United States foreign aid policies to human rights (the Harkin Amendment) and the Jackson-Vanik Amendment (most-favored-nation status is dependent upon the Soviet Union's willingness to permit emigration).

THE POLITICS OF REPRESENTATION AND CONSTITUENT SERVICE:
THE LEGISLATOR AS OMBUDSMAN

One of the main obstacles preventing an effective (read "classical") ombudsman in most American cities is the vociferous opposition of the locally elected officials (see chapter 4). Urban city councilmen perceive their job as including the role of being the ward's conduit to city hall and thus appear to the voters as the main benefactor of whatever largesse the city may be able to deliver. The lawmaker's function in this area of the redress process does *not* include complaints from population about alleged violations of central personal liberties or about criminal behavior by the bureaucrats. Complaints or charges of this nature are best handled by the formal judicial process, since questions of law, liability, and punishment are involved. Rather, the locally elected official sees himself as a quasi-ombudsman: transferring information from city hall departments to the individual, attempting to secure (or excuse) the delivery of municipal services, providing his "good offices" within the administrative process (permits, licenses, and so on), and mediating political conflict.

A recent study by Ronald J. Busch examined this changing nature of the locally elected politician.[2] The municipal legislator—in this example an urban city councilman—has in the past been seen as a "lawmaker" who spends his time in the law-making function (that is, detailed committee work, public hearings, the drafting and passing of city ordinances). This may have been the traditional perception, but the actual behavior and functions of the municipal city councilman has been altered greatly over the past two decades or so. The major role of the local politician has moved away from the legislative function and has turned towards the service function.

The traditional view of the urban city councilman as a "legislator" no longer reflects the realities of actual political behavior, for now the city councilman's activities, especially in a relatively poor urban area, come very close to those performed by an ombudsman. As discussed in chapter 4, the ombudsman is seen to be a line of defense against arbitrary administration and against bureaucratic insensitivity. The ombudsman's main function is to insure that postindustrial public administration has a personal face and to employ his good offices to resolve disputes and mediate conflict. Since the ombudsman seldom has the ability to overrule the decisions of an administrative agency or to substitute his judgment for others or to initiate judicial proceedings, a heavy premium is thus placed upon his skills of persuasion and interpersonal relations. These skills, although applicable to the ombudsman, also are rapidly becoming characteristic of the American city councilman.

This increasing ombudsmanlike role of the city councilman is a result of two related trends: the changing nature of constituency interests and the changing perceptions that the voters have of the local politician. Busch wrote that constituency demands within the central city are different in the late 1970s-early 1980s from what they were only twenty years ago.[3] Constituency demands have become much more frequent and more intense, and the population now expects these demands to be heard and acted upon. Two reasons for this increased popular activity are financial exigencies and the rise of consumerism.

The shrinking tax base of central cities outside the sunbelt, accelerated by decreasing population and encouraged by tax abatements, combined with the massive inflation of the 1970s, have led to severe reductions in municipal services. What formerly was free (that is, funded out of general tax revenues)—an ice skating rink or a swimming pool, for example—has now shut its doors or charges an admission fee; the city no longer hauls away bulk refuse—the individual has to cart the item away himself; the health department no longer has a rat control program—the caller is told to hire an exterminator. But service reductions have not brought financial stability. The voters are constantly badgered to approve additional taxes just to pay for the reduced service levels. The population is becoming "irritated"—California's Proposition 13 is a good example—and we do not like to pay more for less. Complaints are being voiced and they are being directed at those closest at hand and to those who are most vulnerable (although not necessarily those who are most responsible): the city councilman.

A second reason for greater constituency demands is the emergence of countless citizen action groups and public interest organizations and the rise of consumerism. Tracing their lineage back to Ralph Nader's battle with General Motors,[4] these citizen groups and consumer organizations are no longer content to suffer in silence. Individuals now are much more conscious of their right to expect polite, humane, and competent service at a fair price, regardless of the source or the goods. Corporations were made liable for their activities; now a city administration was perceived likewise. The voters became consumers of municipal services and they began to fight city hall in the 1970s when incompetent services were offered at exhorbitant prices.

The city councilman is attuned to this changed constituency. Busch's interviews found that most of the councilmen "knew" the ward's interests and had a good idea of what the voters expected of him. A full 83 percent of those interviewed identified "service" themes as being what the people wanted ("they just want me to do things for them, all kinds of things—and especially where the police are involved" and "I am the dogcatcher"). Some councilmen also listed various "legislative" themes, but the traditional law-making function was not seen as the constituency's major demand or expectation.

An interesting distinction, however, can be made between black and white councilmen on this "service" vs. "legislative" role. All of those who thought that their constituents wanted them to "make laws" were white, but not one black politician thought that his constituents were interested in his acting as a legislator. Most of the black councilmen perceived their own job role as "legislative," and the whites were evenly split between the two. Busch offered a reasonable explanation of these differences:

[A]n . . . interpretation may exist in the greater tendency among blacks, in general, to view politics and public institutions as a means for redressing long-standing grievances and needs of the black community. If black legislators also think of political institutions as mechanisms for addressing and correcting the injustices of the black community, then black legislators may be less likely than whites to make a sharp distinction between those activities they view as "legislative" and those they essentially see as "service."[5]

The councilman also perceives the constituency as expecting, as well as defining his own role as including, the mediation of conflict. Conflicts frequently occur between individuals and various city officials over a wide range of issues—fire hazards, stray dogs, derelict buildings, condemnation proceedings, refuse collection, liquor licenses, snow removal, health inspections, housing code violations, abandoned cars, police behavior—and the ward expects the councilman to mediate and/or expedite the issue. Busch cited one unnamed councilman as saying, "when the police don't come, or there is a bitch about the behavior of a municipal employee, my people expect me to take the initiative and intervene." Disputes between private parties are also brought to the councilman. As one legislator remarked: "I don't know how often I am called on to iron out a problem between a tenant and his landlord, but it is too often." Busch wrote that some of the interviewed councilmen reported they get close to fifty telephone calls a day—both at their office and at home—from constituents with various types of requests and complaints. The urban councilman is thus seen as a facilitator of services and a major participant in extrajudicial conflict resolution.

Busch's interviews of the councilmen also contained questions on how they actually spent their time without reference to how they thought their time should be allocated or how they thought the constituency wanted them to spend the time. The councilman's actual behavior clearly placed constituent service as the primary function. Even for those who thought they were primarily "lawmakers," the amount of time devoted to nonlegislative activity underscored the importance of constituent service.

Eighteen of the councilmen (62 percent) reported that at least a full two-thirds of their work was devoted to taking care of service requests, handling problems in the ward, and communicating with city employees about various problems. Twenty-six of the councilmen (90 percent) said that such activities consumed at least 50 percent of their time. When one adds in the time spent on the necessary political functions of fence mending and campaigning—these particular councilmen devote about two months every two years to the election process—it is evident that these urban "legislators" spend little time with the law-making process.

From the analysis of actual behavior, it appears that these councilmen act more like an ombudsman than a lawmaker: they *are* facilitators of municipal services, mediators of disputes, and initiators of inquiry when bureaucratic insensitivity is alleged. This ombudsmanlike role is further evidenced by those skills or assets identified as necessary by the councilman for his job. The interview process generated responses from the councilmen that suggested skills similar to those needed by an ombudsman. When asked what they thought the primary skills of a councilman should be, twenty-one (72 percent) mentioned "interpersonal skills." A full 27 (93 percent) mentioned assets such as "knowing what it is the people want," "getting along with others," and the "ability to work with people." Those skills, although of course helpful to a lawmaker, are more relevant to an ombudsman. Moreover, most of the councilmen listed "more staff" and "help in handling constituent complaints" as primary support needs. *The councilmen look, act, and think like an ombudsman!*

What is equally significant is the *total* absence of any reference to specific legal skills: not one of the interviewed councilmen thought that skills as a lawmaker or legal training and experience were needed to be an effective councilman.[6] Busch offered several reasons to explain why legal skills are not seen as particularly important. The first reason is the above-described change in expectations and behavior: the councilman is more and more involved in areas that simply do not require any legal training. One need not know the law to deal with a voter whose garbage has not been picked up or whose street has not been cleared of snow. The "ability to get along with others" is more important here, and attorneys never had sole claim to this skill. Those trained in the law would probably bring a too formal and institutionalized approach to constituency service, and as long as the councilman's major function is not lawmaking, legal training is not needed.

Related to this reason is the changing nature of the councilman's career. Twenty or so years ago, most members of this particular city council *were* attorneys. The job as city councilman was part time: the $12,000 the council post paid supplemented a larger salary from professional practice. Now, however, the position is full time, with a salary close to $20,000. Attorneys have opted for full-time private practice, and this has allowed other occupational groups into council. These people are now full-time councilmen, and many do not have supplemental income.

The third reason for the decline in legal expertise of council has been the concurrent growth of the city's law department (this, of course, may be a function of the decreasing ability of council in legal matters). It is the law department that now has the expertise, and council seeks advice and guidance on legal questions and municipal law from it.[7]

Given the nature of the councilman's work load and the expectations that the individual councilman will provide service and solve problems, most proposals to establish a municipal ombudsman are usually met with strong opposition from the urban legislator. No longer a lawmaker, the urban city councilman perceives the ombudsman as a direct infringement on personal responsibilities and prerogatives. If constituent service and problem solving were to be transferred to an ombudsman, the urban councilman would become superfluous. Thus, at least for many American cities, the ombudsman is a long way from existence. But this is not to criticize the role of the councilman in the redress procedure. A classical ombudsman may be able to function more effectively (and less politically) than a councilman, but the point remains that the councilman *does* perform these services. The population does have an ally to represent their interests vis-à-vis city hall, and, although not the best avenue of redress, it at least provides individuals with a place to complain and, hopefully, to receive satisfaction.

The city councilman is the best example of constituent service, since his proximity and visibility to the voters make him very vulnerable to these pressures and demands. But the "errand boy" or "dog-catcher" chores of elected representatives exist at all levels of government in the United States: city, county, state, and even in Congress. The ombudsmanlike role of a member of Congress may not be as compelling or as time consuming as that of the local politician, but congressmen, too, are expected to provide—and actually do provide—constituent service. Two recent books analyzed certain perceptions and activities within congressional life, and it is clear that constituent service is an important congressional function.[8]

Richard F. Fenno, Jr., in his original study of what the congressman does in the home district, found that many House members emphasize their "service" activities to the voters back home. One such incident on the campaign trail was reported by Fenno, and, although perhaps not reflective of all House members, it is illustrative of many:

I'm not identified as a person interested in national problems. I'm identified for my interest in local problems. This is what we're going to make the theme of our campaign.

*   *   *

We took a poll and the one image they had of me was that I was a hard worker. So I got a broad base of votes. I think I get a lot of votes because of casework.[9]

Fenno described this particular congressman's printed campaign literature, and it is all too obvious that these handouts and placards emphasize the service aspect of the congressman:

His campaign brochure listed not a single issue position. At the top, it headlined, "X works for Us!" At the bottom it said, "X works hard to serve his constituents in _____." In between, it listed . . . summary results of his [six] years in office: 14,000 individuals helped "with problems involving the federal government," 25,000 "incidental requests" filled, 20,000 letters . . . answered. . . .[10]

The politics of representation and consituent service in this example is totally directed at the reelection process—the House member himself thinks his votes are the result of casework—and one can only surmise about the degree of real concern shown in the problems brought to his attention. But this may be an unfair criticism—even after discounting the figures above as somewhat inflated, this particular congressman *did* resolve thousands of problems that individuals had with the federal government.[11] These constituents have a conduit in Washington—their elected representative—and his activities in constituent service do provide an additional avenue in the redress process and information dissemination.

The second study, an analysis of congressional staff activity by Harrison Fox and Susan Hammond, also commented on this service function. Part of the reason that congressional staffs have grown so much in the past twenty years is that legislative work loads have greatly increased, and constituent demands are on the verge of being unmanageable. Fox and Hammond cited one senator who receives about three thousand letters a week, each wanting a response or additional activity. Large numbers of people are now employed on the Hill just to deal with constituent problems, casework, and requests for information.

The constituent service or casework performed by Congress may not be as detached from the law-making function as the two are at the local level. In some congressional offices, important links are made between casework on individual problems, administrative oversight, and the legislative process. Fox and Hammond commented:

> Some Congressmen use a constituent's complaint regarding an individual problem with a Federal program as a method of agency oversight. While the Congressman and his staff are in the process of solving the individual situation, they will also examine agency administration of the law in general and on occasion will bring about change in agency procedures. Constituent casework may also lead to legislation. One Congressman, for example, was alerted by a constituent to problems in the payment of medicare claims. After investigation, an amendment remedying the situation was . . . subsequently . . . passed by Congress[12]

Summary figures presented by Fox and Hammond clearly show that "casework"—handling constituent problems—occupies a good deal of staff time.[13] Approximately 188 Senate staffers were interviewed, and 33 (17.6 percent) said they work on constituent problems at least once every hour; an additional 44 staffers (23.4 percent) said, at least once a day or more. The representatives and senators may be less involved in "dog catching" as are the local city councilmen, but these legislators also play an important role in the redress process.

United States congressmen perceive their job as containing ombudsmanlike characteristics: they facilitate, they provide information, they are a conduit, they can hasten a bureaucrat's lethargy. They do not deal with allegations of criminality or with violations of central personal liberties—these grievances are for the courts—but neither does the ombudsman. The politics of representation has the politicians actively engaged in constituency service, and they lend their good offices to resolve individual problems.

THE POLITICS OF OPPOSITION:
THE QUESTION PERIOD AT WESTMINSTER

The Question Period at Westminster is no longer in vogue as a subject of serious study by political scientists.[14] But since the process continues to operate, and is relevant to this chapter, this section presents a short discussion of this particular political avenue of redress. The Question Period is approached in terms of the "politics of opposition": the chief beneficiary of the process is seen to be the politician and/or his party. Although a private individual with a legitimate grievance or complaint against the state or bureaucracy *may* ultimately receive satisfaction, such redress is usually only a spillover—a side effect—of the real political central focus. But if one approaches the situation from the individual's point of view, that redress and satisfaction *are* achieved, then it is perhaps not too crucial if there are political payoffs for the politician as well.

A system of redress that operates only as long as political gains can be made is not on a firm foundation; the politician will soon lose interest in such activity if payoffs no longer exist. A system of redress must be rooted in a concern for the individual and not in the career patterns of the grievance officer. But this is not the situation with the Question Period, because the Question Period plays an incidental role in the redress process. The Question Period could disappear entirely, and British citizens would not suffer state mistreatment since the courts would protect them; the redress of grievances could be removed from the Question Period, and few people would notice, since the process has more important political functions that would continue. The point is that the Question Period may be able to provide an *additional* avenue of redress while the politicians are pursuing other goals. The process has enjoyed a long and honorable history; it performs several functions at the same time, and, in certain circumstances, it may provide instantaneous redress to an individual who has a grievance against the state.

The Question Period, in brief, is the institutionalized and hoary political process by which members of the British House of Commons at Westminister put written and oral questions to members of the government on practically *any* subject and receive a subsequent public response from the relevant cabinet minister.[15] The origins of the process can be traced well back into Parliament's history: a government spokesman announced the future business of Commons in response to a question put by the opposition leader. By the late 1700s, this question and answer process was being applied to matters other than the future agenda. The process was spontaneous: members of the House would ask questions whenever they felt the urge. This ad hoc situation was changed in 1835 when written notice of the intent to ask a question was required. The process was institutionalized around 1850 when the Question Period was given a regular assigned time slot in the parliamentary agenda.

As it now operates, it is obvious that the process fulfills a parliamentary need, because approximately six-thousand oral questions are asked each session.[16] For about one hour a day, Monday through Thursday, members of the House query the ministers; written notice (about a week) of the question must be given to allow the minister time to have an answer prepared. The list of questions are set out for the day: the Speaker calls upon the member to ask his question (read from prepared copy), and the concerned minister or a junior minister answers (again from prepared copy). But this is not the entire matter; if it were, the Question Period would be dull. Rather, the member of the House of Commons who asked the (written) question is now permitted to ask an oral "supplementary" question based on the prepared reply just heard. Prior notice of the content of these supplementary questions is *not* given—they are spontaneous—and the minister must have his wits about him to make an immediate and cogent reply. Usually two or three supplementary questions arise for each prepared answer, but if the Speaker of the House thinks the matter is important, he can allow additional oral questions before moving on to the next prepared question and anwer. These additional oral questions are not limited to the member who asked the original question, and all House members are eligible to enter the fray.

The cabinet ministers are questioned on a revolving basis (the rota). Each large ministry, along with two or three smaller departments, are allocated a particular day (or days) of the week. When it is a particular ministry's day, the minister is questioned first and often will have to hold down the fort for the entire hour. But then the minister will be at the bottom of the list and is unlikely to be questioned at all until the rota system puts him back at the top of the list. The one exception to this rhythm is the prime minister. The prime minister is open to questioning twice a week for a total of approximately forty minutes. This arrangement was introduced in 1961, and it provides an excellent opportunity for House members to question the prime minister directly—compare former President Nixon's statement that neither he nor any executive branch employee would testify in front of a congressional committee—as well as providing the prime minister with frequent opportunities to pronounce official views on various matters.

The process is relatively expensive, however, and only a minority of the members actually ask questions. Kenneth Bradshaw and David Pring[17] cite some data from 1970: each question answered orally costs about £14, and each written answer costs about £10. The total direct costs in 1970 ran to about £300,000, but this amount does not include the indirect costs—the salaries and overhead for all of the civil servants who have to prepare the responses (as well as to anticipate the content of the supplementary questions) for their ministers. In addition, the 1970 data show that 33.5 percent of all questions were asked by only 4.3 percent of the House membership. It is remarkable that the British sense of parliamentary procedure and democratic government tolerates such an expensive process that aids so few of the members. But no movement is made to restrict the system, and it is, indeed, an integral part of the legislative process at Westminister. The role of questions in this legislative process is three-fold: politics, information, and a call for action.

The use of the Question Period for *political* purposes constitutes by far the largest category, and three types of questions fall under the rubric of political: questions that opposition back-benchers ask to embarrass the government and thus enhance the image of their own party, questions that are "inspired" by the majority to allow the minister to expound on a favorite subject, and questions that are asked by all members to generate more publicity and recognition for their own political careers. The dividing line between the first and third type of question is vague, however, and one question can achieve several goals.

Questions of "opposition" are obvious to all who hear them. Partisan political concerns are stated in question form ("Is the Minister aware that . . . unemployment has increased; . . . inflation is at x percent; . . . the balance of payments is not in balance?"), and the government is then expected to defend and justify its policies. It is usually the back-bencher who asks these questions since the opposition front-bench has ample time in debate to air its views. But the opposition front-bench is not always aloof from the process: sometimes a detailed and concerted campaign is orchestrated by the front-bench to harrass a particular minister or government program.[18] The back-benchers ask the written question, but the Shadow Cabinet members enter the fray with carefully prepared oral supplementary questions. The minister is thus subjected to thorough questioning, and the government's policies must be defended.

"Inspired" questions are similar in function to a United States president's opening remarks before a press conference. Inspired questions are asked of a minister at the request of the minister. The back-benchers of the majority party are listed as the author of the question—it is seen as "improper" for party leaders or whips to ask them—and the minister usually has no difficulty in finding someone to "ask" the question. Inspired questions are used for a variety of purposes: to announce a major governmental appointment, to publicize some change in policy, to correct or answer some statement reported in the media, to offer a statement in advance of some anticipated criticism to deflate the situation. D.N. Chester and Nona Bowring commented[19] that the use of inspired questions derives from the long-established British tradition that governmental announcements should first be made to the House of Commons. If a ministry wants greater publicity, duplicated copies of the question and answer are made available as press handouts.

Questions that seek publicity for the questioner are also numerous. The average back-bencher receives little recognition for his work in Parliament: the front-benchers receive most of the time allocated to debate as well as most of the headlines. The back-bencher has a much greater likelihood of being mentioned by the media—at least in the local paper—if he is able to ask a series of questions. The problem with this, however, is that the subject matter of such questions seldom deals with "important" or "significant" issues. Significant issues are taken over by the front-bench, and the publicity seeker is left with matters of limited interest, which are then seen as trivial.[20] But for the back-bencher who can mount a campaign on a matter tinged with the public interest, the resulting publicity may often advance his political career.

The second major type of question is one that seeks information, statistics, and precise factual answers, and such questions are not necessarily asked to embarrass the government, although the information so received may at a later date be employed in political attacks against a minister or the government. Members of the House require information for a variety of purposes: precise knowledge about public policy might make the member of Parliament (MP) more effective; the MP might be preparing a speech or an article; he might want to be kept informed in his area of specialization. In addition, the House of Commons does not have as specialized a committee system as does the U.S. Congress, and, for example, no House Committees exist in Commons on agriculture or foreign affairs. MPs employ questions to get at specialized information. Even when there are House committees, moreover, only a small percentage of the House membership sits on them—most MPs do not belong to any committee, and for the back-benchers, the "information" question is the only means by which they can keep informed of developments in their area of interest.

Information questions are often asked by MPs on behalf of a third person or group.[21] A British ministry has the legitimate authority to refuse to give information to people outside the government—an individual, an interest group, a labor union, private corporations. But the ministry is reluctant to refuse such information if requested by question by a MP. Chester and Bowring commented that many university professors, in need of specific (but nonclassified) information, have called upon a MP to ask the desired question in Parliament and thus have access to the necessary data. Chester and Bowring also said that a ministry, upon refusing to give some information to an interest group, will advise the group to have a MP ask the same question in Parliament. The overwhelming majority of information questions are solely that—a device to get information—and they are not intended for partisan political activity.

The third type of question concerns a "call for action"—asking the minister whether he will take a certain course of action on various aspects of public policy. The intent of such questions is to try to exercise some influence on government policy or action. Few major changes in policy, however, result from the Question Period. Public policy is made at cabinet level, and questions from the floor of Parliament have little influence on the cabinet.

Questions are also used by individual MPs to investigate and, if necessary, provide redress to individuals who have brought some grievance or complaint to the MP's attention. Few individual grievances reach the question stage because they are usually resolved—although not always to the satisfaction of the individual—before the floor of Parliament. The normal process is similar to that of the ombudsman: the MP writes to the concerned minister about the complaint, and the correspondence and/or conversations may stretch on for months. The department may make a concession, or it may convince the MP that it acted reasonably and that nothing more can be done. In these situations, the matter is closed. But in several instances the MP is not satisfied with the government's response, and he can then resort to the Question Period.

The department is not likely to change its decision once it receives notice of the question—it had ample opportunity to do so before the question. But the use of the question puts the department in the spotlight: the grievance now becomes public rather than hidden away in interoffice memos; if the question is interesting enough, the media will publicize it; the individual with the grievance may be interviewed, and all of the "lurid" details may be printed. This publicity does not necessarily mean the minister automatically concedes, but it will make him reconsider the strength and justification of the decision and prepare an explanation that will sound acceptable.

But a MP giving notice to ask a question may result in the individual receiving immediate redress for a long-standing grievance. The following example may be infrequent, but it does illustrate the effectiveness of the Question Period in a system of redress:

Sir W. Smithers asked the Minister of Health if he is aware that Mr. E. Bowen, of Altham Cottage, Knockholt, who has had both legs amputated, is still awaiting information as to his future treatment and the supplying of a mechanical chair; and if he will take the necessary steps to see that Mr. Bowen's disabilities are attended to forthwith.

Mr. Bevan: No Sir. Mr. Bowen is perfectly satisfied with his treatment, which is almost completed, and knows that he will be provided with a mechanical tricycle as soon as possible.

Sir W. Smithers: Is the Minister aware that when this Question was put down he was not satisfied and that it is only because I threatened to put down a Question that Mr. Bowen got immediate treatment?

Mr. Bevan: That may reveal that efficacy of Questions in Parliament, and I have never underestimated their importance. Why the Hon. Member should reproach himself because on one occasion he has been useful, I do not know.

Sir W. Smithers: On a point of Order, may I ask for your protection, Mr. Speaker? I object to being called "vermin" in other words.[22]

The above exchange is concerned more with the political sparring between Bevan and Smithers and less with the disabled Bowen. But the fact remains that Bowen's complaint against the National Health Service was instantaneously resolved once the MP gave notice of the question. Redress of grievances against the state can be achieved through the Question Period, although this avenue of redress is only secondary.

The Question Period, in all of its functions, works well in the United Kingdom. It is an integral part of the parliamentary democratic process, and it is ideally suited to the Westminister style. But as mentioned above, it is only of secondary importance in the redress process from a general viewpoint; from the perspective of people such as Bowen of Knockholt, this process far surpasses any other. Redress of grievances through parliamentary political activity, as illustrated in the Question Period, cannot be the major avenue of redress in a society; as a backup to the primary system(s), it is an honorable and sometimes effective watchdog.

THE POLITICS OF BELIEF AND EXTRA-CONSTITUENCY ACTIVITY

The third area of parliamentary activity to be discussed falls under the category of the "politics of belief" and extra-constituency behavior. The major focus here is to protect individuals from being mistreated by governments, and this desire derives from a sincere and deeply rooted belief in the value of people and human rights. Any political payoff that might accrue to a politician is only incidental: politicians in these examples are concerned with protecting other people rather than furthering their own political career. The attempts in this section are "extra-constituency": the legislature in one country attempts to employ its power and influence to protect—or facilitate redress for—citizens of another country from the latter's own government.

This section concerns three (of many) extra-constituency attempts to protect people from state abuse. The first attempt is the recent linkage of American foreign policy—especially foreign aid decisions—to the status of human rights in the recipient countries. It was the Harkin Amendment that began this process, but it has since moved beyond Congressman Harkin's honorable legislation. Second is the Conference on Security and Cooperation in Europe (CSCE), popularly known as the Helsinki Agreement. It is "basket three" of the CSCE, humanitarian activities, that relates to the lives of private individuals and that seeks to resolve the humanitarian problems arising from a divided Europe and East-West tensions. The third is the Jackson-Vanik Amendment. This amendment "requires" the Soviet Union to permit large-scale emigration, mainly of Soviet Jews, before the United States will grant "most-favored-nation" status to the Soviets in their trade relations with the United States.

I agree with the goals—philosophical, political, humanitarian—of the above three attempts by the U.S. Congress and successive administrations to protect people beyond our boundaries from mistreatment by oppressive governments.

But the real effectiveness of these redress avenues and other similar attempts not discussed (for example, the attempt to control private United States investment in South Africa) is yet to be fully documented or even understood. It is possible that the potential beneficiaries of all of this activity—poor farmers in Chile, Poles with relatives in the United States, Soviet Jews and dissidents—may have seen their situation become worse rather than ameliorated.

Human Rights and Foreign Aid

One of the more consistent images put forth by President Carter is that of morality and concern for oppressed peoples throughout the world. A great deal of public emphasis and political rhetoric have been placed on human rights objectives in the conduct of United States foreign policy and in the administration of economic assistance programs. Much of the groundwork, however, was done before the Carter administration, and it is Congress—and not the president—that deserves whatever merit may accrue to such activities.

It is Congress, in fact—Carter's pronouncements notwithstanding—that is showing a lot more misgivings and doubts about loans and foreign aid to repressive regimes than is the administration, and some conflict has arisen, particularly between the Department of State and a congressional subcommittee. The Department of State appears to view American foreign policy and economic assistance programs from the perspective of American "national interest," and the administration believes the United States could be more effective in advancing the cause of human rights by quiet diplomacy and persuasion. Congress, on the other hand, and particularly the International Organizations Subcommittee of the House Foreign Affairs Committee, seems to approach foreign policy and economic aid from the perspective of the mistreated Chilean and Ethiopian peoples. Congress is more inflexible than the administration: the United States should be required by law automatically to oppose aid to any regime that does not protect human rights.

In a real sense, the Carter administration has been forced into an embarrassing political position: the administration wants to link human rights to foreign aid, but it is also attempting to defuse the efforts of some congressmen who translate Carter's words into formal public policy. It all began in 1976 with Thomas R. Harkin, a Democratic congressman from Iowa. In a routine bill authorizing funds for the Inter-American Development Bank (IADB), Harkin was able to insert a human rights amendment. The Harkin Amendment to the Foreign Assistance Act stated that a "principal goal of the foreign policy of the United States shall be to promote the observance of internationally recognized human rights," and it required the American director of the IADB to oppose any loan to countries that "engage in a consistent pattern of gross violation of internationally recognized human rights" unless such a loan "directly benefits the needy."

In 1977 Harkin continued and got approximately the same language in a bill concerning several institutions, including the World Bank, the Asian Bank and Fund, and the African Development Fund. In the spring of 1977, Harkin extended such language to almost all of the American representatives on the boards of such multinational economic development funds and banks. This legislation applied to international financial institutions where the American representative is only one of many in the decision-making process. Some of these institutions oversee an enormous amount of resources—the World Bank, for example, loaned about $9 billion in fiscal 1979—and Congress wanted some review over their international loans, many of which were going to regimes not noted for their protection of human rights (especially Argentina and Uruguay).

This early legislation had some immediate effects.[23] The original 1976 legislation required that the American director of the IADB vote against a $21 million industrial credit loan for Chile in June, although in December 1976 the United States agreed to a loan to Chile for a water project. This latter loan was permitted since it was seen "directly to benefit the needy." In early 1977 Harold Reynolds, the American representative on the World Bank's board, abstained on human rights grounds from voting on two loans to Ethiopia. In June 1977 the staff of the World Bank indefinitely postponed submitting to the bank's governing board a $24 million loan project for grain storage and marketing facilities in Ethiopia. The bank's "official" explanation was that the disruption of rail lines between Addis Ababa and Djibouti prevented effective economic administration of the project. A *New York Times* article, however, commented that many analysts believed the real reason was the bank staff's disapproval of the human rights record of the new Ethiopian regime of Colonel Mengistu Haile Mariam.

This early legislation applied only to United States participation in international development banks and multinational economic assistance programs. These multinational programs, although large, represent only a fraction of the total amount of United States foreign aid and economic assistance. More recently, Congress enacted similar legislation mandating that human rights considerations be taken into account in decisions on foreign aid, and a broad range of statutes now define and restrict the flow of such assistance to countries with a poor human rights record. These new statutes apply to unilateral American programs, including (but not limited to) the Agency for International Development (AID), the Export-Import Bank, Food for Peace Programs (PL-480 food aid), and the various United States military assistance and sales programs. What Congress is doing here is attempting to employ its power—the denial of economic assistance—to protect people in other countries from being mistreated by their own government. It is being done in the hope that these repressive regimes will reduce the amount of human rights violations, but whether the legislation has achieved its goals remains to be seen.

Although the Carter administration would have preferred "quiet diplomacy" in place of this automatic requirement, the U.S. government appears to be carrying out both the letter and the spirit of these laws. One of Carter's first acts as president was to establish the Interagency Group on Human Rights and Foreign Assistance. This executive interagency group is the forum where human rights issues are discussed in relation to the economic assistance programs. The group is composed of representatives from the Departments of State, Defense, Labor, Treasury, Commerce, and Agriculture and from the National Security Council and the Agency for International Development. The human rights aspects of purely military assistance programs are considered by the Arms Export Control Board.

In testimony before the International Organizations Subcommittee of the House Foreign Affairs Committee in May 1979, Deputy Secretary of State Warren Christopher identified the factors that this Interagency Group on Human Rights and Foreign Assistance considers when applying the statutes to a particular loan or program:

> The present human rights situation in the recipient country and any positive or negative trend;
> The political, economic, and cultural background of the country and the level of human rights performance that can reasonably be expected of the country in light of that background;
> The other fundamental U.S. interests with respect to that country;
> The extent to which a loan will directly benefit the needy; and
> The effectiveness of a decision to defer or oppose a loan in comparison or in combination with any of the available diplomatic tools for indicating our concern about human rights violations.[24]

Christopher listed what he termed some basic principles or guidelines that the Carter administration has followed over the past few years in foreign assistance decisions:

> [T]he most effective strategy for obtaining human rights improvements is one that combines the full range of diplomatic approaches with a willingness to adjust our foreign assistance programs as required. No element in the overall strategy can be as effective alone as in combination with others. In addition, the use of these various elements must be calibrated and sequential, conveying our concerns in a steady, even way while avoiding sudden escalations.
> [B]ilateral or multilateral economic assistance that directly benefits the needy is rarely disapproved, even to governments with poor human rights records. Disapproval could penalize the poor because of their government's misdeeds.
> [O]nly compelling considerations of national security can justify providing security assistance to countries with very serious human rights problems. Even where these considerations require us to go forward with military sales to such a country, we still restrict sales to the police or others involved in human rights abuses. And we take particular care to convey our human rights concerns through other diplomatic instruments.[25]

This entire situation has mixed reviews. On the one hand, it represents an admirable political attempt by the U.S. Congress to put pressure on foreign governments so these governments, hopefully, will reduce human rights violations. In a real sense, Harkin and his colleagues *are* concerned with the poor Chilean or Ethiopian farmers and want to improve their status and condition vis-à-vis their governments. But only the government itself in these countries can affect real change and the United States is on the sidelines, encouraging progress or discouraging continued repression.

The problem, however, is that the United States cannot do this alone—other Western powers can provide a lot of this aid if it is not given by the United States. But what is more frightening is the real possibility that the United States will lose whatever influence it may have over these governments if it denies too many assistance programs. The Soviet Union and other Eastern bloc countries—countries not noted for protecting their citizens from state mistreatment—are all too ready to jump into the breech left by the United States. This happened with Nasser in the 1950s with financing of the Aswan Dam complex; Colonel Mengistu, rebuffed by the United States, has since turned to the Soviet Union for needed economic and military assistance. The abstract goal of this legislative attempt to protect other peoples from their own governments is admirable; its effectiveness in the real political world has yet to be demonstrated.

The Conference on Security and Cooperation in Europe (CSCE): The Helsinki Agreement

The Conference on Security and Cooperation in Europe (CSCE), more popularly known as the Helsinki Agreement, is not strictly a unilateral parliamentary activity as is the Harkin Amendment. Rather, it is a multilateral international agreement—thirty-five nations signed the Final Helsinki Act—but the CSCE can be approached within the framework of this section. The CSCE from this perspective is seen as an attempt by the U.S. government, including the administration and Congress, to employ its power, prestige, and influence to protect and help people in Eastern Europe from being mistreated by their own governments. But as is the case with restricting American economic assistance to regimes with poor human rights records, the real effectiveness of the CSCE for the people it is designed to help is still under review.

The CSCE is both a result of and a contributor to the process of East-West detente, which began with the Nixon administration. The agreement is designed to decrease tension in a divided Europe and to extend the policy of detente and cooperation in military, economic, political, and scientific fields. It is also designed, at least from the West's viewpoint, to strengthen the status of the individual vis-à-vis the state and to protect basic human rights. The CSCE's final act was signed after long negotiations in Helsinki in 1974, and an important follow-up meeting was held in Belgrad (October 1977 to May 1978). Another meeting, designed to conduct a second full-scale joint review of the progress in implementing the act's provisions, was held in Madrid in late 1980.

Three major chapters, or "baskets," make up the CSCE agreement. The first "basket" of the Final Helsinki Act is titled "Questions Relating to Security in Europe," and it includes a section on "Declaration on Principles Guiding Relations Between Participating States." Basket one also includes a subsection on giving effect to certain of the principles as well as a document on military confidence-building measures and certain aspects of security and disarmament. The ten principles of basket one express the basic precepts of international behavior that have traditionally been accepted in the conduct of international relations. Some of these principles concern the peaceful settlement of disputes, nonintervention in internal affairs, and the recognition of human rights and fundamental freedoms. The sections on confidence-building measures and certain aspects of security and disarmament also call for more cooperation and tension-lessening activities. The signatory states are expected to give each other prior notification of major (more than twenty-five thousand troops) military maneuvers, smaller scale military maneuvers, and major military movements. The increased exchange of observers and military visits are also included in basket one.

Basket two is titled "Cooperation in the Fields of Economics, of Science and Technology, and of the Environment." The thirty-five nations are expected to improve the quantity and quality of useful, published economic and commerical information: output statistics, export-import figures, trade laws, foreign trading organizations, and so on. Scientific exchanges and joint research efforts were to be encouraged, and a high-level multinational meeting was envisioned to deal with transnational air pollution.

Basket three of the Final Helsinki Act contains a wide range of provisions with a common objective—the freer flow of people, ideas, and information among the signatory states. It is this particular basket that relates to the lives of private individuals and that seeks to resolve the humanitarian problems arising from a divided Europe. The specific human rights provisions of basket three are discussed in somewhat more detail below, but the provisions of this section of the Final Act relate to the reunification of families, contacts, and regular visits on the basis of family ties, marriage between citizens of different countries, travel for personal or professional reasons, religious contacts, cultural exchanges, and the dissemination of information (journalists, book publishing, journals, films, and broadcasting).

Even though principle six of basket one ("nonintervention in internal affairs") was used by the Soviet Union and other Warsaw Pact countries in an attempt to stifle Western insistence upon full implementation of all provisions (especially those in basket three), the West maintains that principle six does not release countries from fully implementing the human rights provisions. The United States' position at the Belgrade meeting can be summarized as follows:

The full implementation of all provisions of the Helsinki Final Act is essential to the successful development of detente and of security and cooperation in Europe;

Human rights and humanitarian issues are a major, integral aspect of the CSCE process as well as of detente;

Individual states will be held accountable for their implementation failures, both at future CSCE meetings and in the eyes of world opinion;

The United States and other CSCE states will not hesitate, and indeed consider it important, to point out specific examples of implementation failures which threaten the health and credibility of the CSCE process; [and]

Efforts to mask implementation shortcomings with the cloak of nonintervention in internal affairs will not deflect legitimate criticism of a country's implementation record.[26]

The specific provisions of the Final Act relevant to the concerns of this chapter are in basket three—the human rights and humanitarian questions. Again, here is an example of extra-constituency activity in the redress process: the United States, via the CSCE, is attempting to protect the status of individuals in Eastern Europe from assaults by their own governments. However, the Final Act is *not* legally binding on any signatory state—whatever commitment exists is only political—and the states are expected to implement the provisions voluntarily (there is no international enforcement process). Unfortunately, most Eastern European countries accepted basket three in principle but have yet to implement its provisions fully, and I seriously doubt whether the status of human rights in Eastern Europe is appreciably better today compared to pre-CSCE times. The United States has made an admirable attempt to try to protect individuals, but, as is the case with applying pressure through the denial of economic assistance, it is the home government that must provide redress and not the United States.

The first few years' results of the Helsinki Agreement relating to basket three have been mixed, but the overall impression is negative. The United States considers family reunification an important aspect of the agreement— so little is required of governments, and such reunification means so much to the individuals concerned—but as of May 1978, some 4,150 individuals still had requests for emigration refused one or more times and cases still were pending between the United States and countries in Eastern Europe.[27] The CSCE notwithstanding, emigration from Eastern Europe, and the Soviet Union in particular, is difficult, and the obstacles appear to have been purposely designed to discourage applicants. A relatively high fee is charged for an exit visa, especially for those people who have suffered economic deprivation on account of requesting such a visa, and many applicants also lose employment and shelter during the long application procedure.

Temporary reunification through visits and regular meetings on the basis of family ties are also encouraged in basket three, but here again, results have been mixed. Poland's record appears to be the best, allowing thousands of

Polish-Americans to return to Poland each year for family visits (although few travel from East to West), but the Soviet Union and Czechoslovakia have strict policies in this area. In general, visits based on family ties have yet to be implemented fully, for many East European governments consider relatives abroad to have emigrated without official permission. Many Warsaw Pact countries refuse entry visas to such former nationals and refuse their relatives permission to visit the West.

Binational marriages also present some problems, since several East European governments either refuse a citizen permission to marry a foreign national or prevent the marriage by denying visas (exit or entry) to one of the prospective spouses. Rumania has the strictest policy in regard to binational marriages, and each individual case must be approved by the Rumanian government. Again, the existence of the Final Helsinki Act really does not help a Rumanian citizen who wants to marry someone from the West.

It is obvious that the Soviet Union and other Warsaw Pact countries, even with the CSCE, have increased the pressure on human rights advocates within their borders and have attempted to limit their activity. Aleksandr Ginzburg and Anatoly Shcharensky were given harsh prison sentences; others are subjected to continual harrassment for their activities; the cellist Mstislav Rostropovich and General Pyotr Grigorenko had their Soviet citizenship revoked because of their opposition to the human rights situation in the Soviet Union. One of the most serious cases was that of Yuri Orlov, a leader of the Moscow Public Group to Promote Observance of the Final Helsinki Act in the Soviet Union. Orlov was sentenced to a seven-year term—with a possible additional five years in internal exile—on charges of being a Central Intelligence Agency (CIA) agent, but the sentence was to punish, and stifle, the monitoring group. The Helsinki monitoring group in Czechoslovakia—Charter 77—continues to be harrassed by their government with jail terms, loss of employment, and revocation of citizenship. More recently, in October 1979, six Czech human rights activists received jail sentences for "subversion." One of the six was playwright Vaclav Havel, and even *l'Humanité*, the French Communist party's newspaper, denounced the trials as a violation of individual human rights.

What can the United States do in face of this noncompliance activity? Unfortunately, very little can be done by the American government to protect the human rights of people in other countries beyond the usual public pronouncements of disapproval or diplomatic representations to the governments concerned. The ability of the United States to influence how the Warsaw Pact countries treat their own citizens is limited to indignant prose:[28] "individual states will be held accountable in the eyes of world opinion"; after the Orlov conviction, both Houses of the U.S. Congress passed resolutions calling for "the release of all unjustly imprisoned members of the monitoring groups"; "we are hoping that the implementation steps announced prove genuine"; "we will continue to make representations on these many cases in the hope of achieving genuine progress"; "we continue our representations to elicit the co-operation of Bulgarian authorities"; "we continued to monitor progress"; and so forth.

The "pressure" exerted by the United States on the Eastern European countries to abide by the CSCE's Final Act and to protect human rights appears to be similar to the village serf, going, hat-in-hand and with bended knee, to the manor lord and respectfully asking him to alter his behavior. The Eastern European governments will alter their behavior only when it is in their national interest to do so; expressions of hope from the United States will not speed the process.

The Jackson-Vanik Amendment

The third and final example of extra-constituency parliamentary efforts to provide redress for other people vis-à-vis their own government is the Jackson-Vanik Amendment, linking most-favored-nation status for the Soviet Union to increased levels of Soviet Jewish emigration. The Jackson-Vanik Amendment was the culmination of a long political process, involving both public and private American organizations, to help the Soviet Jews. Space does not permit a full description of the entire process, and this section is thus limited to the amendment's role in a system of redress.[29]

The Jackson-Vanik Amendment had its roots in the American refusal to accept in silence the way the Soviet government treated Jews. Although Jewish cultural and political life in Russia has a long history, especially during the Revolution, the late 1940s saw the beginnings of the Soviet government's concerted campaign against Jewish life. The November 1952, Soviet-inspired purge trials in Czechoslovakia (Rudolf Slansky and others) had Jews as the prime defendants; the so-called Doctors' Plot against Stalin in 1953 again featured Jews; Jews were being characterized in official pronouncements as "international parasites," and baking matzos was forbidden; Jews were being systematically squeezed out of the universities, professions, and other jobs; religious activity was curtailed—Yiddish and Hebrew publications were sharply limited, the training of rabbis was limited, and Jews were the only Soviet group that had their religion stamped on the internal passport for nationality. When Jews complained about the treatment received, they were economically harrassed; when they applied to emigrate, they were either refused an exit visa or were subjected to exhorbitant fees (exit visa fees, an "education tax" to reimburse the government for the costs of their education). The American Jewish community had been aware of the situation and was quietly attempting to alleviate it; the blatant mistreatment of the Jews, however, began to arouse the non-Jewish American consciousness as well.

Through a convoluted process involving public and private groups—Jewish and non-Jewish—the U.S. Congress entered the controversy. Led by Charles Vanik of Ohio in the House and by Henry Jackson of Washington in the Senate (both non-Jews), both Houses showed overwhelming support to employ their power and influence to protect the Soviet Jews from their own government. The amendment was tacked on to the East-West Trade Bill, a bill describing the conditions of trade between the United States and nonmarket economies (that is, Communist states). The House approved Vanik's amendment by a vote of 319 to 80 in December 1974, and the entire Trade Bill passed 272 to 140. The Senate approved Jackson's amendment 88–0, and the entire Trade Reform Act passed 77–4. On December 18, 1974, a House-Senate Conference Committee resolved the different language in the two versions, and on December 20 the final bill, including the amendment, passed. On January 3, 1975, President Ford signed the Trade Reform Act.

The Jackson-Vanik Amendment thus remains law and in operation, linking American trade benefits to the emigration policies of nonmarket economy states. The amendment prevented the administration from granting most-favored-nation (MFN) status—the conditions of trade will be identical to the country most favored by the United States—long-term, government-guaranteed credits and investment guarantees to states that denied their citizens the right to emigrate or charged more than a "nominal" fee for an exit visa.[30]

The Soviet reaction was predictable. They rejected the entire concept as undue interference in a country's internal affairs and claimed the United States had no legitimate right to try to influence their domestic policies.[31] The Soviet Union, however, was put in a bind: to receive the needed credits, they would have to allow unhindered (Jewish) emigration, but such emigration would upset their relationship with the Arab states if too many Jews went to Israel. The Soviets have taken a middle position: permit enough Jews to leave to prevent more restrictive American legislation but refuse to institute unhindered emigration. The amendment is still in effect, and the Soviets have yet to receive MFN status. But as is discussed below, the total number of Jews allowed to leave each year from the Soviet Union is *less* in the postamendment years than in the preamendment years.

Why did the American Congress pass such legislation? William Orbach summarized a few of the many reasons:

> Americans . . . remain wary of Communism. Detente, in middle America, arouses distrust. The Jackson-Vanik Amendment, in one stroke, satisfied all American demands: it represented toughness, it allayed the Christian conscience, and it demanded Soviet concessions, especially after the 1972 wheat deal fiasco.[32]

The Jackson-Vanik Amendment has had mixed results for the people it was designed to protect—the Soviet Jews. No doubt the approximately seventy-three thousand Jews who emigrated between 1975 and 1978[33] were at least tangentially aided by the American action. One cannot say with any certainty that the amendment "caused" the Soviets to let them leave, but its influence cannot be discounted. However, as mentioned above and as note 33 shows, fewer people emigrated in the four postamendment years (seventy-three thousand) than during the four preceeding years (approximately one-hundred-thousand Jews arrived in Vienna from 1971 through 1974). The amendment has not increased emigration; it has had the opposite effect. The status of a Soviet Jew who wanted to emigrate was better before the amendment, and, to avoid appearing as "giving in" to the Americans, the Soviets have tightened up the movement. Nonetheless, seventy-three thousand is more than zero, and even if only one person a year is allowed to emigrate, the Jackson-Vanik Amendment would be a success in protecting people from being mistreated by their own government.

The problem is, however, not with what the amendment is designed to accomplish; the problem is that it is a limited "solution" to a complicated situation. The American response via the amendment might possibly aid only a (relatively) small number of Soviet Jews—those who want to emigrate. The amendment totally ignores, and perhaps even exacerbates, the situation of the millions of Jews who do not want to emigrate but prefer to remain and live as Jews in the Soviet Union. The majority of Soviet Jews are *not* being helped by the amendment, and it appears that the Soviet government is not relenting in its treatment of Jews.

The amendment is not permitting an extension of Jewish cultural and religious life; it is not allowing the baking of matzos; it is not encouraging the building of synagogues or the training of rabbis; it is not permitting publishing in Yiddish or Hebrew; it is not helping to open up the universities; it is not preventing Jews from being tried and convicted on trumped-up charges of subversion and espionage. To be truly effective—to have *really* aided the Soviet Jews—the amendment also should have included the way the Soviet government treated the Jews, and every other religious and national group, that wanted to remain in the Soviet Union with full enjoyment of all individual human rights. But this is asking too much since it would be blatant interference in another country's "domestic" affairs. The Soviet response to such American legislation would be no different from the American reaction to a Politburo "demand" that we immediately give all political and human rights to blacks, Chicanos, women, Indians, and so on.

An attempt by one parliamentary body to protect people in another country from those people's own government is a difficult undertaking. The Jackson-Vanik Amendment may not represent the ideal solution, but it is, at least, a beginning to the crucial recognition that individual human rights *is* everyone's concern. The United States Congress cannot wipe out Soviet anti-Semitism, nor can it protect the Soviet individual from being mistreated. Nevertheless, Senator Henry Jackson and Congressman Charles Vanik, and their colleagues in the House and Senate, have performed their role to bring some measure of redress to some 73,276 individuals.

NOTES

1. See Theodore L. Becker, ed., *Political Trials* (Indianapolis and New York: The Bobbs-Merrill Co., 1971). Becker's book reviews "political" trials in eight countries

(West Germany, India, The Philippines, Nigeria, Ghana, Cuba, the Soviet Union, and the United States) where the defendants—in the authors' views—were tried not for criminal behavior but for questioning the dominant political values of the ruling elite.

2. The discussion of the city councilman's role in constituent service and the politics of representation rests upon Ronald J. Busch, "The Urban Legislator as a Municipal Ombudsman," unpublished manuscript (February, 1978), 31 pp. The data contained in this study were derived from open-ended personal interviews of twenty-nine (out of thirty-three) members of the council in a large midwestern city. The findings, although valid only in relation to this city, nonetheless reflect the situation in many other large American cities.

3. Ibid., pp. 6–7.

4. See Ralph Nader, *Unsafe at Any Speed* (New York: Grossman Publishers, 1965).

5. Busch, "The Urban Legislator," p. 12.

6. Three of the city's thirty-three councilmen were attorneys at the time of the interviews, although Busch did not indicate whether these three were among the twenty-nine who were interviewed, among the four who where not, or split between the two groups. It is possible that even those who were trained in the law do not regard such skills as relevant to the job; conversely, it may be that only nonlawyers felt this way.

7. The particular council studied by Busch has even retained legal counsel to represent its interests in its acrimonious relations with the city administration.

8. Richard F. Fenno, Jr., *Home Style: House Members in Their Districts* (Boston: Little, Brown, 1978), esp. chapter 4, "Home Styles: Presentation of Self II," pp. 101–35; Harrison W. Fox, Jr., and Susan Webb Hammond, *Congressional Staffs: The Invisible Force in American Law-Making* (New York: The Free Press, 1977), esp. chapter 6, "Activity and Jobs of Staff," pp. 88–101. Fenno's book is the first real scholarly analysis of how congressmen behave in their home district rather than the usual analysis of what they do in Washington. The book by Fox and Hammond, based on extensive questionnaires, is an empirical analysis of House and Senate staffs.

9. Fenno, *Home Style*, p. 107.

10. Ibid.

11. Fenno does not specify these "problems," but they are probably similar to those received by all House members. An acquaintance of mine was informed by post office personnel to contact her congressman if she wanted "expedited" service from the Department of State on a passport application. This example, of course, does not involve alleged criminality or the protection of human rights, but it does underscore the service function.

12. Fox and Hammond, *Congressional Staffs*, p. 91.

13. Ibid., table 22, "Professional Staff Activities Performed Within the Senate Office," pp. 186–87.

14. The analysis of the Question Period, as well as other similar institutionalized legislative procedures, refers to a bygone day when "traditionalism" was the dominant approach to the study of political science. For an extended discussion of the changing paradigms in political science, see Leon Hurwitz, *Introduction to Politics: Traditionalism to Postbehavioralism* (Chicago: Nelson-Hall Co., 1979). The literature on the Question Period is not really current; nevertheless, some accounts of the process are excellent. See, for example, Kenneth Bradshaw and David Pring, *Parliament and Congress* (Austin: University of Texas Press, 1972), esp. chapter 8, "Scrutiny and

Control over the Executive," pp. 355–412; D.N. Chester and Nona Bowring, *Questions in Parliament* (Oxford: The Clarendon Press, 1962); the classic by Sir Ivor Jennings, *Parliament* (Cambridge: Cambridge University Press, 1969 [originally published in 1939]), esp. chapter 4, "The Framework of Oratory," pp. 95–131; and R. W. McCulloch, "Question Time in the British House of Commons," *American Political Science Review* 27, no. 4 (December 1933): 971–75.

15. The House of Lords also has a Question Period, but it is much more limited than that in the Commons because the cabinet ministers do not sit in the House of Lords, the Lords are not elected, and the members do not have a constituency. Only four questions a day are allowed in the House of Lords, but much more time for discussion is allocated to these questions than to each question in the Commons.

16. Approximately eighteen-thousand additional questions each session are asked, and answered, in written form only. Bradshaw and Pring, *Parliament and Congress*, p. 362.

17. Ibid., p. 368.

18. R. W. McCulloch, "Question Time in the British House of Commons," p. 974.

19. Chester and Bowring, *Questions in Parliament*, p. 222.

20. One such question of extremely limited political interest was the one asking why "father-in-law" was charged as three words in a telegram by the Post Office, whereas "mother-in-law" was treated as one word. Cited in ibid., p. 224.

21. Ibid., p. 202.

22. H. C. Deb. (1948–49), 457, C. 1018: citied in ibid., pp. 203–4.

23. These accounts are from Clyde H. Farnsworth, "Linking Aid Plans to Human Rights," *New York Times*, June 19, 1977, section 3, p. 5.

24. Deputy Secretary of State Warren Christopher, testimony before the International Organizations Subcommittee of the House Foreign Affairs Committee, May 2, 1979; reproduced as "Implementing the Human Rights Policy," Current Policy No. 67, United States Department of State, Bureau of Public Affairs (June, 1979), p. 3.

25. Ibid.

26. Contained in "Fourth Semiannual Report by the President to the Commission on Security and Cooperation in Europe; December 1, 1977-June 1, 1978," *Special Report*, U.S. Department of State, Bureau of Public Affairs, Office of Public Communication No. 45 (June, 1978), p. 5.

27. The pending cases are as follows:

	Immediate Families		Nonimmediate Families	
	Total Cases	Individuals	Total Cases	Individuals
Bulgaria	8	14	13	32
Czechoslovakia	16	31	3	16
German Democratic Republic	1	1	8	21
Hungary	3	6	3	5
Poland	167	283	919	2882
Rumania	34	64	185	431
Soviet Union	128	371	—	—

An immediate family is comprised of spouse plus their minor children. A nonimmediate family includes brothers, sisters, adult children, parents of adult children, and so on. It was not possible to make this distinction in the case of the Soviet Union, the figures for which include both immediate and nonimmediate families. Ibid., p. 18.

28. Ibid, pp. 5, 8, 17, 19, 21.

29. For a detailed discussion of the entire process, including the back-room politicking and tensions among all the concerned people and organizations, see William W. Orbach, *The American Movement to aid Soviet Jews* (Amherst: University of Massachusetts Press, 1979).

30. The Soviet Union, as of Summer 1980, has yet to receive MFN status. The Carter administration, however, in October 1979, proposed that MFN status be granted to the People's Republic of China.

31. The legislative process leading to the amendment was during the height of the Watergate crisis. The Soviet Union constantly played down the affair, and little was published on it in *Pravda* or *Izvestia*. The Soviets felt that detente should not be affected by "domestic" politics, and thus they would not comment on or take sides in Watergate; in exchange, the United States should not seek to influence Soviet "domestic" policies such as their treatment of the Jews. See Leon Hurwitz, "Watergate and Detente: A Content Analysis of Five Communist Newspapers," *Studies in Comparative Communism* 9, no. 3 (Autumn 1976): 244–56.

32. Orbach, *The American Movement to Aid Soviet Jews*, p. 154.

33. The figures on arrivals of Soviet Jewish emigrants in Vienna (the first stop in the West on the "Chopin Express" train) are approximately:

1967—1,400	1971—13,000	1975—13,459
1968— 230	1972—31,600	1976—14,216
1969—3,000	1973—34,933	1977—16,737
1970—1,000	1974—20,695	1978—28,864

These figures are from Orbach, *The American Movement to Aid Soviet Jews*, pp. 159–60, and confirmed by the "Fourth Semiannual Report by the President to the Commission on Security and Cooperation in Europe," p. 18.

PUBLIC SUPRANATIONAL INSTITUTIONS: The European Convention on Human Rights

6

Even though several societies have made available "domestic" avenues of redress against the state, as described in chapters 2 through 5, unfortunately, more than a few situations exist in which individuals still believe their own government has violated their civil-political-human rights, and the prescribed domestic procedures have not been able to validate their complaint. Such situations involve more complex issues than, say, an interpretation of a contract or a request to the ombudsman to secure an apology and/or additional information from the bureaucratic structures. These situations involve human rights questions, but the individual is unable to secure redress from his or her own government because the action of the government was entirely legal and thus permissible under domestic legislation.

Recognizing the inherent limitations of a country's domestic procedures, however impartial and effective they may be—even the ombudsman cannot investigate complaints directed at parliamentary decisions—some societies have progressed one step beyond these domestic avenues into the area of collective international guarantees of the individual right to expect humane treatment from one's government. If, after all domestic avenues have been exhausted, the individual still believes his rights have been violated by governmental action, such a person can then "appeal" to a "higher authority," for example, a supranational institution. This chapter discusses one such process: the European Commission on Human Rights and the European Court of Human Rights, created by the European Convention on Human Rights.

These institutions and avenues of redress, although dealing specifically with "human rights" and not with bureaucratic impoliteness, nonetheless are an important and significant part of any discussion on the role of the state as defendant and the ability of an individual to press complaints against the state or to seek redress for alleged maltreatment. As is shown below, the European Human Rights Court has in several instances placed a sovereign national state in the position of defendant and has ruled that an individual has priority over sovereign immunity. The European process has effective power, especially in relation to those states that have accepted the compulsory jurisdiction of the European Human Rights Court.[1]

THE PROTECTION OF HUMAN RIGHTS IN EUROPE: THE EUROPEAN CONVENTION ON HUMAN RIGHTS

The legislative history of the European Convention on Human Rights and the institutions established by the convention—the European Commission on Human Rights and the European Human Rights Court—formally began just before the creation of the Council of Europe in 1949. Its point of departure was the Congress of Europe, held at The Hague in May 1948, with approximately seven-hundred delegates from sixteen countries and observers from ten others. The purpose of the congress was to provide encouragement to the nascent European unification and cooperative process and to offer recommendations to achieve such cooperation. Adopted at the final session, the congress' *Message to Europeans* contained, among others, the following goals:

We desire a Charter of human rights guaranteeing liberty of thought, assembly and expression as well as the right to form a political opposition . . . [and] a Court of Justice with adequate sanctions for the implementation of this Charter.[2]

The recommendations of The Hague congress were then submitted to the newly created Consultative Council of the Brussels Treaty Organization and, in due course, led to the signing of the Statute of the Council of Europe in May 1949. This statute had a direct and immediate impact on the soon-to-be European Convention on Human Rights. Article 1 of the Statute of the Council of Europe specified that one of the means by which its (the council's) aims were to be pursued would be "the maintenance and further realization of human rights and fundamental freedoms," and article 3 placed the maintenance of human rights and respect for the rule of law as a condition of membership in the Council of Europe.[3]

The Council of Europe strongly endorsed the protection of human rights at that time for two fundamental reasons. Each of these reasons could have stood alone, but acting together, they were a powerful stimulus. One stimulus was the then acute and dangerous ideological conflict between East and West. Not only was European "unity" seen as desirable goal in itself, but it was also a defensive mechanism directed at the then very real Communist threat. It must be recalled that during the short space of time between The Hague congress (May 1948) and the signing of the Statute of the Council of Europe (May 1949), several events occurred, including the Communist coup and seizure of power in Czechoslovakia, the Greek civil war, and the Berlin blockade. It was with these overt actions that the European nations became aware of the Communist challenge and thus the need to reassert their own ideological standards.

As one of my students once mentioned, "it was the real danger of dictatorship that made Western Europe cognizant of the value of democracy and of human rights."

The second reason evolved more from the stream of historical consciousness than from immediate contemporary facts. Europe had just emerged from the neobarbarism of Auschwitz and Treblinka and the utter absence of any concern whatsoever for individual human rights and the protection of the individual from state actions. One of the first steps in the march toward a totalitarian system is the denial of individual rights, and it is difficult to reverse this process before it reaches its inevitable end point: the path to Auschwitz began with the Nazis stripping the Jews of citizenship, removing their status as individuals before the law, and denying their civil and human rights. One of the strongest safeguards to such a repetition was to make the first step more difficult: totalitarianism and the infinite woes of Treblinka would be that more difficult to achieve if the individual human personality was defended.

Those Europeans who drafted, signed, and abided by the European Convention on Human Rights believed that if they specified in advance what basic human rights were to be protected and what governments could not do to individuals, the first step might not ever arise again. The envisaged protection of individual human rights involved the establishment of an international mechanism to monitor the protection of human rights, and if any state should violate such rights, this international mechanism could then be put into operation to restore the rule of law and the protection of individuals. The European Convention did not meet these envisaged goals—no "monitoring" device and no means of automatic international protection was created—although these goals were influential in the creation of the actual institutions and processes.

When the Council of Europe met for its inaugural session in August 1949, the Consultative Assembly placed on its agenda the item titled "measures for the fulfillment of the declared aim of the Council of Europe, in accordance with Article I of the Statute, in regard to the maintenance and further realization of human rights and fundamental freedoms." The council's Committee of Ministers was called upon to authorize the drafting of a convention to provide a collective European guarantee designed to secure the rights and freedoms contained in the Universal Declaration of Human Rights, adopted by the UN General Assembly in December 1948.[4]

General debate on the question began in August 1949, and the entire matter was referred to the Committee on Legal and Administrative Questions. Using the UN Universal Declaration on Human Rights as a basis for its own deliberations, this committee identified a list of fundamental rights that it proposed as the content of this collective European guarantee. The committee then proposed how this guarantee would be established and enforced. First, all members of the Council of Europe would commit themselves to respect the fundamental principles of democracy and to hold free elections at reasonable intervals, employing universal suffrage and secret ballots. It was, however, to be left to each state, subject to certain guidelines, to determine the rules and processes by which these guaranteed rights would be protected within its territory. Second, to implement this collective guarantee, the committee proposed the establishment of a Commission and Human Rights Court. These institutions would administer the guarantee and adjudicate alleged violations of the rights contained in the convention.

A revised draft of the convention was adopted by the council's Committee of Ministers during its fifth session in August 1950. This revised text was, however, considerably weaker in two major areas compared to the original text proposed by the Committee on Legal and Administrative Matters. First, the revised draft made the rights of the individual conditional upon certain processes rather than as absolute, and second, the jurisdiction of the proposed court was made optional at the discretion of each state rather than as compulsory jurisdiction for any state that signed the convention. This revised draft was signed in Rome on November 4, 1950, and the European Convention on Human Rights entered into force on September 3, 1953.[5]

The formal title of the convention is "Convention for the Protection of Human Rights and Fundamental Feedoms," but it is commonly called the European Convention on Human Rights.[6] The rights and freedoms cited below are not, however, absolute: practically every article has its disclaimer, exception, exclusion, or condition. Be that as it may, the convention is an honorable document that does pay more than lip service to the rights of individuals and the protection of individuals from state behavior. Most of the described rights are in the nature of what governments "shall not do" to individuals, although, as mentioned above, these prohibitions are not absolute due to the presence of the exclusions and exceptions.

Citizens of those countries who have signed the convention have their right to life protected by law, and no one shall be deprived of his life intentionally except in the execution of a court decision (article 2); no one shall be subjected to torture or to inhuman or degrading treatment or punishment (article 3); no one shall be held in slavery or servitude or be required to perform forced or compulsory labor (article 4); everyone has the right to liberty and security of person, and anyone who is arrested shall be informed, in a language he understands, of any charge against him and is entitled to trial within a reasonable time (article 5); everyone charged with a criminal offense shall be presumed innocent until proved guilty and shall have the right to legal counsel or be given it free (article 6); states shall not enforce ex post facto laws (article 7);[7] everyone has the right to respect for his private and family life, home and correspondence (article 8); everyone has the freedom of thought, conscience, religion, expression, and peaceful assembly (articles 9, 10, 11); everyone has the right to marry and to found a family (article 12); and article 14 reads that the above rights and freedoms shall be secured without discrimination on any ground such as sex, race, color, language, religion, political or other opinion, national or social origin, association with a national minority, property, birth, or other status.

Even the concept of sovereign immunity is restricted, for the convention explicitly requires each country to have an avenue of redress available for its citizens to complain against the state. Article 13 states that everyone whose rights and freedoms are violated shall have an effective remedy before a national authority notwithstanding that the violation has been committed by persons acting in an official capacity. Article 13 thus strengthened the position of the individual in relation to his own government and, at least for Europe, was perhaps the final blow against sovereign immunity and recognized that the king and/or his agents could do wrong, and, therefore, they were to be held accountable for their actions.

The original convention had five protocols. The first protocol, "Enforcement of Certain Rights and Freedoms not included in Section I of the Convention," was signed in Paris on March 20, 1952, and became effective on May 18, 1954. These additional rights are that every person is entitled to the peaceful enjoyment of his possessions (article 1); no person shall be denied the right to education (article 2); and the signatory states are required to hold free elections at reasonable intervals by secret ballot, under conditions that will insure the free expression of the opinion of the people in the choice of the legislature (article 3).

The fourth protocol, "Protecting Certain Additional Rights," was signed in Strasbourg on September 16, 1963, and became effective on May 2, 1968. These additional rights state that no one shall be deprived of his liberty merely on the ground of inability to fulfill a contractual obligation (article 1); everyone within the territory of a state shall have the right to liberty of movement and freedom to choose his residence, and everyone shall be free to leave any country, including his own (article 2); and collective expulsion of aliens is prohibited (article 4).

The rights and freedoms contained in the convention and the protocols are, however, not absolute. The rights are most of the time qualified by statements such as "except in accordance with law and justified by the public interest in a democractic society" or "except when is necessary in a democractic society in the interests of national security, public safety, or territorial integrity." Thus, if any individual does want to pursue a complaint under the terms of the convention, he might be faced with the "national security" defense. But if such acts are not "justifiable by the public interest in a democratic society"—as some complaints clearly demonstrated—the state is indeed the defendant and is to be held accountable for its actions and treatment of the individual.

INSTITUTIONS

To insure the observance of the rights contained in the convention, two bodies were established: the European Commission on Human Rights and a

European Court of Human Rights. These two institutions, along with the Council of Europe's Committee of Ministers, compose the formal organizations.

The Committee of Ministers was not created by the convention but derives its existence from the Statute of the Council of Europe. The committee, however, was given a substantial role to play in the protection of human rights, and it is an integral part of the process. The Committee of Ministers is the basic executive organ or "governing board" of the Council of Europe. Each member of the council has one seat and vote on the committee, and thus some countries participate in the application of the convention through this Committee of Ministers even though the country has not yet signed the convention. The specific ministers are to be the ministers for foreign affairs, although representatives may participate. In fact, as Louis Sohn and Thomas Buergenthal commented, the presence of all ministers of foreign affairs at a meeting of the committee is the exception rather than the rule.[8]

The convention itself provides the actual powers of the committee in relationship to the application of this collective guarantee of human rights. The committee is responsible for electing members of the commission from a list provided by the council's Consultative Assembly. The committee also has the responsibility to decide whether a violation of the convention has occurred if a case, after being deemed admissible by the commission, has not been settled by the commission itself or referred to the court by the commission. Sohn and Buergenthal[9] believe this authority was granted to the committee because the governments refused to establish a court whose jurisdiction would be compulsory, and the court itself did not come into existence until some time after the convention became applicable. A decision by the Committee of Ministers is stated (article 32) to be binding on the signatory states. Such a decision requires a two-thirds majority vote, but the committee has, in the past, seldom agreed to censure one of its own number.

The commission is the workhorse of the system, for it is the recipient of all complaints. The number of commissioners is equal to the number of states that have signed the convention, and no two members can be nationals of the same state. Elected by the Committee of Ministers, members sit for six-year terms and can be reelected. Article 23 states that the commissioners shall sit in their individual capacity; thus they are to be independent of the committee that elected them as well as their governments. The commission decides by majority vote, determines its own rules of procedure, sits in Strasbourg, and is funded by the Council of Europe.

As mentioned above, the original draft of the convention envisaged the court as having compulsory jurisdiction, but this concept of compulsory jurisdiction provoked strong opposition. The very idea of having a court also brought about some opposition. Thus the jurisdiction of the court was made optional. The court could not be established formally until at least eight convention signatories declared that they "recognize as compulsory *ipso facto* and without special agreement the jurisdiction of the Court in all matters concerning the interpretation and application of the Convention" (article 46). This requirement of eight was not attained until September 3, 1958—five years after the convention entered in force and eight years after the signing of the convention. Thus the activity that was done in applying the convention from 1953 to late 1958 did not involve the court.

The judges[10] of the court are elected for a nine-year term and can be reelected. The Consultative Assembly of the Council of Europe does the actual electing from a list of nominations submitted by the council's members, and the number of judges is equal to that of the members of the council, but no two judges can be nationals of the same state. Thus two judges on the current court are nationals of states that have not ratified the convention, and an additional four judges are nationals of states that have not accepted the compulsory jurisdiction of the court itself.

The convention is relatively silent on the degree of judicial independence the court possesses, although it appears that the judges act in their "individual capacity," and little criticism has arisen about the court being only the outward extension of the various governments. The judges may be nominated by their governments, but the Consultative Assembly appoints them; the court chooses its own president and vice-president; it draws up its own rules and determines its own procedure; and in place of an annual salary, the judges receive a per diem fee. Thus the position is in reality part-time, and the judges are not dependent on the few pounds or francs or marks they may receive. One would have to conclude that the court and judges are "independent," and they have not hesitated to rule against a government when, in fact, a violation of the convention had occurred.

The full court does not usually hear the cases referred to it: the actual hearing is performed by a seven-judge chamber.[11] This chamber is chosen by lot before the case begins, except "there shall sit as an *ex officio* member of the Chamber the judge who is a national of any State party concerned" (article 43). Similar to the procedure with the U.S. Supreme Court, a majority vote is required, with an allowance for concurring and/or dissenting opinions. No appeal from the court's decision is permitted—it is final—and it is the responsibility of the Committee of Ministers to supervise the execution of the court's decisions. The court also sits in Strasbourg and is funded by the Council of Europe.

PROCEDURES

The formal procedures employed in the handling and disposal of a complaint filed under the convention are relatively straightforward, although they do not readily lend themselves to speedy decisions, and an individual petitioner must overcome several obstacles before the merits of the complaint can actually be argued. Since the convention makes the commission the "gate-keeper" or the primary decision-making unit in the process, the commission is thus the "workhorse" of the system and is the recipient of all complaints and petitions. Petitions cannot be submitted directly to the Committee of Ministers and/or the court. Any person, nongovernmental organization, or group of individuals who allege to have been a victim of a violation are entitled to submit a petition. However, this applies only in alleged violations by countries that have signed the convention; it does not apply to the Council of Europe's entire membership.

Governments themselves also have the right to submit complaints to the commission. Article 24 of the convention entitles any signatory government to complain about a violation of the convention by any other signatory government. Governmental complaints are not as numerous as individual complaints, but because of their nature, they receive far greater publicity and media coverage than individual petitions.[12] The best-known of these governmental complaints was *Denmark, Norway, Sweden and The Netherlands* v. *Greece* in 1967. These four countries' complaint against the Papadopoulos regime was broad and far-reaching: it did not refer to a particular law or administrative procedure, but, rather, the complaint was directed at the entire "legal order," including the Greek government's refusal to hold free elections. The commission judged this complaint to be admissible but, obviously, could not achieve a "friendly settlement." The commission referred the case to the Committee of Ministers, which also ruled that the Greek "legal order" was in violation of the convention. But the Greek government renounced its adherence to the convention and withdrew from the Council of Europe. The existence of the convention and the decisions of the commission and committee may have brought unwanted publicity to the Greek situation, but it had little actual influence on the protection of human rights in Greece under Papadopoulos. One would be hard put to argue that the process in Strasbourg by the commission and the Committee of Ministers had any linkage to the eventual restoration of democratic government and civil liberties in Greece.

Summary figures through 1973 show that approximately 6,400 complaints and petitions had been filed with the commission since its establishment.[13] However, out of these 6,400, only 107 or 1.7 percent were judged "admissible" by the commission, and the commission routinely rejected 98–99 percent of the petitions it received. I am not privy to the internal deliberations of the commission and thus cannot comment on the *sub rosa* reasons, if any, employed in the rejection of most petitions as inadmissible. Only the overt grounds for such rulings as contained in the convention can be cited here.

The grounds for mandatory inadmissibility are numerous. As mentioned above, article 25 requires that the government being complained against be a signatory of the convention; the commission cannot, for example, receive complaints directed against the Spanish and Portuguese governments. Article 25 also requires that the signatory government against whom the complaint is lodged "recognize the competence of the Commission to receive such petitions." Thus no complaints by individuals can be received by the commission if they are directed against one of the five states that have yet to allow such individual petitions. However, for those thirteen countries that do recognize the commission's competence in receiving individual's petitions, such countries have the added obligation of not "hindering in any way the effective exercise" of this right of petition. One application of this right is that, even though certain countries maintain some censorship over prison inmates' correspondence, a request to the commission must be forwarded by the prison administration.

Article 26 specifically mandates as inadmissible any petition that has not progressed through all domestic avenues of redress or review. This means that any individual who believes his rights as contained in the convention have been violated must have exhausted all avenues of review and appeal within the state itself before turning to the commission for relief. The commission is thus not perceived to be a parallel structure for the redress of grievances, but, rather, the state itself, through whatever process it makes available, is an independent process of review that has to run its entire course before the commission can be involved. I have no criticism of this exclusionary clause, for it does strengthen and, hopefully, make more viable the avenues of redress available to the population. Article 26 does require, however, that a petition must be submitted to the commission within six months from the date on which the final domestic decision was taken.

Article 27 mandates as inadmissible any petition that is anonymous or that is substantially the same as a matter previously examined by the commission. This exclusion of "previously examined" questions can include those that have been ruled either admissible or inadmissible. Thus, for an individual who submits a petition claiming a violation of the convention, if a similar case in the past were accepted and a decision reached against a state, this petition would be ruled inadmissible, and the individual could not rely upon the commission for redress. In such situations, the individual either does not receive redress or, depending upon the way commission and court decisions are seen to be part of domestic legislation—a question dealt with below—is dependent upon the goodwill of his national government to once again review its actions in light of court decisions. Article 27 also categorizes as inadmissible a petition that has already been submitted to another international procedure of settlement but only if the petition contains no relevant new information. If a petition does contain "relevant new information," the fact that it was previously submitted to a different international review process will not automatically render it as inadmissible.

The above grounds for inadmissibility may be broad, but at least they are precisely stated and they have meaning. However, article 27 also contains some vague and nondefined grounds for mandatory inadmissibility, which I regard as a political obstacle placed in front of the individual petitioner. These additional obstacles read that the commission shall view as inadmissible any petition that it considers "incompatible with the provisions of the Convention, manifestly ill-founded, or an abuse of the right of petition." It is my view that a petition that meets the requirements of articles 25, 26, and 27 (1) cannot be "manifestly ill-founded" or an "abuse of the right of petition." Be that as it may, for the above reasons (and, perhaps, for unstated reasons), the commission routinely rejected as inadmissible approximately fifty-nine of sixty petitions received.

The commission as gatekeeper thus had a very small gate through which petitions must squeeze, and, as figures show through 1973, only 107 of 6,400 petitions were judged admissible. What is the next stage in the process, once the eye of the needle has been successfully negotiated? The first goal of the commission, after accepting a petition and ruling it admissible, is to appoint a seven-person subcommission (each of the parties involved in the complaint can appoint someone of their own choice to this subcommission) to investigate the "facts" and to attempt to reach a "friendly settlement." With our figures above, of the 107 petitions ruled admissible, 71 were resolved at this stage through a "friendly settlement." The friendly settlement, however, must be based on "respect for human rights" as defined in the convention.

However, with our figures, this leaves thirty-six cases in which the commission was unable to use its good offices to reach a "friendly settlement." The entire commission now has an important option: it can submit the unresolved dispute either to the Committee of Ministers *or* to the court.[14] Of these thirty-six, the commission referred twenty-six cases to the committee and ten to the court. If sent to the committee, a decision about whether the convention has been violated is made by a two-thirds vote of the entire committee. If a violation is deemed to have occurred, the Committee of Ministers prescribes what has to be done by the state. The signatory states to the convention have "undertaken to regard as binding on them any decision" of the committee, although the convention recognizes that this may not be automatic. If the "guilty" state does not take the prescribed measures, as defined by the committee, the committee may meet again to decide how to effect its original decision, and publicity is one of the methods mentioned in the convention. The committee is hesitant, however, to censure one of its own members, and a "friendly settlement" is usually attained at this stage in the process.

Our figures leave ten petitions that were not resolved at the commission level, nor were they referred to the committee: these were the ten cases the court heard through 1973. The individual petitioner does not bring the case to the court, but, rather, it is the commission or the signatory state against which the complaint has been lodged. Once a case leaves the commission—either referred to the committee or the court—it cannot be withdrawn by the individual petitioner and/or the signatory state. The arguments—oral and written—are presented to the court from each party in the dispute, and it is the commission that usually acts as the "prosecuting attorney," and the state is the "defendant." The court's decision is sent to the Committee of Ministers, which supervises the execution of any decision. No situation has yet occurred where a state has refused to abide by the court's decision, although only a few of the cases that did reach the court ruled against the state. Be that as it may, the state is certainly a "defendant" in the court, and it is held liable for its behavior.

SOME CASES

Space does not allow for a full discussion of all of the cases heard by the court or, for that matter, of those cases where a "friendly settlement" was reached by the commission or the committee. The following comments, therefore, touch upon only a few of the early court decisions and a somewhat greater discussion of more recent decisions. The figures cited above (6,400 petitions, 107 ruled admissible, 97 "friendly settlements," and 10 court decisions) were over the period through 1973. The case load has increased remarkably since then, including the number of petitions, rulings of admissible, and cases heard by the court. From 1973 to 1977, the court ruled on 10 more cases, and in 1977 alone, 6 cases were argued. Thus in the four years between 1973 and 1977, the court ruled on 16 cases compared with 10 in its first fifteen years of operation. Similarly, the commission is investigating more petitions: 30 petitions were ruled admissible in 1977 alone.

This increase is due to several factors. The increased court ability is primarily a result of the commission ruling more petitions as admissible and, if unable to achieve a "friendly settlement," choosing the option of referring the case to the court rather than to the Committee of Ministers. The commission is choosing the court over the committee because as Marc-Andre Eissen, the commission's registrar, said: "The Commission and the governments both feel these days that alleged human rights violations should be judged by the Strasbourg Court and not by politicians."[15] Another factor in this increased activity is the increased salience that human rights enjoys: the protection of human rights has been raised to a meaningful international level, and more people are becoming aware of the convention and the commission, especially with President Carter's and the current U.S. administration's human rights campaign. All of this may be only a passing fad, and it is possible that the current spate of activity will ebb, but, at least at this time, the commission and the court are much more active when compared to previous years.

One of the first cases heard by the court was the *Lawless* case, decided in 1961.[16] R. G. Lawless, an Irish national, was arrested in July 1957 and detained without trial until December 1957. The detention was by an order of the Irish minister of justice, and Lawless was held on suspicion of being a member of the IRA (Irish Republican Army), an organization defined as illegal under the Irish Offenses against the State Act (1940). Lawless argued that the detention, without formal charges and without a trial, violated articles 5 and 6 of the convention. The petition was ruled admissible, but the commission, unable to achieve a "friendly settlement," referred the case to the court. The court ruled against Lawless and thus in favor of the Irish government. The court held that a state of emergency existed in Ireland, and, therefore, the protection of articles 5 and 6 were conditional upon article 15 (in time of public emergency threatening the life of the nation, a government may take measures "derogating" from its obligations under the convention to the extent required by the exigencies of the situation). For the same reason, the court also held that the 1940 Offenses Act was not contrary to the convention. The *Lawless* case clearly decided that the protected rights were not absolute if a democratic society, in the interests of national security, saw the necessity of violating these individual rights.

The *Belgian Language* case,[17] decided in 1968, concerned a group of French-speaking Belgian nationals who petitioned the commission, alleging that several Belgian legislative acts (1932, 1955, 1959, and 1963) dealing with language matters and education violated their rights under several convention articles and protocol 1. The situation arose when six families were denied access to Frengh-language schools outside Brussels. In an extremely long and complex decision, the court held that the application of the Belgian Act of 2 August 1963 (on the use of language in administrative matters) did violate article 14 of the convention (the rights contained in the convention are to be secured without discrimination on grounds of language) and article 2 of protocol 1 (no person shall be denied the right to an education, and the state shall respect the right of parents to insure that such education is in conformity with their own religious and philosophical convictions).

The court thus ruled for the individual(s) in this case against the state, but, and this is important for a full understanding of the process, the court did not (could not), as if it were the U.S. Supreme Court, rule that the Belgian Act was "unconstitutional." Its ruling was limited to the specific application of the act to the above families involved, although the court did add the provision that the individuals could file for "compensation." The court had no authority to *enforce* a change in Belgian internal legislation, since the enforcement process is one of moral suasion, and no real safeguard exists to prevent Belgium from repeating the activity—actions deemed contrary to the convention—with respect to other people. But an enforcement process does exist: those states that have signed the convention and that have recognized the court's jurisdiction (and Belgium has) are legally bound by the convention to accept the court's decision. The Belgian Parliament did write a more equitable law in light of the court's decision, and the French-speaking community scored a victory in language and education matters. The decisions of the court are enforced because the states have agreed to enforce them; if states do not want to enforce the decisions, as was the situation with Greece and the imminent committee decision, no real avenues are available to secure enforcement.

The 1971 (and 1973) *Ringeisen* case[18] defined the right of the court to grant "just satisfaction" or compensation to an individual whose rights have been violated. Ringeisen, an Austrian national, alleged that the Austrian government violated his rights under articles 5 and 6 of the convention. He was arrested for fraud and was detained from July 1963 to December 1963. He was arrested a second time and detained from March 1965 to March 1967—a two-year period. The court based its decision in relation to Ringeisen's second arrest in 1965. The court ruled that the two-year period Ringeisen was in jail did violate article 5 (the right to a "speedy" trial or bail pending trial), particularly when the Austrian court had all of the relevant information from Ringeisen's first trial. The court also ruled that Ringeisen had the right to "just satisfaction," and he filed for such in 1972. Ringeisen was awarded 20,000 DM as compensation, but the Austrian government contested the payment and attempted to "attach" the award. In the 1973 decision, however, the court ruled that the compensatory award was to be paid directly to Ringeisen and was not to be attached by the Austrian government. The Austrian government did not dispute this ruling, and the award was paid to Ringeisen.

Some of the more recent cases heard by the court have involved Great Britain as the "defendant," and the court has found Great Britain "guilty" in two decisions and "innocent" in the third. The first case heard by the court that involved Great Britain was the *Golder* case,[19] decided in 1975. Sidney Golder was sentenced in 1965 to fifteen years for "robbery with violence." While he was imprisoned at Parkhurst, in 1969, a prison riot took place, and Golder was accused by a prison guard of being a participant in the riot. As a result of this initial implication, Golder was put in solitary confinement. Ten days later, however, the prison guard who made the original charge against Golder admitted that he was not sure that Golder was, in fact, a participant. All charges were dropped, and Golder was returned to his normal confinement area.

Five months later, Golder sought permission from the prison authorities to contact his attorney to bring a libel charge against the guard as well as to hold an inquiry to determine that no mention of his alleged role in the riot remained on his record. Golder thought that with any mention of his alleged participation, his chances in a forthcoming parole hearing could be adversely affected. Golder had to request permission because of rule 34 (8) of the 1964 Prison Rules, which touched upon the whole question of a prisoner's access to the outside world, especially in relation to legal advice. Rule 34 (8) stated: "a prisoner shall not be entitled to communicate with any person in connection with any legal or other business, or with any person other than a relative or friend, except with the leave of the Secretary of State." The ramifications of the rule were widespread. *The Times* (London) reported that the rule could effectively stifle any action a prisoner wanted to take to assert his rights inside a prison as well as his outside interests. In a real sense, a prisoner had to get permission from the secretary of state merely to see a lawyer, let alone to sue.[20] The Prisons Department and the home secretary had no criteria to follow in granting or refusing such permission, and *The Times* saw no reason to believe the officials were being overly obstructive, but at the same time some observers thought the approach was too restrictive.[21]

Golder's request, following rule 34 (8), to the home secretary, then James Callaghan, was denied in April 1970. Golder was also denied the opportunity even to write a letter to his attorney. The Home Office state that the whole incident was a mistake—a simple "error in perception" by the guard—and since no real material damage was done to Golder (except, of course, the time spent in solitary confinement and the possibility of his parole hearing being affected), no reason could be found to permit Golder either to see or write his lawyer. Golder eventually petitioned the commission, arguing that the rights guaranteed him by article 6 (a fair and impartial hearing) and article 8 (right of personal correspondence) were violated by the Home Office's refusal to grant his original request.

The progress of Golder's petition through the system until it reached the court is reflective of the internal workings of the convention's apparatus. The petition was initially examined by three members of the commission who also solicited the views of the British government about its admissibility. The British government challenged its admissibility on grounds that it was "ill founded;" that is, being a prisoner convicted under due process of law, Golder was not entitled to the complete enjoyment of convention-protected rights, particularly (in this case) the right to a fair hearing and the right of personal correspondence. The three-person subcommission ruled the petition admissible, however, and it was forwarded to the next stage for consideration of its merits, if any.

Golder was granted legal aid at this point, and written arguments on his behalf, as well as from the British government, were filed with the commission. A commission hearing, lasting for two days, was held in Strasbourg in December 1971. Both sides, each represented by counsel, reiterated the arguments that were previously submitted in written form. As always, the commission attempted to achieve a "friendly settlement," but the British government chose not to settle. The British government was understandably concerned about prison discipline, an area firmly within the English common law tradition. Golder was paroled from prison before the commission's finding, but the parole did not affect the process. In June 1973 (eighteen months after the hearing), the commission decided in favor of Golder and then had the option of submitting the case to the Committee of Ministers or to the court. The commission opted for the committee, but Great Britain then decided to invoke its right to take the case to the court. Accordingly, the committee relinquished jurisdiction to the court. Golder as an individual was no longer a formal participant at this stage; at the level of the court, the two formal parties were the commission and the British government.

The court heard arguments for two days in October 1974. The British government's position was that under English common law, some convention-protected rights did not necessarily apply to all people; in this specific situation, the right to an impartial hearing and personal correspondence did not apply to prison inmates. The government argued, as reported in *The Times* (London),[22] that it would be impossible to run a prison and have effective discipline if the prisoners had unlimited access to lawyers, especially as many of them, with time on their hands, "would inevitably abuse the right and indulge in vexation and frivolous litigation or other legal action." Golder's position was just the opposite: in the absence of a national emergency or a situation threatening the existence of a democratic society (a position the government did not argue), the status of prison inmate does not mean such an individual no longer has the right to an impartial hearing and private correspondence.

The court announced its judgment in February 1975, holding that the British government *did* indeed violate two separate articles of the convention. The court ruled that the Home Office's denial of Golder's request to see a lawyer violated article 6 (right to a fair trial), for the court held that access to a lawyer was an "essential and inherent" part of the right to a fair trial. The British government really did not argue that a person did not have the right to legal advice once a trial had begun; the government argued that, in Golder's situation, since no trial was held, Golder did not need access to a lawyer. The court did not accept this reasoning either: by application of rule 34 (8) the government could determine whether there even would be a trial! The court wrote that "the fair, public and expeditious characteristic of judicial proceedings are of no value at all if there are no judicial proceedings."

Article 8 (right of correspondence) was also judged to have been violated. The court rejected the British government's argument that prohibiting Golder to correspond was necessary to prevent disorder and crime or to maintain prison discipline and that preventing someone from even initiating correspondence constituted the most far-reaching interference with that right: "it was not for the Home Secretary himself to appraise the prospects of the action contemplated; it was for a solicitor to advise the applicant on his rights and then for a court to rule on any action that might be brought."[23]

The court's decision received wide publicity in Great Britain—*The Times* (London) carried six items, one a front-page lead story—and the court, following the procedures specified in the convention, referred it to the Committee of Ministers to supervise its execution. But the British government did not require additional prodding from the committee. Approximately two weeks after the court's decision, the then Home Secretary, Roy Jenkins, when queried about amending rule 34 (8) of the 1964 Prison Rules by another member of

Parliament (MP), responded with these comments: "I shall naturally give effect to the Court's ruling in the Golder case and I am actively studying the means by which this should be done. . . . I assure [the M.P.] that I shall see that the Court decision is given effect."[24] The court decision, and the comments by Jenkins, obviously did not help Sidney Golder—he had been paroled from prison two years previously—but the court's judgment did have some real impact upon future Golders in British prisons. The state was a defendant and was held accountable for its actions and its treatment of individuals.

One of the most bitterly contested, longest, and politically explosive cases decided by the court was an interstate complaint, *Ireland* v. *United Kingdom*. The Irish petition to the commission was formally submitted in December 1971, but the process was not completed until January 1978, when the court announced its decision—seven years after the original submission of the petition. This seven-year period witnessed investigations, recriminations, hostile international propaganda, secret rendezvous, charges of obstructing justice and countercharges, and a chilled relationship between Ireland and the United Kingdom. Although the Irish petition contained a series of charges and demands, the most important and significant component of the Irish petition was the allegation that the British security forces in Northern Ireland "tortured" suspected IRA internees.

The major issue concerned the techniques employed by the British security forces in the "interrogation" of suspected IRA internees: these techniques were termed "sensory-deprivation" methods, and, obviously, they were designed to elicit desired information from the internees. The "sensory-deprivation" method involved prolonged wall standing, loud noises, hooding, and deprivation of food, water, and sleep.[25] The interrogations took place at an undisclosed security facility somewhere in Northern Ireland in August and October 1971, against fourteen internees. The British government did not deny the application of such techniques, and thus one of the major issues was not whether these techniques occurred but, rather, whether such behavior and additional actions by the British government constituted a violation of the European convention.

The 1971 Irish petition to the commission contained allegations of several convention violations, as well as demands that the British government take further action to "atone" for or rectify such violations. The Irish government charged that the "sensory-deprivation" techniques violated article 3 (no one shall be subjected to torture or to inhuman or degrading treatment or punishment); that such treatment was a formal administrative policy of the British that was applied beyond the documented fourteen individual cases; that the British practice of interning IRA suspects violated article 5 (detainees are entitled to a trial within a reasonable time or to be released on bail); that article 50 should be invoked ("just satisfaction" or compensation to the injured party); and, not least, that the British government prosecute those people responsible for the actual violations (the police and security forces) *and* those people responsible for the decision to violate the convention (the politicians themselves, starting with the British prime minister). These were indeed serious allegatiöns and demands, particularly when most of the "facts" were not in dispute (the British *were* interning people and they *were* practicing "sensory deprivation" on at least fourteen individuals).

The petition was ruled admissible by the commission in 1972, but it did not announce its findings until 1977. The investigation into the merits of the charge was long, costly for both sides, and contained elements of grade-B espionage novels with a secret rendezvous and unidentified witnesses. Approximately one hundred twenty witnesses appeared before the commission, and their testimony ran to forty-five hundred "closely typed" pages.[26] Some members of the commission accused the British government of deliberately obstructing the investigation to minimize adverse publicity. Such a charge arose out of Britain's initial refusal to allow members of its security forces to appear as witnesses.[27] Several three-sided meetings (Ireland, the United Kingdom, and the Commission) were held, both public and private meetings, and controversy dominated and chilled Irish-British relations.

As usual, the commission attempted to achieve a "friendly settlement" between the two parties, and, for a while, it appeared that a settlement could be reached because Great Britain "confessed." The British government admitted fault, stopped the practice of sensory deprivation, gave assurances that it would not be restored, and made compensation of up to £25,000 to those subjected to the special interrogation techniques. But the Irish government was not prepared to negotiate a "friendly settlement," although the commission did, in no uncertain terms, label the sensory-deprivation techniques as torture, and, moreover, the British government did *not* contest the commission's finding (in a sense, the British government pleaded "guilty" to the commission on the charge of "torture"). The commission thus finally ruled in favor of Ireland, and the controversy might have ended at this point if Ireland had accepted the "friendly settlement." But Ireland did not, and an editorial from *The Times* (London) commented on the British perception and interpretation of the Irish government's decision:

It was difficult to avoid the supposition that the Irish Government (it was not Mr. Lynch's but its predecessor) persisted for domestic political reasons and in order to maximize a propaganda advantage over Britain. The reasons which it published or supplied were of course higher sounding: the implication of the case for the security of human rights were of an order that *called for the authoritative judgment of a court over and above the findings of a Commission*; and there were other claims arising out of the proceedings with which it did not succeed before the Commission and which it wished to pursue before the court in the name of justice.[28]

Accordingly, the Irish government made use of its prerogative under the convention and appealed the case to the court. The court received written and oral arguments in 1977, and the Irish position basically was identical to its original petition and arguments before the commission. The British government, however, did not contest the commission's finding of "torture" in front of the court, although, since the Irish argued that it was torture, the British government did defend itself at the court hearing. The court announced its verdict in an eighty-three-page decision on January 18, 1978. The court's decision, given what had been decided previously and given that Great Britain really did not contest the commission's findings but, rather, had admitted the offense and had compensated the victims, came as a crude shock to the Irish government (and, in my perception, a surprise to the British government).

Seventeen judges participated in the decision (including both the Irish and British judges) and, either unanimously or by an overwhelming majority, *rejected* all but one of the Irish claims and demands. The sole allegation upheld by the court was that "sensory deprivation" was inhuman and degrading treatment, *not* torture, and Great Britain was "cleared" of all other charges. The initial reaction of the Irish government was one of muted disappointment, and the British government and its elite press demonstrated glee at the Irish government's loss of prestige and embarrassment.

As mentioned above, the decision ran to eighty-three pages and space allows for only a summary of the court's findings[29] and some of the reasoning behind the decision. To Britain's immense (but unexpected) satisfaction, the court unanimously ruled that, although certain violations were not contested (the unanimous finding of the commission that the administrative practice of sensory deprivation did indeed constitute "torture"), the court nonetheless should rule on the merits of such posited violations. This meant the court would re-open the question of whether sensory deprivation was, in fact, torture, although Ireland, the United Kingdom, and the commission all previously accepted it as such.[30] The court thus examined the issue of torture and by a vote of thirteen to four found that "sensory deprivation" did not constitute torture, but it did, by a vote of sixteen to one, find that it constituted a practice of inhuman and degrading treatment and, therefore, was a violation of article 3.

Majority opinion held (by a vote of thirteen to four), in rejecting the allegation of torture, that the techniques of sensory deprivation did not cause "suffering of the particular intensity and cruelty implied by the word 'torture.'" The practice was, however, by a vote of sixteen to one, judged to be "inhuman" treatment and thus a violation of article 3. It was the British judge who dissented from the "inhuman" treatment decision; for this judge, sensory-deprivation techniques weren't even inhuman or degrading. The majority view on the torture issue apparently was that "torture" is reserved for acts such as having electrical shocks applied to one's genitals or having one's fingernails torn out one at a time; being forced to stand against a wall for twenty-four hours was, in the court's view, essentially something else—something not nice and "inhuman" but definitely not "torture."

Such reasoning was immediately accepted and praised by the jubilant British government and the press. In a lead editorial titled, "A Dispassionate Judgment," the usually staid *Times* (London) rushed to endorse the view that "torture" could only take place under the Spanish Inquisition in some dark smelly dungeon or by the SS in Auschwitz; if such activity were done at other times by other methods, it could not be torture. The *Times* editorial neatly made this distinction, and it reflected the court's opinion:

"Torture" never was the right word for the treatment. . . . "Torture" is an ultimate word. It denotes those practices, like the rack, electric shock, beating to the point of sur-render, the purpose of which is to inflict such pain that terror of its continuation or repetition breaks the victim's will to resist interrogation.

That is not the purpose of . . . sensory deprivation. . . . The purpose is to induce a state of temporary disorientation and distraction of the will in which the victim may be more easily led by his interrogator. *It induces stress, it inflicts pain, its effects may not wholly disappear when the pressure is lifted . . . but it is less than torture,* and it is a good thing the Court . . . has said so.[31]

Four judges dissented from this verbal legerdemain: the Austrian, Greek, Cypriot, and, not surprisingly, the Irish judge. In a separate opinion against the majority view, Philip O'Donoghue, the Irish judge, stated:

One is not bound to regard torture as only present in a medieval dungeon where the appliance of rack and thumbscrew, or similar devices were employed. Indeed, in the present-day world, there can be little doubt that torture may be inflicted in the mental sphere.[32]

Sensory deprivation may indeed not be torture *à la* the Gestapo or the Inqui-sition, but Judge O'Donoghue is on the right track with his view that torture may be mental or psychological. Raised to new heights in the second half of the twentieth century, brainwashing and other psychological techniques have, in the main, replaced the rather crude rack or portable electrodes. Such practices do induce stress, do inflict pain, and do not always disappear when the pres-sure is lifted, and with these practices the will is distracted: great pain can be deliberately inflicted to the mind, and it is unfortunate that the court refused to look beyond the thumbscrew and, in the words of the Northern Ireland Civil Rights Association, refused "to call a spade a spade." Britain could no longer be accused of *torturing* the internees—a term that is headline material—but only for engaging in the more acceptable and less interesting practice of "inhuman" and "degrading" treatment.

The Irish government was understandably surprised and disappointed with the court's decision, especially since the commission previously ruled by a unanimous vote on the torture issue and since Great Britain did not contest the commission's ruling. The official Irish position, however, was that its view was indeed upheld, since the practices in question *were* a violation of article 3 (inhuman treatment). The court's verdict was a very hollow "victory" for Ireland.[33]

As mentioned above, all of the other allegations and demands in the Irish petition were rejected by the court, each by an overwhelming majority. The court ruled that it was not established that the practice in question (sensory deprivation) continued beyond the autumn of 1971, nor was it established that other ill treatment occurred at the unidentified interrogation centers. By a unanimous decision, the court ruled that it could not direct Great Britain to institute judicial proceedings against those security personnel who actually administered the sensory deprivation or against those who "tolerated" the practice (for example, the British politicians). Thus, although Britain was "guilty" of inhuman treatment, the court declined to press for any punishment of those who committed the violations. The court also ruled unanimously that article 50 (just compensation to the victims) was not to be applied, and whatever compensation Great Britain might have offered in the past was sufficient. Ireland also alleged a violation of article 14 (religious discrimination), since most of the people interned by the British were Roman Catholics. The court simply ruled (fifteen to two) that no such discrimination existed. Finally, it was the unanimous decision that whatever measures Britain applied (excepting sensory deprivation) in Northern Ireland, especially the practice of interning suspected IRA sympathizers, were not in violation of articles 5 and 6. For almost the identical reason employed in ruling in Ireland's favor in the *Lawless* case, the court cited article 15 as Britain's justification for the activities. Article 15 is the escape clause: in time of public emergency threatening the life of a nation, measures derogating from the convention to the extent required by the situation are permissible. The court, including even the Irish judge, ruled that, indeed, a public emergency existed, and the measures taken by Great Britain were required by the situation.

But what can be said about the protection of an individual's rights vis-à-vis state behavior after a reading of the *Irish-British* case? The existence of the commission and the court obviously did not help the fourteen people subjected to sensory deprivation, except, perhaps, international publicity was given to their experience, and Britain was chastised for its behavior. Perhaps the real impact of the case will be in the future, and similar situations may be avoided. The British government gave its assurance that the practice will not be repeated, and no reason can be found to doubt the government's promise. But other European countries face a public emergency threatening the existence of the nation to, of course, a less immediate degree than do the British in Northern Ireland. The Italians have their Red Brigade; the Germans, their Baader-Meinhof Gang; the Dutch, their South Moloccan terrorists; even the French, a nascent Breton movement claiming the responsibility for several bombing incidences. These governments might be more hesitant to employ techniques such as sensory deprivation, knowing full well that it has been condemned as inhuman treatment and, as well, is a violation of the convention. The real impact of the British case lies in the future.

One of the more recent cases (April 1978) decided by the court was *Tyrer* v. *United Kingdom*, with the commission acting as "prosecuting attorney" and the British government once again placed in the role of defendant. Although far less explosive and emotional, less publicized, and less "political" than the Irish allegations of torture, the *Tyrer* decision may in the long run have more far-reaching and significant consequences for Great Britain than any of the cases previously cited. The *Tyrer* decision directly intrudes into British "domestic" processes and its traditional modes of administrative organization and constitutional practices. The future of devolution—granting internal self-government to Scottish and Welsh assemblies—will most certainly be affected by the *Tyrer* decision.

In 1972 Anthony Tyrer, then fifteen-years-old and a resident of Castletown on the Isle of Man, was convicted of assaulting a schoolmate and was sentenced to three strokes of the birch. The Manx teenager's rights of due process were scrupulously observed: the appeal process ran its course; he was offered the choice between birching or a period of detention; the birching was eventually carried out in private, and, being a minor, Tyrer's name was not made public. The imposition of the punishment took place in a room attached to the Court in the presence of his father and a physician. Tyrer's trousers and underpants were lowered, and while two policemen held him, a third administered the three strokes. The birch raised welts but did not cut the skin. Soon thereafter, in September 1972, Tyrer, with the help of the British National Council for Civil Liberties, filed a petition with the commission, alleging that the punishment violated article 3 of the convention (degrading and inhuman treatment or torture).

Although judicially imposed corporal punishment was abolished in England, Scotland, and Wales in 1948, and in Northern Ireland in 1968, such punishment was still "legal" on the Isle of Man. The maintenance of the birch on the Isle of Man was a result of two closely related factors: the constitutional status of the Isle vis-à-vis the United Kingdom's Parliament in London and Manx public opinion. The Isle of Man is a crown dependency with its own Parliament (Tynwald), responsible for its own laws and internal self-government. To be sure, the British government is responsible for the island's external affairs (defense, treaties, international relations), and London also maintains the ultimate authority to legislate on all matters for the Isle of Man. But historically and traditionally, London has allowed the Manx MPs complete internal autonomy. The penal code falls within the Tynwald's jurisdiction, and Westminister has not interfered with the penalties, including the birch, meted out by the Manx judicial process.

Thus, although such punishment was abolished in the rest of the United

Kingdom, it still existed on the Isle of Man (and the Channel Islands), because it was an "internal" affair, and overwhelming popular support existed for birching juvenile offenders. *The Times* (London) reported that a petition in favor of the practice had been signed by approximately thirty-one thousand of the total adult Manx population of forty-five thousand,[34] and general island opinion was that the practice deterred juvenile crime. Birching was considered right, proper, legitimate, and in the best interests of society as defined by the democratically elected Tynwald MPs.

Tyrer's petition was ruled admissible by the commission, and hearings were held. Tyrer attempted to withdraw the petition in 1976 when he turned eighteen, but the commission, applying its prerogative, refused to permit its withdrawal because of the general issue involved. The commission announced its decision in March 1977: by a vote of fourteen to one it was held that birching was "degrading" treatment and, as such, a violation of article 3 of the convention. The commission urged the complete abolition of corporal punishment, and Love Kellberg, a Danish lawyer on the commission, described[35] birching as an "arbitrary and cold-blooded act"; the arguments that judicially imposed punishment "had any redeeming social value or that it was an effective deterrent" to crime were dismissed. The commission, with only one dissenting vote, stated that the "inviolability of a person's physical integrity" was a basic human right protected by the convention, and birching violated this right.

The commission was obviously unable to achieve a friendly settlement before its decision mainly because of the Manx insistence that the birch remain. Some concessions were made, however: the punishment was to be restricted to males between fourteen and twenty (Manx law permitted a maximum of six strokes for a child between ten and fourteen), and the offenders would no longer be hit on bare flesh (they could keep their trousers up). Such concessions were not enough for the commission and thus its decision. The commission, as always, had the option of referring the case to the Committee of Ministers or to the court. For reasons mentioned above, the commission chose the court and acted as "prosecuting attorney" with the United Kingdom and Isle of Man as the "defendant."

The court held hearings in January 1978. The commission repeated the arguments against birching that it used in arriving at its March 1977 decision: a court-ordered beating of a juvenile violates his human rights, and such practices ought to be stopped. The British government was in a strange position: being responsible for the Isle's external affairs, it was the "defendant" but argued against birching; the Manx delegate then argued in favor of it. Louis Blom-Cooper, head of the British delegation, made it clear in his presentation to the court that the United Kingdom government was present only because it was responsible for the Isle of Man's external affairs, and he severely criticized birching (he frequently used the term *whipping*). The British position supported the commission, and Blom-Cooper told the court that the "United

Kingdom Government, like virtually every other country to which the Convention applied, believes that judicial corporal punishment is not effective for any internationally acknowledged penal purpose."[36]

It then fell to Jack Corrin, the Manx attorney-general, to argue the merits of beating ten-year-old children and to attempt to convince the court that such beatings were not "degrading" to the individual. Corrin argued that birching was a deterrent to crime, and it did not degrade the individual in the eyes of other people because it did not "outrage public opinion" on the island. Since the punishment was administered in private without the offender's name publicized, such punishment could not be degrading. The Manx argument was quite simple: we like it, it deters juvenile crime, and it is not degrading in anyone's eyes.

The Manx attorney-general also argued that birching be allowed to continue on account of article 63 of the convention. It was through article 63 that the convention became applicable to the Isle of Man. Article 63(1) states that the "Convention shall extend to all or any of the territories for whose international relations it (the signatory State) is responsible"—the status of the Isle of Man—upon notification to the Council of Europe. Great Britain filed such notification, but, and this was the crux of Corrin's argument, article 63(3) states that the "provisions of this Convention shall be applied in such territories *with due regard, however, to local requirements.*"[37] The Manx position was that "local requirements" included the birch, and it should be permitted, or, in other words, article 63(3) should take precedence over article 3 (degrading treatment).

A big show of popular support for birching on the Isle arose on the same day the court heard the oral arguments. Four thousand people marched through Douglas, and a Manx government spokesman addressed the crowd:

You have shown that the retention of the birch is not just something that your government is trying to impose, but that it is the wish of the great majority of the people of this island. We are determined to maintain law and order. This is our top priority. We believe in human rights on the Isle of Man: the right of everyone, young and old, to walk on the streets of our community without fear of being molested.[38]

The court announced its decision in April 1978 and, by a vote of six to one, held that the practice of birching juvenile offenders on the Isle of Man was "degrading punishment" and thus a violation of article 3.[39] The court rejected all of the Manx arguments and thus gave article 3 precedence over article 63(3). The court opinion said that, for punishment to be "degrading" and thus in violation of article 3, "the humiliation or debasement involved must attain a particular level, higher than the usual element of humiliation involved in punishment in general." The nature and context of the punishment itself and the manner of its administration was also considered by the court—birching had a ritualistic process to it—and the opinion stated the "the Court cannot but be influenced by the development and commonly accepted standard in the penal policy in the member states of the Council of Europe in this field."

The court rejected the Manx argument that birching was not a violation of the convention since it did not "outrage" public opinion on the island. The six judges said it was not firmly established that birching was not considered degrading punishment by those people who supported it; rather, it was possible that one of the reasons why they did support it was precisely the element of degradation it involved. The court also rejected the argument that it could not be degrading since the whipping was done "in private" without Tyrer's name being published: "(P)ublicity may be a relevant factor in assessing whether a punishment is degrading . . . but the Court does not consider that absence of publicity will necessarily prevent a given punishment from falling into that category: It may well suffice that the victim is humiliated in his own eyes even if not in the eyes of others." Also considered irrelevant was the argument that the punishment was for an act of violence, or that Tyrer "chose" birching over a period of detention.

The court also rejected the argument on the deterrent effect of birching even though Manx public opinion believed it to be such. The court saw no evidence that law and order could not be maintained without birching, and, furthermore, even if law and order could not be maintained without the birch, that would not make the punishment allowable under the convention: "it is never permissible to have recourse to punishments which are contrary to Article 3 whatever their deterrent effect may be."

The one dissenting judge was, once again, Sir Gerald Fitzmaurice of the United Kingdom. Sir Gerald simply did not agree that the humiliation and debasement involved reached the level necessary to make it "degrading punishment," and it was vastly different, in terms of degradation, for a juvenile than for an adult to drop his trousers to receive a punishment. The British judge regarded the court's view, which implied that any judicially imposed corporal punishment on a juvenile was degrading, as "far too dogmatic and sweeping," although he confessed that his view was biased by the fact that he "had been brought up and educated under a system in which the corporal punishment of schoolboys was regarded as the normal sanction for serious misbehavior." He could not recall that any boy felt degraded or humiliated by such beatings, and the beatings were often seen as preferable to alternative punishments.

Birching might not have "outraged" Manx public opinion, but the court's decision most certainly did, and the island had a strong angry initial reaction.[40] Howard Simcocks, a Tynwald member, accused Great Britain of ignoring article 63(3) and the special Manx "local conditions" at the court hearing; Peter Craine, the only Manx Nationalist in the House of Keys, Tynwald's lower House, said the island "should tell the court to go to hell and mind their own business"; the chairperson of the Manx Nationalists, Audrey Ainsworth, said, "if the Isle of Man is a nation, let us act like one." The Channel Islands, another crown dependency, had a different reaction, however. The attorney-general of Jersey, Vernon Tomes, said the court's decision was both morally and legally binding on his government, and the refusal to abolish birching would put Jersey's internal independence in question.

The impact of the *Tyrer* case goes far beyond a fifteen-year-old youth receiving three strokes of the birch on his bare buttocks, although Tyrer's individual situation should not be deemphasized. Tyrer as an individual did complain against his government for alleged mistreatment, and his complaint was upheld by the European court. Of course, Tyrer still had his three strokes—the court will not issue an injunction or a restraining order while an appeal is made—but, probably, no more Anthony Tyrers will be found on the Isle of Man or the Channel Islands now that birching (and probably all forms of juvenile corporal punishment) has been categorized as "degrading" treatment under article 3 of the convention.

The real importance and significance of Tyrer's case involved the relationship of court decisions to domestic law as well as the future constitutional framework of the United Kingdom. The *Tyrer* case solidified a process that started previously: if a country's domestic legislation and/or administrative procedures are found to be in violation of the convention, such procedures then must be revised to prevent future violations. The United Kingdom is not by any means the only country in this situation with the *Golder* and *Tyrer* cases: Austria and Germany have reduced pretrial detention periods; the Belgian vagrancy laws have been revised; military discipline in the Dutch army has been relaxed; and a current case before the court deals with the United Kingdom's "contempt of court" legislation. The decisions of the European court are impinging on domestic legislation to protect the individual from his government.

The *Tyrer* case also has significant implications for the future relations between London and the Isle of Man, on the status of all crown dependencies with their up-to-now almost complete internal autonomy, and most important, on the contemporary process of devolution in the United Kingdom, especially in regard to Scotland. In view of the state of public opinion regarding birching in the Isle, and in view of the public position already staked out by the Manx government, it would be difficult for Tynwald to pass abolishing legislation (one possible face-saving device would be to leave the legislation alone but never apply it). However, if Tynwald refuses to act, it is then the United Kingdom's government in London that has the responsibility to see that the court's decision is obeyed. This can easily be accomplished by Westminister simply abolishing birching on the Isle of Man and the Channel Islands, but past tradition has not seen London meddling in Manx internal affairs. Such interference, at best, would question the status of crown dependencies and might lead to their demise; at worst, such interference could exacerbate Manx nationalism and present a whole new set of problems that would far surpass Tyrer's buttocks.

The current process of devolution is also affected by the *Tyrer* decision. Devolution would not make Scotland a crown dependency in the formal sense, but the Scottish Assembly would have full internal autonomy (finances, social legislation, judicial process), and Westminister would be responsbile for its external relations and treaty obligations. When and if Scotland receives its autonomy and internal sovereignty, it will remain London's responsibility to insure that domestic Scot legislation is in harmony with international treaty obligations such as the Human Rights Convention. But, and this is what is significant, the most recent Scotland bill did *not* expressly give to London the right to legislate in areas reserved to Scotland if Edinburgh refuses to bring its domestic legislation into harmony with international treaty obligations. The long-term effect of Anthony Tyrer's case against birching will reach right into the future constitutional arrangements in the United Kingdom.

SOME CONCLUDING COMMENTS

Although the institutions and processes described above are not daily household concerns with widespread media coverage, and although few individuals are directly affected by the commission and the court, the European Convention on Human Rights system has nonetheless had some impact. Avoiding spectacular or dramatic actions, the process has influenced the relationship of the individual vis-à-vis the state, has provided an additional avenue for the individual to complain about state behavior, and has enhanced the individual's ability to place the state in the role of defendant and thus be held accountable for its actions. The European Convention was the first real international agreement giving specific legal content and protection to the individual in relation to his or her government as well as establishing the necessary machinery for its supervision and enforcement. The European system may very well serve as a model for other geographical groupings of states that want to set up a similar process.

The European system has strengthened the position of the individual by clearly requiring the establishment of domestic avenues of redress and thus reducing sovereign immunity to a concept whose time has passed. Article 13 of the convention rejects the notion that official acts are immune from accountability (everyone should have "an effective remedy before a national authority notwithstanding that the violation has been committed by persons acting in an official capacity"), and this alone would be a significant and important contribution. In addition, article 57 authorizes the secretary-general of the Council of Europe to receive an explanation of how the internal domestic law of any signatory state "ensures the effective implementation" of the convention. The convention and its institutions thus may question domestic law, uncover those segments of domestic law that are possibly in violation of the convention, and prevent further occurrences (English prisoners *can* correspond with legal counsel, birching *will* be stopped). The anomalies in domestic law regarding human rights are being "exposed," and, at least in some recent cases, national legislation has been amended. The court, as long as the states continue to recognize its jurisdiction and accept its decisions as legitimate, will insure that national legislation is coherent with the provisions of the convention.

The commission itself has an important function that is similar to the ombudsman. The process of a "friendly settlement" within the commission serves to mediate conflict and, rather than punishing past behavior, attempts to prevent a future reoccurrence. This low-key and muted conflict-management process serves the individual well and protects him or her from governmental and/or bureaucratic mistreatment.

But the above comments are not to be interpreted as saying no problems or shortcomings exist with the European convention system. The formal proceedings are, to say the least, ponderous and time consuming. Several years may elapse between an original filing of a petition and a final decision. The *Golder* case described above illustrates part of this problem: the same arguments were repeated at six stages (oral and written arguments on the petition's admissibility, in front of the commission, and then before the court) without any new information added in steps two through six. Recent attempts to streamline and therefore shorten the process have been made, but the unduly lengthy process does not serve the individual's interest.

The most serious shortcoming is that the protected rights are not absolute; that is, ample leeway exists for states to violate the convention and not be held accountable for its actions. Article 15 can be invoked (such as in the *Lawless* case and the *Ireland v. United Kingdom* "torture" case) as a justifiable defense to what would otherwise be a clear violation of the convention. Article 15 allows the states, in time of war or other public emergency threatening the life of the nation, to take measures derogating from its obligations under the convention. It is, however, *precisely* during such "public emergencies" that individuals need added protection from state treatment rather than allowing the state to do as it sees fit. If the "exigencies" of the situation justify the need for a "national emergency," the mistreatment of individuals can be justified by the vague notion of a "public emergency."

In conclusion, the European convention process represents a later developmental stage in the slow transformation of the nature of the relationship between a private citizen and the state. The relationship began with sovereign immunity without any effective avenues of redress, passed through national processes, and now has arrived at international avenues of redress. The European Commission and Court of Human Rights presents an extraterritorial jurisdiction and is slowly eroding national juridical self-sufficiency. An extraterritorial process now exists that provides for an appeal beyond the domestic legal system. The individual is well served by the European Convention on Human Rights.

NOTES

1. A UN Commission on Human Rights also exists, but it is not nearly as effective as the European commission. The UN commission may have lofty ideals and good intentions, but it has little real power or influence in protecting an individual from state behavior.

2. Cited in A. H. Robertson, *Human Rights in Europe* (Manchester: Manchester University Press, 1963), p. 24.

3. Article 3 of the Statute of the Council of Europe reads, *inter alia*: "Every Member of the Council of Europe must accept the principles of the rule of law and of the enjoyment of all persons within its jurisdiction of human rights and fundamental freedoms, and collaborate sincerely and effectively in (their) realization. . . ."

4. The UN Universal Declaration of Human Rights proclaimed all human beings "free and equal in dignity and rights." Invoking many inalienable rights and consisting of some thirty articles, the declaration emphasized the right to life, liberty, security, nationality, property ownership; freedom of thought, conscience, religion; freedom from arbitrary arrest, detention, exile; freedom of movement, residence, and freedom of peaceful assembly and association. Although an admirable document, the declaration's practical effect in protecting human rights has been minimal at best and non-existent at worst.

5. The twenty members of the Council of Europe are Austria, Belgium, Cyprus, Denmark, France, Federal Republic of Germany, Greece, Iceland, Ireland, Italy, Luxembourg, Malta, The Netherlands, Norway, Portugal, Spain, Sweden, Switzerland, Turkey, and the United Kingdom. Thus the Committee of Ministers and the court each have twenty members, one from each of the council's members. All members have ratified the convention, with the exception of Spain and Portugal; thus the commission's membership is eighteen (ratification being necessary for commission membership). However, only fourteen countries have recognized the court's jurisdiction; the exceptions being Cyprus, Greece, Malta, Turkey (and, obviously, Spain and Portugal). In addition, only thirteen countries have recognized the right of individual petition to the commission, the exceptions being Cyprus, France, Greece, Malta, Turkey (and, obviously, Spain and Portugal).

6. Its French title is "Convention de Sauvegarde des Droits de l'Homme et des Libertés fondamentales." An official copy of the convention and protocols 1 through 5 are available upon request from the secretary to the European Commission of Human Rights, Council of Europe, 67006 Strasbourg.

7. Although article 7(1) prohibits ex post facto legislation, article 7(2) reads that 7(1) "shall not prejudice the trial and punishment of any person for any act or omission which, at the time when it was committed, was criminal according to the general principles of law recognized by civilized nations." It is obvious that article 7(2) refers to Nazi war crimes, and the convention thus permits the prosecution and punishment of such crimes. It is significant, however, that the German Federal Republic made the following reservation when ratifying the convention: "[The German Federal Republic] will only apply the provisions of Article 7(2) of the Convention within the limits of Article

103, Clause 2, of the Basic Law of the German Federal Republic. This provides that 'any act is only punishable if it was so by law before the offense was committed.' "

8. Louis B. Sohn and Thomas Buergenthal, *International Protection of Human Rights* (New York: The Bobbs-Merrill Co., 1973), p. 1099.

9. Ibid., p. 1100.

10. Article 39(3) lists the necessary qualifications: "the candidates shall be of high moral character and must either possess the qualifications required for appointment to high judicial office or be jurisconsults of recognized competence."

11. Recent practice by the court, however, has had the full court hearing a greater number of cases. In addition, article 3(1) of protocol 2 has the full court responding to the committee's request for an advisory opinion.

12. Approximately ten such interstate complaints have been filed. One of these, *Cyprus* v. *Turkey* (1974), illustrates a shortcoming of the process. Cyprus filed the petition, alleging that Turkey violated numerous convention articles when Turkey invaded Cyprus in 1974. However, since neither Cyprus nor Turkey recognize the court's jurisdiction, the case was referred to the Committee of Ministers, which usually shies away from such "political" decisions.

13. *Yearbook of the European Commission on Human Rights* (The Hague: Council of Europe, 1973), Statistical Charts.

14. Article 32 requires the referral of the case to the committee if the commission does not send it to the court within three months or if one of the states involved does not recognize the court's jurisdiction. A state always has the prerogative, however, to refer a commission decision to the court.

15. Marc-Andre Eissen, cited in the *New York Times*, November 27, 1977, p. 9.

16. *Yearbook of the European Convention on Human Rights* (1961), pp. 430–88.

17. Ibid., 1968, pp. 832–1018.

18. Ibid., 1971, pp. 838–64.

19. *The Times* (London), February 20, 22, 25, and 28 and March 7, 1975, contains a good summary description of the *Golder* case.

20. As reported by Peter Evans and Marcel Berlins, *The Times*, February 20, 1975, p. 5.

21. Ibid.

22. Ibid.

23. Twelve judges decided the *Golder* case. The court unanimously ruled on article 8 regarding correspondence as well as on the view that a fair trial necessitated the right to counsel. However, three judges dissented from the majority opinion that the convention provided any right to go to court in the first place. "Letter to Editor" from Sir Gerald Fitzmaurice (British), judge of the European Court of Human Rights, ibid.

24. Roy Jenkins, cited in *The Times*, March 7, 1975, p. 9.

25. *The Times*, January 19, 1978, p. 5, presented a brief description of sensory deprivation: "Some of the Irish witnesses demonstrated to the Commissioners how they were spreadeagled against a wall, their legs spread apart and their weight forced on to their fingertips. One man said to have remained like that for 29 hours. The hoods used on the 14 men were described as black or navy-blue bags and the noise to which they were subjected as 'a continuous, loud hissing sound.' They were denied sleep and given a restricted diet consisting of a round of bread and a pint of water every six hours."

26. The commission's document was and still is cloaked in secrecy: only two copies

exist, and all parties have agreed not to publish the full document; in the commission's 500-page public report, witnesses are identified by code names only.

27. Some of the proceedings appear to have been lifted from the cloak-and-dagger script of the "Mission Impossible" TV series: several members of the British security forces were flown by the RAF to Sola on the Norwegian coast to be interviewed by the commission, and the witnesses appeared behind screens to protect their identity.

28. "A Dispassionate Judgment," Editorial, *The Times*, January 19, 1978, p. 17; emphasis supplied.

29. *The Times* of January 19, 1978, contains an excellent summary of the decision, esp. p. 5.

30. The British judge, Sir Gerald Fitzmaurice, severely chastised the British government for not contesting the commission's original finding that sensory deprivation was torture. Sir Gerald stated: "Had the Court accepted the United Kingdom contention that it need not and should not pronounce upon the non-contested allegations, the Commission's findings as to torture would have constituted the last word on the subject and . . . the United Kingdom would have stood convicted . . . of that grave charge." Cited in ibid.

31. Ibid., p. 17; emphasis supplied.

32. Philip O'Donoghue, cited in ibid., p. 5.

33. The Irish government attempted to retrieve the situation by issuing several platitudinous statements about "inhuman" treatment, but its real reaction was probably summed up by an unidentified Irish spokesman in reference to Britain not contesting the commission's finding of torture but having the court decide otherwise: "it is akin to someone pleading guilty in court and being overruled."

34. *The Times*, January 18, 1978, p. 1.

35. As reported in ibid., p. 2.

36. Louis Blom-Cooper, QC, as cited in ibid.

37. Emphasis supplied.

38. Jan Anderson, Manx MP (Glenfaba, Ind.), as cited in *The Times*, January 18, 1978, p. 2.

39. As reported in *The Times*, April 26, 1978, pp. 1–2.

40. As reported in ibid.

PRIVATE TRANSNATIONAL AGENCIES: Amnesty International

7

The real political world, characterized by the traditional independent, sovereign nation-state system, is still beset by controversies and conflicts. Not only do expected conflicts arise among states that have yet to form a security community (for example, the United States-Soviet Union, Israel-Syria, Greece-Turkey), but controversies also arise among states that have at least nominally friendly or cordial relations (for example, Ireland and the United Kingdom over Northern Ireland, Mexico and the United States over natural gas imports and prices). An attempt by one government to change the policies of another is usually seen as undue and unwarranted interference in the domestic concerns of a sovereign state.

Many governments often work at cross-purposes, and open clashes are frequent. These clashes and political differences among states are not always the result of one set of decision makers being "evil" and the other having "justice" on its side—many are the inevitable result of fundamental differences in the perceptions of reality and political goals. Given this state of affairs—and it appears that the international situation will remain as such for the foreseeable future—the work and contribution of private transnational agencies in protecting an individual from his government and in securing redress for individual grievances have become more relevant, important, and successful in the second half of the twentieth century.

Formal political attempts by institutionalized political entities—whether a single state or a collection of states in an intergovernmental organization—to influence and change a government's domestic behavior meets with apathy at best and with resistance at worst. However noble and well meaning one country's concerns may be—as discussed in chapter 5 in relation to the U.S. Congress' attempts to aid the potential Russian emigrés—they are often ignored as an illegitimate intrusion in internal policies. One is hard put to document empirically the effects, if any, that United States activity has had in alleviating the situation of the Russian dissidents and potential emigrés. Pressure by one state on another is sometimes effective when the respective power status is vastly different (for example, the United States and Nicaragua), but it is seldom effective when the respective power status is equal (the United States and the Soviet Union).

Public intergovernmental organizations run the range from reasonably effective institutions to those somewhat less effective in securing redress for the individual against his government. As discussed in chapter 6, the European Convention on Human Rights system can and does protect the individual but only vis-à-vis those governments that have voluntarily recognized the competence and jurisdiction of the system. The European convention system would be powerless if it tried to extend its activities to, say, the governments of Latin America or Africa. Agencies within the United Nations are composed of formal representatives of political governments, and these agencies are not immune from political pressures—governments are wary and hesitant to cede any authority to an international agency.

The doctrine of sovereignty is strictly maintained, and most nations, especially those with a poor record regarding the treatment of individuals, simply do not allow any external political entity to control or influence internal policy. Countries such as the Soviet Union and South Africa, for example, even refuse entry to information-gathering groups. Given this unfortunate international political atmosphere, it is precisely at this stage that private (nongovernmental) transnational agencies can enter and enlarge the scope of the redress system. These private agencies often work in a low-key and muted atmosphere, although some are anything but muted; publicity is used with discretion, and they are ostensibly nonpolitical and nonideological. The activities of these private transnational agencies can often lead to success when all other avenues of redress have failed the individual.

We are not dealing here with international social welfare operations in the charitable and humanitarian areas. This is not to imply that agencies such as Amnesty International do not engage in humanitarian services and activities, but—and this is the crucial distinction—Amnesty International is primarily concerned with protecting the individual from mistreatment by overt actions of governments. The international social welfare agencies, on the other hand, deal primarily with *la condition humaine*; that is, they work to alleviate the suffering caused not by state action but from the impersonal forces of life, nature, circumstances, and the environment (famine, health, community development, the care of refugees, the aged, natural disasters, and so on).

Hundreds of such international social welfare agencies and voluntary charitable organizations exist.[1] These agencies and organizations can be classified into four general categories: agencies of international governmental organizations, private (nongovernmental) organizations of an international character, national public governmental agencies whose activities are in the international area, and private national organizations whose activities in welfare services extend beyond their borders.

The first category—agencies of international governmental organizations—

include most of the specialized agencies within the United Nations. The major ones are the UN Economic and Social Council (ECOSOC); International Labor Organization (ILO); World Health Organization (WHO); UN Educational, Scientific, and Cultural Organization (UNESCO); UN Development Program; UN International Children's Emergency Fund (UNICEF); UN High Commissioner for Refugees (UNHCR); Food and Agricultural Organization (FAO); and International Bank of Reconstruction and Development (IBRD). Other agencies in this first category would be several activities of the European Community—the Social Fund, the European Agricultural Guidance and Guarantee Fund, the European Investment Bank, the Regional Development Fund—and certain activities of the World Bank.

The specialized UN agencies have a vastly different record from the political agencies such as the UN Commission on Human Rights. These social welfare agencies have been able to bring some measure of success and hope to those they are to serve. But the reason behind whatever success they have achieved is that they are dealing with the forces of nature and the human condition—they are not attempting to control or alter the *political* behavior of sovereign governments.

The second category—private organizations of an international character—are numerous, and only the more important ones can be listed here: International Red Cross and its national units; International Council on Social Welfare; World YMCA and YWCA; HIAS (Hebrew Immigration Aid Society); International Conference of Catholic Charities; Catholic International Union for Social Service; Boy Scouts World Bureau; World ORT Union; World Council of Churches; International Union for Child Welfare; *Terre des Hommes* (Switzerland); Oxfam (Oxford Famine Relief); and *Aktion Sühnezeichen* (symbol of atonement), a German-based organization that facilitates volunteers to work in Israeli kibbutzim.

The third category—national governmental agencies—would include the U.S. Peace Corps; the U.S. Agency for International Development (AID); and the U.S. Office on Child Development. The last category—private national agencies whose welfare services extend to the international area—includes Swiss Aid to Europe; Dutch Interchurch Aid; Unitarian Service Committee; British and American Friends Service Committee (the Quakers); American Jewish Joint Distribution Committee; U.S. Bishops' Fund; Institute for International Education; United Jewish Appeal; and Cooperative for American Relief Everywhere (CARE).

All of these agencies and organizations, as well as the hundreds not mentioned, are primarily engaged in social welfare activities, and they emphasize the charitable and humanitarian aspect of their services. They are not locked in political combat with governments; they do not monitor the political behavior of states; they do not attempt to control or alter domestic political decision making. The focus of this chapter is on a private transnational agency that attempts to do what the social welfare agencies shy away from. Such an agency, although of course having unquestionable social and humanitarian concerns, is engaged in overt political activities. These activities include the constant monitoring of how governments treat their citizens; the attempt to protect specific individuals from being mistreated by their governments; and, with varying levels of success, the attempt to provide an additional avenue of redress for an individual who wants to complain against his government. The private transnational agency involved in the redress of grievances system to be discussed in this chapter is Amnesty International.[2]

AMNESTY INTERNATIONAL

Recipient of the Nobel Peace Prize in 1977, London-based Amnesty International is an unincorporated nonprofit organization that has as its primary objective the observance, throughout the world, of the provisions of the United Nations Universal Declaration of Human Rights and of the United Nations Standard Minimum Rules for the Treatment of Prisoners. Founded in 1961 by Peter Benenson in the belief that every person has the right to hold and to express his convictions and has an obligation to extend the same freedom to others, it is now a worldwide human rights group that is independent of any government, political, ideological, economic, or religious entity. Amnesty International's basic objective is well stated in the opening paragraph of its own statute:

Considering that every person has the right freely to hold and to express his convictions and the obligation to extend a like freedom to others, the objects of Amnesty International shall be to secure throughout the world the observance of the provisions of the Universal Declaration of Human Rights, by:

(a) irrespective of political considerations working toward the release of and providing assistance to persons who in violation of the aforesaid provisions are imprisoned, detained, restricted or otherwise subjected to physical coercion or restriction by reason of their political, religious or other conscientiously held beliefs or by reason of their ethnic origin, sex, colour or language, provided that they have not used or advocated violence (hereinafter referred to as "Prisoners of Conscience"). . . .[3]

The operating statute continues and places Amnesty International as an advocate of fair and early trials for all political prisoners and works on behalf of people detained without charge or without trial. Amnesty International also opposes the death penalty and torture or other cruel, inhuman, or degrading treatment or punishment of *all* prisoners, whether or not such prisoners have used or advocated violence. The organization's international appeal is increasing, and it is a recognized transnational group. It even has consultative status with ECOSOC, UNESCO, and the Council of Europe; it has cooperative relations with the Inter-American Commission on Human Rights of the Organization of American States; and it has observer status with the Organization of African Unity (Bureau for the Placement and Education of African Refugees).

In brief, Amnesty International is governed by an International Council that meets once a year. This council is composed of representatives of the organization's national sections and members of the International Executive Committee. The committee is responsible for the implementation of the decisions of the council by the International Secretariat in London. Almost entirely dependent upon voluntary contributions, it is financed by dues from its national sections throughout the world, by individual contributions, and by donations. Its publishing department runs at a loss—only nominal sums are charged for its publications—and the almost £80,000 it received from the Nobel Peace Prize was a welcome infusion for the budget.

Amnesty International has approximately two hundred thousand members with about twenty-one hundred local adoption groups. National sections are found in thirty-five countries, with individual members and supporters in seventy-six additional countries. These local adoption groups work for three "prisoners of conscience," each in countries other than their own—these three countries are chosen to reflect geographic and political balance to insure impartiality. In addition, the International Secretariat arranges missions to countries where concern is evident and sends representatives to talk with government officials. Whenever worthwhile (and possible), it also sends observers to trials. Most of the funds dispensed by Amnesty International provide relief for prisoners of conscience and their families. This relief may be money, clothes, books, other material needs, or help with legal, educational, or other expenses.

The Framework of Organization

The organizational arrangements of Amnesty International (AI) are relatively straightforward, and the international character of the organization is maintained throughout. The three decision-making units are the International Council, the International Executive Committee, and the International Secretariat. The International Council is the chief authority for the general conduct of AI's affairs; the International Executive Committee is responsible for AI's affairs between meetings of the council and is also responsible for implementing the council's decisions; the International Secretariat is a permanent body under the general direction of the executive committee and is responsible for AI's day-to-day affairs. The membership consists of national sections and affiliated local groups, individual members and supporters, and corporate members.

The International Council, responsible for the overall direction of Amnesty International, does not meet frequently—about once a year or at least once every two years. It is a large group: the eleven members of the International Executive Committee are on the council as well as representatives from each of the national sections. All national sections can appoint at least one council member (thirty-five as of June 1978) as well as additional representatives according to the number of local adoption groups affiliated with the national section; national sections composed mainly of individual members rather than organized local groups can appoint additional council members according to the size of their membership.[4] The national sections can vote in council deliberations only if their annual fee to AI has been paid, but this rule is lax—sections having financial problems are not automatically shut out of council decisions. Finally, representatives of groups not affiliated with AI can, upon invitation, attend council meetings as observers without voting rights.

The International Executive Committee is elected by the council by proportional representation to insure a balance from the national contingents, and not more than one member of any national section or group can be a member of the executive committee.[5] The committee meets not less than twice a year, and it is responsible for overseeing the implementation of the guidelines established by the council. As with the council, the committee can determine the location of its meetings.

The everyday work of Amnesty International is performed by the International Secretariat. The executive committee appoints a secretary-general (the current secretary-general is Martin Ennals) who is the effective administrative executive. The secretary-general has the ability to hire a staff, and the number of full-time employees at the secretariat's London office is substantial.

The membership of AI is composed of national sections, individual members and supporters, and corporate members. As mentioned above, the executive committee has the authority to admit corporate entities as AI members upon payment of an annual fee. In countries where no formal national section exists, individuals can become AI members, again by paying an annual subscription fee. At present, about eighty-five countries have individual AI members-supporters, including countries such as the Soviet Union, South Africa, Chad, and Vietnam. The national sections and affiliated local groups constitute, however, the bulk of AI's membership and financial resources.

Thirty-five countries have national sections, with a total of approximately twenty-two hundred adoption groups and two hundred thousand members. Such national groups fund AI by paying an annual fee fixed by the International Council, and the local adoption groups do most of the work concerned with appealing for the release of prisoners and maintaining the relief program. The annual fees are often oversubscribed by the national sections, and inability to pay is not an immediate cause for termination or membership—the prize money from the 1977 Nobel Prize was earmarked by AI to aid the less financially secure national sections.

The American national section—AIUSA—is one of the largest and best funded of all national sections. Its main office is in New York, but offices are also found in Washington, San Francisco, Los Angeles, Cambridge, and Chicago. As of March 6, 1979, AIUSA had 167 officially chartered local adoption groups, with some having a membership of over 100 people.[6] The activities of the International Secretariat and the national sections and local adoption groups are discussed in more detail below.

Amnesty International maintains close and cordial relations with other international and national organizations, including both intergovernmental organizations (IGOs) and nongovernmental organizations (NGOs). AI has consultative status with ECOSOC, and this has allowed it to submit information to various United Nations bodies and to have an official representative at meetings dealing with human rights questions.[7] AI also has consultative status with UNESCO, and, in fact, AI was reelected, in 1977, at the Conference of International NonGovernmental Organizations having such status with UNESCO, to the NGO Standing Committee. AI also has consultative status with the Council of Europe and organized a Council-funded NGO seminar on "Torture and Human Rights." In addition, Amnesty International has close contacts with the Organization of American States (OAS), and an AI delegation attended the Eighth General Assembly of the OAS at the invitation of the OAS Permanent Council. AI also continues to work with the Inter-American Commission on Human Rights (IACHR) and frequently provides information to the IACHR on prisoners of conscience, the use of torture, the lack of legal safeguards, and the failure to bring political prisoners to trial throughout the Americas. Finally, AI is a member of the Coordinating Committee of the Organization of African Unity's Bureau of Placement and Education of African Refugees.

Amnesty International also maintains close cooperation and collaborates with other nongovernmental organizations. It is a member of the Bureau of the Conference of Non-Governmental Organizations in Consultative Status with the United Nations, and AI's secretary-general is a vice-president of the bureau. It is also a member of the special Non-Governmental Organization Committee on Human Rights in Geneva and New York as well as a member of the Alliance of Non-Governmental Organizations on Crime Prevention and Criminal Justice (New York). AI has also strengthened its contacts with the International Association of Penal Law (IAPL), and an AI representative attended several IAPL conferences. AI works with the Inter-Parliamentary Union and is beginning to work with a number of international union organizations—the International Confederation of Free Trade Unions (ICFTU), the World Confederation of Labor, and the World Federation of Trade Unions. AI's goal in working with these trade union organizations is to increase the effectiveness of their efforts on behalf of workers imprisoned and/or tortured by their governments.

Amnesty International is thus a worldwide, transnational, nongovernmental organization whose prestige—at least among several countries and governments—is increasing year by year. Its nonpartisan and nonideological voice has enabled it to gain admittance to governments and to international authorities, and it has become a strong defender of the individual vis-à-vis his government.

The Major Activities

Several major areas of activities and programs have been identified and emphasized by Amnesty International over the years. The International Secretariat in London sets the tone for them, but much of the day-to-day work for the first two programs below is done by the national sections and the local adoption groups. Amnesty International has six major areas of activity:

1. The release of political prisoners and prisoners of conscience.
2. A relief program designed to aid those political prisoners who remain in detention or who have been released but still require such aid—this relief program extends to the families of political prisoners.
3. A concerted campaign for the abolition of the death penalty.
4. A concerted campaign for the abolition of torture (CAT) and all forms of inhuman or degrading treatment of *all* prisoners, not just prisoners of conscience.
5. The support of conscientious objectors' opposition to enforce military service— Amnesty International regards jailed COs as prisoners of conscience.
6. A worldwide research and information effort—this includes a strong and visible publicity department as well as missions and observers sent to various countries.

The primary goal of Amnesty International has always been its work directed at securing the release of prisoners of conscience. AI has estimated— a rough approximation, of course—that the number of political prisoners and prisoners of conscience that exist worldwide at any time ranges well into the hundreds of thousands. Numbers alone preclude a universal approach, and the organization deals with about five thousand cases each year. An extensive research and documentation effort is undertaken before an individual is classified as a prisoner of conscience, for AI continually attempts to work for those who have been jailed *only* on account of their beliefs. A person who employed or advocated violence—a terrorist with some plastique, for example—does not qualify for AI's efforts. But AI will work, however, for such prisoners' right not to be subjected to torture or mistreatment while in jail, and the organization will also extend, to this terrorist, its opposition to the death penalty; what AI will not do with people who have used violence is to work for their release.

The research and documentation effort is carried out by a variety of means: observers' reports, press clippings, official announcements, and letters from friends, families, and sometimes the prisoner himself. Once AI is satisfied that a specific individual is indeed a "prisoner of conscience" and that he should be "adopted," his name is then circulated and assigned to the national sections and the local adoption groups. Certain mandated conditions—general guide-lines—are set out by London, and these guidelines must be adhered to by the local groups. To begin with, the maximum number of cases any local group can deal with at any time is limited to three, although many will handle only one or two at a time. This limit has served AI well in the past: the resources of each local group can be concentrated and thus have a greater chance of success in the individual cases. This maximum obviously limits the total number of prisoners that are helped by AI, but at least effective use is made of limited resources.

The second guideline is a political rather than economic restriction, and it relates to the country in which the adoptees are detained. This guideline has also served AI well in the past. The adoption groups *cannot* adopt a prisoner of conscience from their own country for this would immediately transform the local group into a political partisan organization rather than a private, "non-political" human rights group. In addition, the local adoption groups must balance the geographical-political nature of their adoptees: one is to be from the West, one from the East, and one from the Third World. This balance is crucial for AI's claim to be nonideological in its selection of political prisoners (this claim has been disputed by some as discussed below), and the organiza-tion's credibility would be severely questioned if this practice were to be abandoned.

The International Secretariat works along with the local groups in attempt-ing to secure the release of the adopted prisoners. The secretariat works through the media to draw attention to the case, and observers and representa-tives are sent to talk with government officials; the local groups embark on an extensive letter-writing campaign to various officials on behalf of the adoptee. One letter from one individual may not accomplish much for the prisoner, but letter after letter from a number of people addressed, say, to the minister of jus-tice *may* result in the release of the prisoner. Unwarranted publicity may do more damage to a country than the release of a specific individual, and although Amnesty International by no means claims an inflated success rate, its intercession in the process has led to the release of many individuals. The release may be for a single prisoner or it may be a wide-ranging general amnesty for a large number of detained political prisoners.

But many (the majority) of these letters, requests, and efforts for release fall upon unresponsive officials, and this carries over to AI's second major and parallel program—the relief program. Recognizing that the actual release of a prisoner is a long-term affair, the local adoption groups also employ their resources on behalf of their adoptees still in prison and their families. Some-times this relief program continues after the individual has been released if his situation requires such assistance. Most of the relief is in the form of cash grants, although other aid is given.

The relief program is handled in a variety of ways. The International Secretariat itself dispenses its own monies—some $400,000 in 1977–78, up from $250,000 the previous year—generated from within its own budget and augmented by the Nobel Prize money. The International Secretariat also dispenses relief funds made available to its Relief Committee by several national sections over and above their normal allocations. In 1977–78 approximately $170,000 was transferred from seven national sections through this process.[8] The International Secretariat is dealing with large sums of money, but it averages out to about $100 a prisoner (the actual amounts received are of course much higher than this $100 since money is not sent to all the adoptees). Amnesty International also is convinced that most, if not all, of the funds dispensed by the International Secretariat eventually reach the people it was designed to help. The nature of the transactions often preclude a signed receipt—prisoners in the gulag, for example—but the accounting firm that has audited the International Secretariat's budget is quite optimistic about the amount of leakage:

Payments of relief are usually made to prisoners or their families via intermediaries. This relief activity involves entrusting persons whom the International Secretariat consider to be responsible with relief monies and relying extensively on their integrity and dedication to ensure that the proper persons benefit from relief. It is not always possible or practicable to obtain receipts from beneficiaries of relief monies, but the International Secretariat does have additional sources of information which, it believes, would report any significant instances where relief monies, for one reason or another, did not reach prisoners or their families. No such significant instances have been reported.[9]

The relief program administered by the International Secretariat is varied. AI's *Annual Report* noted that well-established relief projects in Southern Africa still constitute a large part of the secretariat's relief effort. In addition, some long-term projects in Latin America and Asia were enlarged, and new channels for relief were established in Tanzania, Chile, Argentina, and Morocco. The *Report* commented that although the scale of relief programs in the Soviet Union and Eastern Europe are severely hindered by travel and currency restrictions, the secretariat was able to provide material relief to some prisoners and their families. This aid is separate from that organized by the local adoption groups and the national sections.

Not all of the relief monies are outright cash gifts to individuals and/or their families since AI also believes in self-help and long-term self-sufficiency projects. Within the last few years, the International Secretariat established a special fund (along with the Spanish national section) to help defray travel expenses of people in "imminent danger of imprisonment" in Latin America; in an attempt to help the families of some "disappeared" Chilean prisoners become self-supporting, AI gave assistance in establishing a bakery and a nursery school as well as in purchasing some fishing boats; money was also given to support several Asian organizations that are involved in rehabilitating and retraining former prisoners by providing loans to set up cottage industries and other self-help projects.

The relief program is also carried out by the national sections and the local adoption groups. The International Secretariat is unable to estimate the *total* amount of relief given since many of the local groups do not report the exact amounts to their national sections, and the national sections do not report the amount of the relief administered out of their own funds.[10] The final total amount of AI's relief program is enormous, however, if the following activity of one local adoption group is indicative of the twenty-two hundred or so worldwide local groups.[11]

In 1975 a then twenty-six-year-old Soviet dentist, Mark Nashpits, was arrested for appealing publicly for the right to emigrate to Israel. He was duly tried and sentenced to five years of "internal exile" in Siberia. Nashpits was seen as a bona fide prisoner of conscience by Amnesty International's research department, and his "case" was assigned to three local adoption groups: one in West Germany, one in the Netherlands, and one in Great Neck, New York. The Great Neck local has about fifteen members, and the chairperson for the Nashpits campaign is Johanna Hurwitz, the well-known author of children's books. This adoption group has attacked along a two-pronged front: attempt to secure the release of Nashpits but at the same time to provide relief and assistance.

The attempt to get Nashpits released before the end of his five-year sentence has not met with success, although it was not for lack of trying. The Great Neck local sent letter after letter to high-ranking Soviet politicians and bureaucrats—Brezhnev, Kosygin, and Podgorny included—respectfully requesting an end to Nashpits's "internal exile." The locals in West Germany and the Netherlands also wrote to Moscow but with the same unfortunate result. Letters were also sent to the Soviet embassy in Washington as well as to their United Nations mission in New York. These letters fell upon unresponsive officials—not one was ever acknowledged. The local even organized a street demonstration at the Soviet mission with the usual placards, but this, too, was ignored.

More than four hundred letters were sent by the Great Neck local to Nashpits in the first three years of the campaign. Many of these were mailed outside the United States to give the impression to the Soviets that Nashpits had worldwide support rather than support from only a small group of people in a Long Island community. The letters have nothing in them that would connect them with Amnesty International—the AI letterhead stationary is never used for such letters—and their content, to pass the scrutiny of the Soviet censors, reflects folksy and nonideological subjects. The Great Neck local has been extremely fortunate in that it has received about a dozen letters written by Nashpits.

This local adoption group has also been sending material relief to Nashpits—some of the packages reached their destination, others were assumed never to have arrived. One such package contained a heavy woolen sweater, two boxes of cocoa powder, and two boxes of bouillon cubes. This small package cost the group $85, with most of the cost going toward postage and prepaid duties. Money has not been sent to Nashpits: an American dollar will not buy much in Siberia, and rubles would probably be intercepted and confiscated. But items such as inexpensive scarves and novelty goods (3-D postcards) were sent so Nashpits could perhaps sell them in Siberia. One member of the Great Neck group is a dentist also, and he has been sending Nashpits copies of an American dental journal.

This relief may not even dull the edge of the Siberian exile, and it certainly is not getting Nashpits released before the five years, but at least it is a link to the outside, and Nashpits—as well as the other prisoners of conscience adopted by local groups—does have the knowledge that he is not forgotten and that people are still concerned for him. Johanna Hurwitz commented on the campaign: "We don't know that we're going to help him get out in less than five years but if it makes the five years pass a little bit easier, then we will have done something."[12] This person-to-person support and relief effort is a hallmark of Amnesty International, and its effect on the prisoners cannot be overestimated. The letters and packages transmit the crucial message: take courage and don't despair for you are not alone.

The third major activity of Amnesty International has been an extensive worldwide campaign for the total abolition of the death penalty. This program has long been a concern of AI, but it began in earnest in December 1977 with an AI-convened international conference in Stockholm. This Stockholm Conference on the Abolition of the Death Penalty was a true international meeting, for over two-hundred delegates from approximately fifty countries participated. The conference was subsequent to several preparatory sessions held in Columbo, Hamburg, New York, Paris, Port-of-Spain, and Ibadan.

The delegates represented a fair balance of disciplines and interests relevant to capital punishment—lawyers, judges, politicians, penologists, sociologists, psychologists, police officials, political scientists, theologians, trade unionists, and journalists. The nongovernmental nature of the conference did not preclude governmental officials from participating—Thorbjörn Fälldin, the prime minister of Sweden, opened the conference.[13] As is customary in such meetings, the work was done in working committees and in plenary sessions. The subjects of six working committees were (1) "The Death Penalty and Public Opinion," (2) "Alternatives to the Death Penalty," (3) "Individual Involvement in the Death Penalty," (4) "The Death Penalty and Discrimination," (5) "The Death Penalty in International Law and Organization" and (6) "Murder Committed or Acquiesced in by Government."

The conference passed what has since been called the "Declaration of Stockholm," and the report was endorsed in its entirety by AI's International

Executive Committee in March 1978. The Declaration of Stockholm unequivocally stated its opposition to the death penalty—capital punishment "is the ultimate cruel, inhuman and degrading punishment and violates the right to life," and the use of it is "brutalizing to all who are involved in the process." The declaration also stated that the death penalty "is frequently used as an instrument of repression against opposition, racial, ethnic, religious and underprivileged groups" and that it has never been shown to have any special deterrent effect. This document concluded with pleas for nongovernmental organizations, both national and international, to work collectively and individually to provide public information material directed toward the abolition of the death penalty; for all governments to bring about the immediate and total abolition of the death penalty; and for the United Nations to declare that capital punishment is contrary to international law.[14]

Amnesty International is not alone in this campaign, for other organizations have entered into the debate. Reaffirming the desirability of abolishing the death penalty, the UN General Assembly, in December 1977, instructed the United Nations-convened Congress on the Prevention of Crime and the Treatment of Offenders—held in Sidney in 1980—to "discuss the various aspects of the use of capital punishment and the possible restriction thereof, including a more generous application of rules relating to pardon, commutation or reprieve, and to report . . . recommendations to the General Assembly. . . ."[15] A more recent development occurred at the June 1978 Council of Europe's Conference of European Ministers of Justice in Copenhagen. Acting on a memorandum from the Austrian minister of justice, Dr. Christian Broda—one of the main speakers at the Stockholm Conference—the conference unanimously adopted a resolution requesting that the Committee of Ministers of the Council of Europe "refer questions concerning the death penalty to the appropriate Council of Europe bodies for study as part of the Council's work program. . . ."[16] This resolution was based on the justice ministers' view that all human beings have dignity and rights such as those contained in the European Convention on Human Rights and that the death penalty does violence to these principles.

Amnesty International's campaign for the abolition of the death penalty is two-sided. It works in the general field with general campaigning and educational activities to bring the issue to a point of discussion and debate. It also takes specific action in individual cases throughout the world—some appeals are successful, others are not.[17] AI also attempts to maintain a dialogue with those states that make extensive use of the death penalty with the goal of reducing the number of offenses that, upon conviction, can result in capital punishment.[18] This is slow and often disappointing work, but Amnesty International is indeed slowly achieving its objective, for the worldwide trend is to reduce the number of crimes that can incur capital punishment, and several countries have abolished the death penalty entirely.

The fourth major activity of Amnesty International is its Campaign for the Abolition of Torture (CAT). The CAT began in 1971, and this has always been a central objective of AI. The CAT has had some success over the years; public awareness of the widespread use of torture has been raised, many specific individuals have been aided, and several organizations—governmental and nongovernmental—are dealing with proposed standards and ways to prevent torture. AI is sanguine, however, about the enormity of its task and it comments that

> ... there is little room for satisfaction. Torture in its cruellest forms continues to be a systematic practice in many countries. Furthermore, in some parts of the world, new, more sophisticated methods of torture are being developed for the interrogation of political suspects or for deterring opposition to the regime. And torture is also being used by anti-government and opposition groups.
>
> So long as the inhuman practice of torture continues, so will this Campaign.[19]

Part of the CAT is the "Urgent Action Network," a program designed to intervene on behalf of specific known individuals who are under the threat of torture. AI members in over thirty countries appealed on behalf of 362 individual victims from June 1977 to May 1978. Exact information is hard to come by concerning these individuals, but AI estimates that positive results were achieved in about one-third of the cases: torture had stopped, the individual was released or "officially recognized" as being a prisoner, visits from families were allowed, or medical treatment was provided. These developments concerned about 120 people, and when this number is compared with the total worldwide number of people being tortured or subjected to inhuman or degrading treatment, the futility of the task becomes evident. But AI refuses to give up, and the Urgent Action network appears to bring some measure of relief to certain individuals.

A second part of the CAT is country-related campaigns to expose and publicize systematic abuses of human rights and the use of torture. In 1977–78 AI focused on Paraguay, South Africa, Argentina, and the Soviet Union in its country campaigns. AI was concerned that the international public had little knowledge about the extent of the use of torture in Paraguay, and it published several pamphlets documenting such mistreatment; the use of torture by the South African security police—involved in the "accidental" death of several detainees—also was investigated and publicized; information campaigns were carried out in relation to the "disappearance" of thousands of people in Argentina as well as in relation to the Soviet practice of incarcerating "political" prisoners in psychiatric institutions.[20]

The third section of the CAT is AI's close collaboration with other organizations to devise standards and an enforcement process. AI has worked with the World Health Organization (WHO), the Council for International Organizations of Medical Sciences (CIOMS), and the World Medical Association (WMA) in drafting a code of ethics for all medical personnel regarding the protection of detainees from torture. The completed draft is to be submitted to the UN General Assembly. AI is also supporting the adoption by the United Nations of an international code of ethics for the legal profession—a profession that has a crucial role to play in insuring that prisoners should not be tortured and that victims should have an avenue of redress. AI also convened a seminar on Violations of Human Rights: Torture and the Medical Profession in 1978 in Athens. Physician members of AI presented findings on their research about questions such as the effects of torture and how one can identify a victim of torture, especially when the more modern varieties leave very few visible marks.

Amnesty International also is concerned with the implementation of international standards already in force. One of the biggest setbacks for AI's campaign was the European Court of Human Rights' ruling—as discussed in detail in chapter 6—on the Irish claim that the United Kingdom "tortured" several people by inflicting "sensory deprivation" techniques of interrogation. It is to be recalled that the court ruled that such techniques were "inhuman and degrading treatment" but not torture. AI severely criticized this interpretation, and it continues to oppose and condemn as torture similar techniques employed by other governments in the interrogation process.

Amnesty International has also expended a lot of activity regarding conscientious objectors (COs)—AI classifies jailed COs as prisoners of conscience and thus qualified for assistance. Many countries allow alternative service or exemptions based upon ethical or religious grounds, but AI is specifically interested in those COs who have been tried on the basis of their *political* opposition to military service. Many of AI's adopted prisoners in Western Europe are COs—all AI adopted prisoners in France are COs, and the situation of COs in Switzerland is a major concern.

AI worked on 34 French cases in 1977–78, and 16 were still under consideration as of June 1978. French law stipulates that any person who has his request for CO status denied but still refuses military service can be tried for draft resistance. Special military tribunals, the *Tribunaux permanents des forces armées*, adjudicate the case, and the convicted CO is liable for up to two years in prison, although most sentences have not been for the maximum. AI is also involved with Swiss COs: in the twelve-month period that ended in June 1978, 345 convictions were for draft refusal in Switzerland. Of these 345 COs, 25 gave *political* reasons—as distinguished from ethical or religious reasons—for their objection. The average length of sentences for Swiss COs is about eight months. Amnesty International is also active with Greek COs—the only adoptees in post-junta Greece are about 50 Jehovah's Witness COs—as well as with the status of COs in West Germany.

The last major area of activity by Amnesty International is a research and documentation effort linked with fact-finding missions and observers. Some of these missions and observation visits result from invitations offered to AI by governments who believe they have been falsely accused in the human rights area and want to have the impartial "investigation" of AI to discover the truth. Recent invitations of this type issued to AI have come from the Mexican government to observe some detention centers and from the Italian government to study conditions in what were termed *special* prisons. Most of the missions, however, result from AI's own initiative, but the team is sometimes denied entry into the country or denied access to the object of the mission (a prison, a courtroom trial, a prisoner). Most AI missions, though, are received courteously by the host government, but this by no means suggests that government policies are immediately altered after the visit. Approximately thirty one-or two-person missions to twenty-six countries were operating in 1977–78.[21]

An extensive publication effort is also being carried out by AI. The organization has cordial relations with most of the media, and its press releases are usually printed and/or broadcast. The list of publications generated under AI's imprint is impressive in terms of both quantity and the degree of scholarship and documentation.[22] The 1977 Nobel Prize recognized this high level of scholarship along with an absence of polemics. The publications are offered at a nominal charge, and AI does not earn a profit from its worldwide sales effort. In fact, the deficit of the publications department in 1977 was approximately $88,000, and for 1978 the loss soared to approximately $200,000.[23] The information conveyed in these documents far surpasses, however, any monetary value, and public knowledge is much richer as a result of Amnesty International's publication efforts.

Some Individual Cases

Some five-thousand prisoners of conscience are currently "adopted" or under investigation by Amnesty International. The basis for selecting the few individual cases discussed in this section follows the guidelines established by the International Secretariat for the local adoption groups: one cannot deal with a prisoner in one's home country, and a fair balance of geographical-political representation must exist. The following examples thus do not include the United States,[24] but do represent one from the West (Brazil), one from the East (Vietnam), and one from the Third World (Bahrain).[25] The descriptions below are those presented to AI members in an AIUSA publication, and each of the three people are classified as prisoners of conscience. AI stated that "each has been arrested because of his or her religious or political beliefs, color, sex, ethnic origin or language. None has used or advocated violence. Their continuing detention is a violation of the United Nations Universal Declaration of Human Rights." Readers are reminded that international appeals can perhaps secure the release of these prisoners or improve their detention conditions, and AI members are urged to write letters to the relevant authorities. The general format of the letters are indicated: they are to be worded carefully and courteously; the writer should stress that the concern shown for human rights is not politically motivated; letters should be signed "Yours respectfully and sincerely."

The first example concerns Edival Nunes da Silva, a twenty-nine-year-old member of the Justice and Peace Commission of the Roman Catholic Church in Recif, Brazil's northeast coastal city. The *Matchbox* description is as follows:

Nunes da Silva is being held in incommunicado detention in the *Quartel de Cavaleria da Policia Militar de Pernambuco*, a military prison. He is reported to be suffering from intestinal problems. Writs of *habeas corpus*, presented to the Superior Military Tribunal requesting an end to his preventive detention, have been rejected.

He was detained without a warrant on May 12, 1978 when armed men kidnapped him in the street on his way home from a church meeting. He was taken to the Federal Police headquarters and held incommunicado for more than a month. During this time he was subjected to electric shock torture, forced standing, and beatings by members of the Operations Section of the *Departamento de Orden Politica e Social*.

Nunes da Silva has been charged with attempting to reorganize a political party, the *Partido Comunista Revolucionario*. Police claim to have found incriminating documents in his prison cell, but Nunes da Silva denies the charges and claims that the documents were planted after his arrest.[26]

The description of Nunes da Silva's case concludes with the request to send courteously worded letters appealing for the immediate release of Nunes da Silva to Presidente da Republica Federativa do Brasil, His Excellency General Joao Figueiredo, Gabinete do Presidente, Palacio do Planalto, 70000 Brasilia D.F., Brazil.

The second example concerns Bui Tuong Huan, a former Vietnamese university professor and political figure, who has been in detention since 1975. The *Matchbox* description is as follows:

During the 1960s, Bui Tuong Huan, who was closely identified with the Buddhist cause, was jailed on several occasions by successive governments in South Vietnam for protesting against religious and political repression in the country. In 1970, however, he was elected a member of the Senate and shortly afterwards he was instrumental in promoting a movement called the National Reconciliation Force, which advocated a negotiated settlement to the war.

On April 29, 1975, when the armed forces of the Provisional Revolutionary Government (PRG) were surrounding Saigon, the administration of President Nguyen Van Thieu was replaced by a new cabinet of which Bui Tuong Huan was a member. The following day, this cabinet handed over power to the PRG.

After the change of government, the new authorities issued a decree instructing all military personnel and civil servants of the former administration to register for "re-education." It was originally announced that "re-education" would last for a maximum of three years and in most cases would be considerably shorter. Four years have now passed. AI has received reports that tens of thousands of people, including both former members of the armed forces and civilians, are still detained in "re-education" camps.

Bui Tuong Huan has now been undergoing "re-education" for three and a half years. He was last reported to be in poor health. The camp in which he is detained in the northern province of Thanh Hoa.[27]

The description of Bui Tuong Huan's case concludes with the request to send courteously worded letters appealing for the immediate release of Bui Tuong Huan to His Excellency Pham Van Dong, Prime Minister, Office of the Prime Minister, Hanoi, Socialist Republic of Vietnam.

The last example concerns Jassim Haddad, a poet who was arrested in 1973 after participating in an Arab Writers' Conference in Beirut and was adopted as a prisoner of conscience by AI at that time. He was released under an amnesty in 1974, but the *Matchbox* description presents some more recent facts:

In August, 1975, Jassim Haddad was again arrested, a few days before the Emir of Bahrain issued a decree which dissolved the country's National Assembly on August 26, 1975. The arrests were apparently intended to stifle any protest about the dissolution, which followed the Assembly's refusal to pass a general security law permitting the government to imprison any citizen whose acts or statements are found objectionable. The National Assembly is still dissolved.

Jassim Haddad was detained until recently at Safra Prison, where most of the country's political prisoners are held. While a prisoner, he has required two medical operations and on January 12 1979, he was transferred to a hospital for treatment of a recurrent ear infection which is reported to be causing him great pain and affecting his general health. It is not known whether he is still in a hospital, or if he has been returned to prison. During his last period of imprisonment, Jassim Haddad was reported to have suffered serious injuries as a result of maltreatment.[28]

The description of Jassim Haddad's case concludes with the request to send courteously worded letters appealing for his immediate release to His Excellency Sheikh Khalifa Bin Sulman al-Khalifa, Prime Minister, Bahrain, Arabian Gulf.

The cases above are but three of the thousands of similar cases that AI is concerned with, and they represent an infinitesimal fraction of the total number of people who are so treated throughout the world. Nunes da Silva, Bui Tuong Huan, and Jassim Haddad may not—probably will not—be released on account of AI's letters, but at least the attempt is made to provide these unfortunate people with another avenue of redress against governmental mistreatment. Given the nature of the political regimes in Brazil, Vietnam, and Bahrain, and given the almost total lack of domestic protection for the individual, the intercession of organizations such as Amnesty International may be the only (and last) effort that can help these people.

Some Problems

The above discussion of Amnesty International has been presented in a positive framework. I am impressed with the philosophical goals of AI as well as with most of their activities and accomplishments and fully support the comments made by the Nobel Committee in presenting the Peace Prize to AI:

In a world of increasing brutality, internationalization of violence, terrorism and torture, Amnesty International used its forces for the protection of human values. Its efforts on behalf of defending human dignity against violence and subjugation have proved that the basis for peace in the world must be justice for all human beings.[29]

Many, however, do not share this view. Serious questions have been raised about Amnesty International's approach to the defense of human rights against governmental mistreatment. AI is seen by many to be biased—as lacking a sense of balance—as well as overstepping the boundaries of its "legitimate" sphere of activity. Some of the opposition is stated in paranoic, hysterical terms, buttressed by a conspiracy view of the universe, and other opposition is a more reasoned and scholarly critique. Both agree, however, that AI is open to the charge of a lack of balance and misplaced priorities.

The more hysterical arguments mainly come from the authoritarian regimes of the Right, especially those countries in South America (for example, Chile, Argentina, Uruguay) that are constantly identified and castigated by AI for frequent and gross violations of human rights. The view from South American is represented by a unsigned (other than "by our Montevideo Office") polemic appearing in a South American journal.[30] The view from Montevideo is that Amnesty International is concerned only with (alleged) violations of human rights in anti-Communist societies, and, therefore, AI serves the Moscow-run international Communist conspiracy, undermining the values of Western civilization.

The authoritarian South American regimes question AI's claim to neutrality and impartiality. They complain that AI publishes "imaginative reports" about torture in Chile under the junta but ignores the situation of people who were mistreated under Allende; they complain that AI investigates "so-called political prisoners" in Uruguay but refrains from even asking permission to inspect the Cuban situation; atrocities by Portuguese military personnel in Mozambique were reported in detail, but genocide by Left-leaning black African rulers was ignored. These examples stretch on and on to the identical conclusion: Amnesty International does not engage in "neutral" acitivity—it ignores *real* violations of human rights in Communist and Leftist countries while manufacturing false charges against the free world.[31]

AI is accused of devoting about 80 percent of its publications space to these "bloodcurdling" and "sadistic" details about Western countries, whereas the few pages on Communist countries are bland whitewashes. The South Americans see this as a conscious act by AI to advance the cause of communism:

> The Soviet Union is obviously the biggest beneficiary of AI activities. As everybody knows very well that political prisoners exist in the East bloc, the specific mention of a case or two does not really hurt their prestige. On the contrary, if one of those prisoners is set free, a clever tactic that is sometimes applied, AI's importance and effectiveness is enhanced. Furthermore, AI is attacked in the communist press as "imperialistic," "Fascist," "reactionary." *This is just a smokescreen that gives AI directors a pretext to claim that they are so fair and objective that they are attacked from the two opposing camps.*[32]

Amnesty International is dismissed by these regimes (its Nobel Prize was called "a bad joke in poor taste") as a willing tool of Moscow to discredit all of those governments not friendly to communism and especially those that are strongly anti-Communist. The view that AI is a willing tool of Moscow needs no further space except to note that it is a view accepted only by the paranoical Right. But the South American charge of a lack of balance and neutrality has been taken up, albeit in terms more reasoned and more reflective of reality, by other people.

In a 1978 article in the United States publication *Commentary*, one of the more respected liberal American intellectual journals, Stephen Miller took Amnesty International to task for a lack of neutrality and for activities that appear to be an indiscriminate application of some basic concerns.[33] Miller echoed the complaint of the Uruguayans: the regimes that seem to be the "most scandalously repressive" are usually on the Right (especially Chile, the Philippines, Argentina, and Uruguay), while those on the Left (except the Soviet Union and Czechoslovakia) generally receive higher marks. Miller analyzed AI's 1977 *Report* and found an overwhelming imbalance in terms of space devoted to specific countries: West Germany has a four-page description, for example, whereas Cuba, Cambodia, and North Korea have a total of four and one-half pages among them. The 1978 *Report* is more balanced in terms of space, but even this latest publication makes Rightist, authoritarian regimes look far worse than the Leftist, totalitarian regimes.

Miller also complained about the nature of what is being reported: specific instances of individual situations, with all the lurid details, are presented in regard to the authoritarian and even fully democratic regimes, but only sweeping generalizations are offered vis-à-vis the Leftist regimes. Miller wrote that AI's literature "tends to exhibit an automatic distrust of all rightist governments and an equal automatic desire to give [most] leftist governments . . . the benefit of the doubt." In fact, as Miller continued, AI allowed the Vietnamese government to give its own explanation of why there were so many political prisoners but never accepted any statement by government officials of Rightist regimes. Amnesty International's political neutrality was questioned by Miller, and although he did not subscribe to the view that AI is controlled by Moscow, he did repeat the Uruguayan complaint that it is

... hard to resist the conclusion that some policy, or at least some conscious set of attitudes, is at work behind AI's increasingly frequent practice of whispering softly when it comes to Vietnam, Cuba, China and Cambodia but shouting vehemently when it comes to Argentina, Chile, the Philippines and South Korea.[34]

Miller also castigated AI for what he saw as an indiscriminate application of principles, especially in regard to the prisoner of conscience category. As mentioned above, a POC is jailed on account of his beliefs and has not used or advocated violence. Such a definition obviously applied to Jassim Haddad, Nunes da Silva, Bui Tuong Huan, and Mark Nashpits, but, as Miller mentioned, such a definition has led AI into muddied waters. AI has worked on behalf of Jehovah's Witnesses who, in many countries, are jailed "not because they refuse induction into the military but because they refuse even to apply for conscientious-objector status." Miller believes that in such situations AI is clearly overstepping the line between "persecuted beliefs" and outright negative actions that a state legitimately can punish.

The *Commentary* article concluded with the fear that AI is coming too close to overt political partisan activity under the guise of human rights. Miller cited a letter that appeared in the *New York Review of Books*—a letter signed, among others, by two members of the governing board of AIUSA. After branding President Carter's human rights policy as "hypocritical," the letter presented a litany of "human rights" that are being violated by the American government: the "right" to an abortion, the "right" to child care facilities, the "right" to affirmative action in housing, education, employment, and so on. Miller saw this as possible politicization of AI and commented:

This blatant enlistment of the language of human rights in the service of a partisan political position is a truly ominous sign. If it were an aberration from AI's habitual practice, there would be little cause to remark upon it. It seems more likely, however, that the organization as a whole is moving away from its original purpose, a concern with violations of human rights all over the world, to a selective and predictable partisanship. If this is really so, it will mark the ruination of an enterprise that has brought hope to many.[35]

Amnesty International has had a mixed reaction to these criticisms—they have ignored some and offered responses to others. They (rightfully) ignored the charge that they are the conscious dupes of the international Communist conspiracy. Such a belief is held only by those hysterics in Latin America and South Africa who, after being de-Christianized, must find a substitute for the devil theory of history. Not only is Amnesty International *not* a puppet on a string—it is master of its own house—there are considerable doubts that such a conspiracy actually exists.

But the criticism of unbalance, of whispering about violations from the Left but shouting about those from the Right, is much more serious, documented, and relevant than the ravings of the Uruguayans. Amnesty International has recognized this criticism and believes it strikes at the core of its stated neutrality and impartiality. The organization has attempted to explain the reasons for its behavior, as shown by the remarks of Thomas Hammarberg, chairman of AI's International Executive Committee:

> . . . Amnesty International is less often attacked for what it publishes than for what it does not report. We are sometimes criticized for being unbalanced, for reporting too little or too much on a certain country or group of countries.
> Balance for the sake of balance would be artificial. We work with realities. If there were gross violations of human rights in one group of countries and only minor infringements in another, we would *not* spend fifty percent of our resources on each. But as the world is today, a human rights organization with an impartial and serious approach must work on all continents and in countries with the most differing political systems. This, too, is a reality and has created a need for work that is geographically 'balanced.'
> That balance is not easy to establish. There are still some few countries where the authorities refuse to have any communication with Amnesty International: they will not admit observers or representatives and our letters and cables receive no reply. These same regimes have a restrictive approach to the international media and little, if any, detailed information on the human rights situation in their countries therefore exists. Our movement has made great efforts to break through such situations; the result for the past year can be seen in this *Report*.[36]

As mentioned above, the 1978 *Report* is less unbalanced than the 1977 issue, but it still emphasizes the activities of the Right and the democracies over the activities of the Left and the totalitarian regimes. It is of course difficult to generate reliable information about, say, people in an Albanian or North Korean jail, but this nonetheless does not cancel the criticism. Far more important than the amount that AI actually publishes on certain countries is the central issue—something that Thomas Hammarberg totally overlooks—of what actually is published: the tone of the comments, the implied meanings, the underlying message AI is giving the reader. It appears that on this score AI is indeed open to criticism.

The reader is reminded of the *Matchbox* descriptions of Nunes da Silva of Brazil and Bui Tuong Huan of Vietnam. The government and special police of Brazil were severely criticized for arresting Nunes da Silva for attempting to organize a political party. The message to me is clear: da Silva did not do anything wrong and should be released immediately by the repressive Brazilian authorities. But what of Bui Tuong Huan? AI is concerned here *not* because he was put into a "reeducation" camp, but, rather, that he was in a camp *for a longer period* than originally prescribed by the Vietnamese government.

The message to some readers may be that the Vietnamese government is also engaged in violating human rights, but to the contrary, that description justifies the very existence of such "reeducation" camps, as if Amnesty International fully believes that anyone connected with the Saigon regime deserves being "reeducated." At no place does AI even question the need for "reeducation" camps in the first place, and they are concerned only because someone stayed longer than three years. This is *not* impartiality by any means, and Amnesty International is indeed whispering softly about certain countries.

The criticism of AI above from Stephen Miller about the indiscriminate application of the POC status also appears valid. AI is slowly turning toward working on behalf of people who take "negative activity" if such activity is based upon "sincere belief." This can lead to a total state of chaos and anarchy, and it is the extreme version of libertarianism, denying a state's legitimate claim to obedience. Refusal to pay income tax would make one eligible to be adopted by AI as a POC; the practice of polygamy because of religious beliefs would seem to be protected; refusal by a parent to allow a child a life-saving operation on account of "beliefs" all would fall under the rubric of POCs. Being "persecuted" for one's beliefs—an area where AI can and should intervene—and being given five years for failure to pay income tax on account of "political" beliefs are different types of action. Amnesty International must recognize this crucial distinction if it is to avoid an untimely and premature demise. In addition, AI's attempt to link its traditional concern with "human rights to "political" rights (housing, employment, and so on) can only backfire and cause the organization to be simply another partisan, political, special-interest group.

These criticisms and problems are important, and Amnesty International must rethink some of its philosophy and behavior. If, however, it continues in the direction it has been taking recently, it will indeed "mark the ruination of an enterprise that has brought hope to many."

SOME CONCLUDING COMMENTS

Amnesty International presents an excellent illustration of what a nongovernmental transnational organization can and cannot do in the redress procedure. That it is nongovernmental and transnational is not open to debate: it is permitted and even encouraged to operate by governments (many governments have given AI tax-exempt status), but it is a purely private organization; its membership and areas of activity cross national boundaries. AI is in a sense a special-interest group but not like the usual lobbies. AI's power (if any) does not rest upon a mass electoral base (for example, trade unions) or upon large financial resources (for example, the American Medical Association). Whatever influence AI may have derives from its access to, credibility with, and influence over governmental elites.

AI's tactics are to work with the elites—the governmental elites, the mass media elites, and the elites within mass public opinion. What makes AI different from other such groups who target the elite is that the latter usually work for the economic and/or political advancement of the group members themselves, whereas AI does not advance their interests but, rather, the interests of the people it considers to have been mistreated by governments.

How effective is Amnesty International in providing an avenue of redress to individuals wronged by their governments? This is a difficult question to answer in precise empirical terms. It is of course effective on one level of analysis: it has been in existence for almost twenty years, its budget and membership is increasing, and it is recognized as an effective organization (the Nobel Committee, for example). But on a more important level—the level of individual situations—the record is less convincing. People are still being tortured and put into jail for their beliefs and no one, not even AI itself, really believes that the organization's efforts will end this barbaric behavior.

But Amnesty International *has* made the world a better place by its very existence. People are becoming sensitized to brutality, and knowledge is always a precondition to action. Amnesty International may be open to serious criticism for specific actions, but the end goal is admirable—people should not be mistreated by governments, and AI will publicize the mistreatment *wherever it occurs* until the rights of man are observed.

Can Amnesty International provide redress to an individual? The answer is no. AI's role in the redress procedure is to rely upon the force of opinion, hopefully, to convince governmental authorities to provide the redress. For many people, Amnesty International is the *only* process left—not the courts or tribunals or lawyers or parliaments or ombudsmen or international governmental organizations—for it is composed of concerned individuals. The strongest bulwark against governmental mistreatment is the stance of each person in a society that refuses to remain quiet in the face of brutality and mistreatment of others. Amnesty International has not remained silent or uninvolved, and this has been its greatest contribution.

NOTES

1. See Walter A. Friedlander, *International Social Welfare* (Englewood Cliffs, N.J.: Prentice-Hall, 1975), for a brief introduction to some of these international social welfare agencies. The *Yearbook of the Union of International Associations* (Brussels: Union des Associations Internationales) lists over a thousand international voluntary organizations.

2. Amnesty International is by no means the only organization that keeps watch on how governments treat individuals and that attempts to protect the individual from official mistreatment. For information on the activities of human rights organizations throughout the world, see the *Human Rights Internet Newsletter* (Washington, D.C.: Human Rights Internet, nine issues p.a.). Hundreds of such organizations exist worldwide, such as the International Sakharov Committee (Denmark); the Latin America Research Group (Canada); the British Institute for Human Rights (UK); International Committee for the Defense of Human Rights in Taiwan (Japan); Paraguay Arbeits-Gruppe (West Germany); and Pax Christi (Belgium).

3. Paragraph 1 of the Statute of Amnesty International as amended by the Tenth International Council meeting, Bad Honnef, Federal Republic of Germany, September 16–18, 1977. Reproduced as appendix 1 of *Amnesty International Report 1978* (London: Amnesty International Publications, 1979), pp. 299–305. Amnesty International has a large publications division—specific country reports, briefing papers, a monthly newsletter, mission reports, an annual report—and these publications are available at nominal sums from the International Secretariat, 8–14 Southampton Street, London WC2E 7HF or from most of the national sections. The United States locations are at 304 West 58th Street, New York, NY 10019 and at 3618 Sacramento Street, San Francisco, CA 94118.

4. The number of additional representatives for national sections with groups is as follows: 10–49 groups—one representative; 50–99—two; 100–199—three; 200–399—four; and 400 groups or over—five additional representatives. For national sections, without organized groups, 500 to 2,499 members can appoint one additional council member, and national sections with over 2,500 members can appoint two.

5. As of June 1978, the International Executive Committee's members were Chairperson Thomas Hammarberg (Stockholm), Andrew Blane (New York), Dirk Börner (Hamburg), Alfred Heijder (Amsterdam), Irmgard Hutter (Vienna), Michael McClintock (London), Marie-José Protais (Paris), Mümtaz Soysal (Ankara), Kevin White (Dublin), Suriya Wickremasinghe (Columbo), and Jose Zalaquett (Santiago).

6. The honorary chairpeople of AIUSU are currently Roger Baldwin, Hanna Grunwald, Sean MacBride, Victor Reuther, and Michael Straight. The board of directors includes David Hinkley, David Weissbrodt, A. Whitney Ellsworth, and Ramsey Clark.

7. During the 1977–78 period, representatives of AI attended sessions of the following United Nations bodies: the thirtieth session of the Sub-Commission on the Prevention of Discrimination and the Protection of Minorities (August 1977); the thirty-second regular session of the General Assembly (September-December 1977); the ECOSOC Committee on Non-Governmental Organizations (January 1978); the Human Rights Committee, second and third sessions (August 1977 and January 1978); and the fifth session of the Committee on Crime Prevention and Control (June 1978).

8. The seven national sections and the amounts contributed are: Britain—£11,650; Switzerland—£10,000; Norway—£10,000; Australia—£464; Canada—£650; Germany—£35,000; and the Netherlands—£17,600.

9. Note no. 2 to Auditors' Report [Arthur Andersen & Co., London, June 20, 1978] of Amnesty International's financial position and balance sheets as of April 30, 1978, *Amnesty International Report 1978*, p. 292.

10. Only the Swedish national section reports the amounts spent on prisoner relief to the secretariat, but even these figures do not include the activities of the local adoption groups.

11. The discussion of this one example is based upon Ron Chernow, "Comrades in Conscience," *Quest/78*, 2, no. 7 (December-January 1978), esp. "One Minute Equals Five Years," p. 47.

12. As cited in ibid.

13. Other well-known participants included Garfield Todd (Rhodesia/Zimbabwe), Olle Dahlen (Swedish ambassador to NGOs), Christian Broda (Austria's federal minister of justice), Krishna Iyer (an Indian supreme court justice), Warren Allmand (Canada's minister of consumer and corporate affairs), Canon Carr (general secretary of the All-African Conference of Churches), and Hipolito Yrigoyen (a former Argentine senator).

14. The Declaration of Stockholm is reproduced as appendix 2, *Amnesty International Report 1978*, p. 306.

15. United Nations General Assembly Resolution 32/61 of December 8, 1977, on Capital Punishment; reproduced as appendix 3, *Amnesty International Report 1978*, pp. 307–8.

16. Resolution adopted unanimously by the Eleventh Conference of European Ministers of Justice, Copenhagen, June 21–22, 1978; reproduced as appendix 4, *Amnesty International Report 1978*, p. 309.

17. The country-by-country reports in AI's 1978 report (pp. 33–277) contain numerous examples of where AI has appealed for the commutation of specific death sentences. Amnesty International does not, however, take any credit in successful cases—the decision is a governmental one, and AI believes that the credit belongs to such governments.

18. One such dialogue has been attempted with King Khalid ibn Abdul Aziz of Saudia Arabia. In a March 1978 letter to the king, AI explained its position in regard to the death penalty (used frequently in Saudi Arabia) and its goal of abolishing capital punishment. The letter concluded with these words: "Islam is, we understand, a merciful religion and the Qur'an in many instances advocates mercy and forgiveness... [and] with this in mind, and in the light of a growing world-wide consensus against the death penalty, we most respectfully request that you give consideration to the question of the death penalty in your country and the possibility of abolishing its use." *Amnesty International Report 1978*, p. 270. AI has yet to receive a reply from King Khalid.

19. *Amnesty International Report 1978*, p. 16.

20. See the pamphlets "Deaths under Torture and Disappearance of Political Prisoners in Paraguay" (1978); "Political Imprisonment in South Africa" (1978); "Prisoners of Conscience in the USSR: Their Treatment and Conditions" (1975).

21. The thirty missions in 1977–78 are too numerous to list, but the following is a representative sample: Huang Wen-hsien of the International Secretariat and Ramsey Clark of the United States went to Thailand for talks with government officials and visits to prisons; Martin Ennals went to Bangladesh for government talks; Wolfgang Aigner went to Czechoslovakia to observe the trial of four people detained in connection with "Charter 77"; and Peter Tak of the Netherlands went to West Germany to observe a trial of several students charged with "the defamation of the memory of a dead person." AI's *Report* (1978) contains a complete and specific listing of all missions in 1977–78 (pp. 278–79).

22. AI's publications are available in Danish, Dutch, English, Finnish, French, German, Greek, Italian, Japanese, Norwegian, Spanish, and Swedish. AI publishes an annual report, briefing papers, leaflets, mission documents, newsletters, and special reports. In addition, AI also translates and publishes *A Chronicle of Current Events*—the *samizdat* journal of the human rights movement in the Soviet Union.

23. Note no. 5 to Auditor's Report [Arthur Andersen & Co., London, June 20, 1978] of Amnesty International's financial position and balance sheets as of April 30, 1978, *Amnesty International Report 1978*, p. 294.

24. This exclusion by no means implies that AI is not concerned with what it believes to be human rights violations in the United States. Several AI missions came to the United States in 1977–78: Luis Reque of Bolivia observed the trial of James E. Grant, an AI adoptee; Liyoko Kakula and Mwangala Kamwanga of Zambia observed the trial of Leonard Peltier, charged with the attempted murder of a police officer; and Brian Wrobel of the International Secretariat observed Peltier's appeal of his conviction. AI has been active in appealing for the commutation of the numerous death sentences pending in the United States. The 1978 report (p. 138) remarked, however, that "It is still difficult to identify prisoners of conscience in the United States. The problem . . . lies in substantiating allegations that people apparently convicted of non-political criminal offences have in fact been 'framed' because of their political activities or ethnic origin."

25. These three cases are taken from *Matchbox* (May 1979), p. 7 and reprinted with the permission of Amnesty International USA. *Matchbox* is AI's thrice-yearly newsletter.

26. Ibid.

27. Ibid.

28. Ibid.

29. The 1977 Nobel Peace Prize Citation, *New York Times*, October 11, 1977, pp. 1, 14.

30. "Is Amnesty International Impartial?" *The Review of the River Plate* 157 (April 10, 1975): 489–91.

31. The article cited above (note 30) says that the people in detention are not prisoners of conscience but, rather, are convicted of crimes of violence such as murder, kidnapping, armed robbery, and bombing. In addition, such people are "treated exceptionally well" while in prison—some are housed in a room with a private bath, reading material, frequent visitors, and even "home cooked food every day." The Uruguayans treat their prisoners so well, continued the article, "the other prisoners rebelled and demanded the same treatment" received by the convicted *Tupamaros*.

32. Ibid., p. 491, Emphasis supplied.

33. Stephen Miller, "Politics and Amnesty International," *Commentary* 65, no. 3 (March 1978): 57–60.

34. Ibid., p. 60.

35. Ibid.

36. Thomas Hammarberg, cited in *Amnesty International Report 1978*, p. 2.

CONCLUDING ESSAY:
The Future of Individual
Redress

8

This book examines the differing processes and methods at the disposal of a private citizen in various selected countries to complain against his or her government and have a reasonable expectation that the complaint will be heard and acted upon without prejudice. The content of such complaints concern either an alleged violation of a central personal liberty by the state or for insensitivity on the part of the faceless bureaucratic structures. This study also is a cross-national comparative analysis of an individual's ability to have his or her basic human rights protected against governmental or bureaucratic interference. The main theme, and unifying element, is the question of how one can bring some measure of justice, concern, and sensitivity to bear on the relationshipsbetween an ever-growing, impersonal administrative technology in the nuclear world—the modern postindustrial state—and the atomized and powerless single individual within this state.

The specific functional areas of redress discussed include a country's regular court system and the doctrine of judicial review to protect individuals; specialized administrative tribunals and courts such as the French *Conseil d'Etat*; the office of ombudsman or "citizens' protector" that is prevalent in the Scandinavian countries; action by politicians and parliamentary bodies that range from constituent service by local city councilmen to attempts by one legislative body protect people in other countries (the Jackson-Vanik and Harkin amendments); public intergovernmental institutions such as the European Convention on Human Rights system; and, finally, private (nongovernmental) transnational organizations such as Amnesty International.

Not all of these processes are available to everyone, since several are specific to individual countries, and some have much more efficacy than others in conflict management and in the resolution of disputes. Each of the procedures is intimately linked to the political culture and values of the society in which it operates, and each reflects the society's past record in providing avenues of redress against the state.

Although each of these avenues of redress differs in effectiveness and operates in different cultures and legal traditions, some common strands of agreement cut across all of them. The most important common thread is the crucial recognition that the state *is* (and not just should be) responsible and liable for its actions. The related doctrines of *rex gratia dei*, the king can do no wrong or authorize his agents to do wrong, and sovereign immunity have become outmoded for the Western democracies. These countries recognize that state power cannot exist without state obligations and that the individual can demand, and expect to receive, sensitive treatment from the public authorities. These democratic societies have accepted the view that the state, in its technocratic and bureaucratic costume of the twentieth century, is dealing with individuals, and that these individuals should not be wronged by the king. This view, and the processes and procedures generated by it, is part of what we mean by a "democratic" system, and the continued existence of these redress institutions appears to be assured.

A second strand of common agreement is the degree to which these societies exalt the redress process and require that the institutions' personnel be competent and dedicated. These redress agencies—the federal courts in the United States, the French *Conseil d'État*, the Scandinavian ombudsman—are at the height of their society's value system, and the prestige of the office is immense. The decisions generated by these redress institutions are legitimate, because the process employed to arrive at these decisions—whether the process is a U.S. Supreme Court hearing or an investigation in a French administrative court—is an integral part of the country's traditional behavior patterns. One should be wary of trying to transplant specific avenues of redress to different societies, for, if they do not dovetail with the political values of the country or if they are not congruent with people's expectations, they will not take root and will be ineffective.

Another thread of agreement among these democratic countries is that the redress system is based on concern for the individuals and not on ulterior political motives or economic concerns. To base a redress system on the benefits that will accrue to the redress officer—votes, time, money, prestige, and so on—will inject a cost-benefit accounting framework into the system. If the cost is too high (for example, not enough votes), redress will not be available, and this certainly does not protect the individual from administrative abuse. A system of redress must be based on a real concern for the individual; it must be based on beliefs, not benefits.

Finally, any system of redress is doomed unless those people, agencies, and governments that actually establish redress procedures firmly believe in the desirability, need, and competence of the oversight agencies and readily submit to, and honor, any forthcoming decision. Regardless of their outward attractiveness, procedures that allow for the lodging of a complaint only with the prior permission of the state or procedures that allow the honoring of the decision only insofar as the content of the decision agrees with the state's prior position do not contribute to the protection of the individual. Such procedures are hollow gestures and maintain bureaucratic abuses of power.

What of the future? It is perhaps asking too much to expect the nondemocratic and authoritarian states of Africa, Asia, Latin America, and Europe to institute redress avenues. Doing so would be admitting that the state no longer has primary control over the individual, and such an admission would negate the philosophical and political base of these societies. The future of individual redress against the state does not appear to be optimistic or promising: the democracies have already provided these avenues, but it is unlikely that other countries will follow suit.

SELECTED BIBLIOGRAPHY

GENERAL WORKS

Anderson, Perry. *Lineages of the Absolutist State*. New York: NLB/Schocken Books, 1978.

Bayley, David H. *Public Liberties in the New States*. Chicago: Rand McNally and Co., 1964.

Cappelleti, Mauro, and William Cohen. *Comparative Constitutional Law*. Indianapolis and New York: The Bobbs-Merrill Co., 1979.

Chalidze, Valery. *To Defend These Rights: Human Rights and the Soviet Union*. Translated by Guy Daniels. New York: Random House, 1974.

Claude, Richard C., ed. *Comparative Human Rights*. Baltimore: The Johns Hopkins University Press, 1976.

Crown Proceedings Act, 1947 (U.K.) 10 and 11 Geo. VI. c. 44.

Dowrick, F. E., ed. *Human Rights: Problems: Perspectives and Texts*. Farnborough, Hants: Saxon House/Teakfield Ltd., 1979.

Flathman, Richard. *Political Obligation*. New York: Atheneum, 1971.

Friedmann, Karl A. *Complaining: Comparative Aspects of Complaint Behavior and Attitudes Toward Complaining in Canada and Britain*. Beverly Hills and London: Sage Publications, 1974.

Hobbes, Thomas. *Leviathan*. Edited with an Introduction by Herbert Schneider. Indianapolis: The Bobbs-Merrill Co., 1958. First published in 1651.

Justice Society (John Wyatt). *Citizens and the Administration: The Redress of Grievances*. London: Sweet, 1961.

Kirchheimer, Otto. *Political Justice: The Use of Legal Procedure for Political Ends*. Princeton University Press, 1961.

Locke, John. *Two Treatises of Government*. Edited by Peter Laslett. New York: The New American Library, 1963. First published in 1690.

Petition of Right Act, 1860 (U.K.) 23 and 24 Vict. c. 34.

Ridley, F. F., and Jean Blondel. *Public Administration in France*. New York: Barnes and Noble, 1964

Shonfield, Andrew. "An Essay on Some Political Implications of Active Government." Part 4 of *Modern Capitalism: The Changing Balance of Public and Private Power*, pp. 383–427. New York and London: Oxford University Press, 1965.

Street, Harry. *Governmental Liability: A Comparative Study*. Cambridge: Cambridge University Press, 1953.

THE REGULAR COURT SYSTEM

Abraham, Henry J. *The Judicial Process: An Introductory Analysis of the Courts of the United States, England, and France*. 4th ed. New York: Oxford University Press, 1980.
Becker, Theodore L., ed. *Political Trials*. Indianapolis and New York: The Bobbs-Merrill Co., 1971.
Cox, Archibald. *The Role of the Supreme Court in American Government*. New York: Oxford University Press, 1976.
deSmith, S. A. *Judicial Review of Administrative Action*. London: Stevens, 1959 and Sweet and Maxwell, 1963.
"Federal Administrative Procedure Act," Public Law 89–554 (September 6, 1966), Title 5, *United States Code*, Part 1, Sections 501ff. and 701ff.
"Federal Tort Claims Act," Title 4, Legislative Reorganization Act of 1946. Title 28, *United States Code*, Section 2674.
Sindler, Allan P. *Bakke, DeFunis, and Minority Admissions: The Quest for Equal Opportunity*. New York: David McKay/Longman, 1978.
Theberge, Leonard, ed. *The Judiciary in a Democratic Society* (Lexington, Mass.: D. C. Heath/Lexington Books, 1979.
White, G. Edward. *The American Judicial Tradition*. New York: Oxford University Press, 1976.

SPECIALIZED ADMINISTRATIVE COURTS

Bodiguel, Jean-Luc. *L'École nationale d'administration*. Volume 2: *Sociologie: Les anciens élèves de l'ENA*. Paris: Presses de la fondation nationale des sciences politiques, 1978.
Brown, R. D. *The Battle of Crichel Down*. London: Bodley Head, 1955.
Christoph, James B. "Political Rights and Administrative Impartiality in the British Civil Service." *American Political Science Review* 51, no. 1 (March 1957): 67–87.
Crossland, H. G. "Rights of the Individual to Challenge Administrative Action Before Administrative Courts in France and Germany." *International and Comparative Law Quarterly* 24, no. 4 (October 1975): 707–47.
Freedeman, Charles E. *The Conseil d'État in Modern France*. New York: Columbia University Press, 1960.
Institut d'Etudes Politiques de l'Université de Grenoble, Centre d'Études et de Recherches sur l'Administration Régionale et Locale. *Administration Traditionnelle et Planification Régionale*. Cahiers de la Fondation nationale des sciences politiques, No. 135. Paris: Armand Colin, 1964.
Kessler, Marie-Christine. *L'École nationale d'administration*. Volume 1: *Historie: La politique de la haute fonction publique*. Paris: Presses de la fondation nationale des sciences politiques, 1978.

_____. *Le Conseil d'État*. Cahiers de la fondation nationale des sciences politiques, No. 167. Paris: Armand Colin, 1968.

Landon, Pierre. *Histoire abrégée du recours pour excès de pouvoir des origines à 1954*. Paris: Librairie générale de droit et de jurisprudence, 1962.

Langrod, Georges. "The French Conseil d'État: Its Role in the Formulation and Implementation of Administrative Law." *American Political Science Review* 49, no. 3 (September 1955): 673–92.

Letourneur, Maxime, and Jean Méric. *Conseil d'État et juridictions administratives*. Paris: Armand Colin, 1955.

Marshall, Geoffrey. "The Franks Report on Administrative Tribunals and Enquiries." *Public Administration* 35 (Winter 1957): 347–48.

Peters, B. Guy. *The Politics of Bureaucracy: A Comparative Perspective* (London: Longman, 1978).

Robson, William A. *Nationalized Industry and Public Ownership*. 2d rev. ed. (London: Allen & Unwin, Ltd., 1962).

_____. "Administrative Justice and Injustice: A Commentary on the Franks Report." *Public Law*, Spring 1958, pp. 12–31.

Thomas, Rosamund. *The British Philosophy of Administration: A Comparison of British and American Ideas, 1900–1939*. London: Longman, 1978.

United Nations. *1962 Seminar on Judicial and Other Remedies Against the Abuse of Administrative Authority with Special Emphasis on the Role of Parliamentary Institutions*. Stockholm, Sweden, June 12–25, 1962. New York: United Nations, 1962.

United States House of Representatives, Subcommittee on Crime of the Committee on the Judiciary. *Hearing on H.R. 6667: The Bureaucratic Accountability Act of 1974*. Ninety-Third Congress, Second Session, March 27, 1974. Washington, D.C.: U.S. Government Printing Office, 1974.

Wraith, R. E., and R. G. Hutchesson. *Administrative Tribunals*. London: Allen & Unwin, Ltd. 1973.

Wraith, R. E., and G. B. Lamb. *Public Enquiries as an Instrument of Government*. London: Allen & Unwin, Ltd., 1971.

THE OMBUDSMAN

Anderson, Stanley V. *Ombudsman Papers: American Experience and Proposals* (Berkeley: Institute of Governmental Studies, University of California Press, 1969).

Gellhorn, Walter. "The Ombudsman's Relevance to American Municipal Affairs." *American Bar Association Journal* 54 (February 1968): 134–40.

_____. *Ombudsmen and Others: Citizens' Protectors in Nine Countries*. Cambridge: Harvard University Press, 1966.

Gregory, Roy, and Peter Hutchesson. *The Parliamentary Ombudsman*. London: Allen & Unwin, Ltd., 1977.

Hill, Larry B. "Defining the Ombudsman: A Comparative Analysis." Paper delivered at the Annual Meeting of the Midwest Political Science Association, Chicago, April 21–23, 1977, 48 pp.

_____. *The Model Ombudsman: Institutionalizing New Zealand's Democratic Experiment*. Princeton: Princeton University Press, 1976.

_____. *Ombudsmen, Bureaucracy, and Democracy*. New York: Oxford University Press, 1976.

_____. "Institutionalization, the Ombudsman, and Bureaucracy." *American Political Science Review* 68, no. 3 (September 1974): 1075–85.

Hurwitz, Stephan. *The Ombudsman: Denmark's Parliamentary Commissioner for Civil and Military Administration*. Copenhagen: Det Danske Selskab, 1961.

Morgan, G. G. *Soviet Administative Legality: The Role of the Attorney General's Office*. Stanford: Stanford University Press, 1962.

Peel, Roy V., ed. *The Ombudsman or Citizen's Defender: A Modern Insitution*. The *Annals* of the American Academy of Political and Social Science 377 (May 1968).

The Position and Functions of the Finnish Parliamentary Ombudsman. Helsinki: Office of the Ombudsman, 1965.

Rowat, Donald C., ed. *The Ombudsman: Citizen's Defender*. 2d ed. Toronto: University of Toronto Press, 1968.

Stewart, Kenneth L. "What a University Ombudsman Does: A Sociological Study of Everyday Conduct." *Journal of Higher Education* 49, no. 1 (1978): 1–22.

Weeks, Kent M. "Members of Parliament and the New Zealand Ombudsman System." *Midwest Journal of Political Science* (currently the *American Journal of Political Science*) 14, no. 4 (November 1970): 673–86.

Wyner, Alan J., ed. *Executive Ombudsmen in the United States*. Berkeley: Institute of Governmental Studies, University of California Press, 1973.

PARLIAMENTARY ACTIVITY

Barker, Anthony and Michael Rush. *The Member of Parliament and His Information*. London: Allen & Unwin, Ltd., 1970.

Bradshaw, Kenneth, and David Pring. *Parliament and Congress*. Austin: University of Texas Press, 1972.

Brown, Peter G., and Douglas MacLean, eds. *Human Rights and U.S. Foreign Policy: Principles and Applications*. Lexington, Mass.: D. C. Heath/Lexington Books, 1979.

Buergenthal, Thomas, ed. *Human Rights, International Law and the Helsinki Accord*. Montclair, N. J.: Universe Books/Allanheld, Osmun & Co., Publishers, 1978.

Busch, Ronald J. "The Urban Legislator as a Municipal Ombudsman." Mimeographed. Cleveland: Cleveland State University, Department of Political Science, 1978, 31 pp.

Chester, D. N., and Nona Bowring. *Questions in Parliament*. Oxford: The Clarendon Press, 1962.

Christopher, Warren. *Implementing the Human Rights Policy*. Current Policy No. 67, United States Department of State, Bureau of Public Affairs. Washington, D.C.: U.S. Government Printing Office, June 1979.

Cohen, Stephen D. *The Making of United States International Economic Policy*. New York: Praeger Publishers, 1977.

DeWitt, R. Peter, Jr. *The Inter-American Development Bank and Political Influence*. New York: Praeger Publishers, 1977.

Dominguez, Jorge I. et al. *Human Rights and International Relations*. New York: McGraw Hill Book Co., 1977.

Fenno, Richard F., Jr. *Home Style: House Members in Their Districts*. Boston: Little, Brown, 1978.

Fox, Harrison W., Jr., and Susan Webb Hammond. *Congressional Staffs: The Invisible Force in American Law-Making*. New York: The Free Press, 1977.

The Helsinki Review Group, David Davies Memorial Institute of International Studies. *From Helsinki to Belgrade*. London: Europa Publications, Ltd., 1977.

Jennings, Sir Ivor. *Parliament*. Cambridge: Cambridge Univeristy Press, 1969.

Johnson, Nevil. "Parliamentary Questions and the Conduct of Administration." *Public Administration* 39, no. 2 (Summer 1961): 131–48.

Kochan, Lionel, ed. *The Jews in Soviet Russia Since 1917*. 3rd ed. New York: Oxford University Press, 1978.

Lauterpacht, Elihu, and John G. Collier, eds. *Individual Rights and the State in Foreign Affairs*. New York: Praeger Publishers, 1977.

Letalier, Isabel, and Michael Moffit. *Human Rights, Economic Aid and Private Banks: The Case of Chile*. New York: Institute for Policy Studies/Transaction Books, 1978.

McCulloch, R. W. "Question Time in the British House of Commons." *American Political Science Review* 27, no. 4 (December 1933): 971–75.

Orbach, William W. *The American Movement to Aid Soviet Jews*. Amherst: University of Massachusetts Press, 1979.

United States Department of State. *Fourth Semiannual Report by the President to the Commission on Security and Cooperation in Europe, December 1, 1977-June 1, 1978*. Special Report No. 45, Bureau of Public Affairs, Office of Public Communication. Washington, D.C.: U.S. Government Printing Office, June 1978.

Van Dyke, Vernon. *Human Rights, the United States and World Community*. Oxford: Oxford University Press, 1970.

PUBLIC SUPRANATIONAL INSTITUTIONS

Bloomfield, Louis M., and Gerald F. Fitzgerald. *Crimes Against Internationally Protected Persons: Prevention and Punishment. An Analysis of the UN Convention*. New York: Praeger Publishers, 1975.

Carey, John. *UN Protection of Civil and Political Rights*. Volume 8: *Procedural Aspects of International Law Series*. Edited by Richard B. Lillich. Syracuse: Syracuse University Press, 1970.

Castberg, Frede. *The European Convention on Human Rights*. Updated and edited by Torkel Opsahl and Thomas Ouchterlony. Leiden and Dobbs Ferry: A. W. Sijthoff/Oceana Publications, 1974.

Convention for the Protection of Human Rights and Fundamental Freedoms with Protocols Nos I and IV and Selected Reservations/Convention de Sauvegarde des Droits de l'homme et des Libertés Fondamentales accompagnée des

Protocoles Nos I et IV et d'un choix de Réserves. Strasbourg: Council of Europe, n.d.

European Commission on Human Rights. *Annual Review.* Strasbourg: Council of Europe.

Fawcett, J. E. S. *The Application of the European Convention on Human Rights.* Oxford: The Clarendon Press, 1969.

Jacobs, Francis G. *The European Convention on Human Rights.* Oxford: The Clarendon Press, 1975.

Robertson, A. H. *Human Rights in Europe.* Manchester: Manchester University Press, 1963 and 1977.

Sohn, Louis B., and Thomas Buergenthal. *International Protection of Human Rights.* New York: The Bobbs-Merrill Co., 1973.

United States Department of State. *Human Rights.* Selected Documents No. 5, Bureau of Public Affairs/Office of Media Services. Washington, D.C.: U.S. Government Printing Office, n.d. Excerpts from the *UN Charter;UN Universal Declaration of Human Rights; UN Convention on the Prevention and Punishment of the Crime of Genocide; UN International Convention on the Elimination of all Forms of Racial Discrimination; UN International Convention on Economic, Social, and Cultural Rights; UN International Covenant on Civil and Political Rights and the Optional Protocol to the International Covenant on Civil and Political Rights.*

United States House of Representatives, Subcommittee on International Organizations and Movements of the Committee on Foreign Affairs. *Hearings on International Protection of Human Rights—The Work of International Organizations and the Role of U.S. Foreign Policy.* Ninety-third Congress, First Session, August 1, 1973-December 7, 1973. Washington, D.C.: U.S. Government Printing Office, 1974.

Weiss, Thomas G. *International Bureaucracy: An Analysis of the Operation of Functional Global International Secretariats.* Lexington, Mass.: D. C. Heath/Lexington Books, 1975.

Yearbook of the European Commission on Human Rights. The Hague: Council of Europe.

PRIVATE TRANSNATIONAL AGENCIES

Amnesty International. *Annual Report(s).* London: Amnesty International Publications.

Anon. "Is Amnesty International Impartial?" *The Review of the River Plate* 157 (April 10, 1975): 489–91.

Chernow, Ron. "Comrades in Conscience." *Quest/78* 2, no. 7 (December-January 1978): 44, 46–49, 100–01.

Davis, Morris, ed. *Civil Wars and the Politics of International Relief: Africa, South Asia, and the Caribbean.* New York: Praeger Publishers, 1975.

———. "The International Committee of the Red Cross and its Practice of Self-Restraint." *Journal of Voluntary Action Research* 4, nos. 1–2 (January-April 1975): 63–68.

Forsythe, David P. *Humanitarian Politics: The International Committee of the Red Cross*. Baltimore, The Johns Hopkins University Press, 1978.

Freymond, Jacques. "Humanitarian Policy and Pragmatism: Some Case Studies of the Red Cross." *Government and Opposition* 11, no. 4 (Fall 1976): 408–25.

Friedlander, Walter A. *International Social Welfare*. Englewood Cliffs, N.J.: Prentice Hall, 1975.

Human Rights Internet Newsletter. Washington, D.C.: Human Rights, Internet, nine issues p.a.

Matchbox. New York: Amnesty International USA, 3 issues p.a.

Miller, Stephen. "Politics and Amnesty International." *Commentary* 65, no. 3 (March 1978): 57–60.

Scoble, Harry M., and Laurie Wiseberg. "Amnesty International: Evaluating Effectiveness in the Human Rights Arena." *Intellect* 105, no. 2377 (September-October 1976): 79–82.

————. "Human Rights and Amnesty International." *The Annals of the American Academy of Political and Social Science* 413 (May 1974): 11–26.

Sommer, John G. *Beyond Charity: U.S. Voluntary Aid for a Changing Third World*. Washington, D.C.: Overseas Development Council, 1977.

Yearbook of the Union of International Associations. Brussels: Union des Associations Internationales.

INDEX